HOME MORTGAGE LAW PRIMER

Third Edition

Revised and Updated by
Margaret C. Jasper

Oceana's Legal Almanac Series:
Law for the Layperson

Oceana®
NEW YORK

OXFORD
UNIVERSITY PRESS

Oxford University Press, Inc., publishes works that further Oxford University's objective of excellence in research, scholarship, and education.

Copyright © 2009 by Oxford University Press, Inc.
Published by Oxford University Press, Inc.
198 Madison Avenue, New York, New York 10016

Oxford is a registered trademark of Oxford University Press
Oceana is a registered trademark of Oxford University Press, Inc.

Library of Congress Cataloging-in-Publication Data

Jasper, Margaret C.
    Home mortgage law primer / by Margaret C. Jasper. — 3rd ed.
        p. cm. — (Oceana's legal almanac series: law for the layperson)
    Rev. ed. of: Home mortgage law primer / Mavis Fowler. 1995.
    ISBN 978-0-19-538616-5 ((hardback) : alk. Paper)
    1. Mortgages—United States—Popular works. 2. Mortgage loans—Law and legislation—United States—Popular works. I. Fowler, Mavis. Home mortgage law primer. II. Title.
    KF695.F69 2008
    346.7304'364—dc22

                                                                    2008037771

Note to Readers:

This publication is designed to provide accurate and authoritative information in regard to the subject matter covered. It is based upon sources believed to be accurate and reliable and is intended to be current as of the time it was written. It is sold with the understanding that the publisher is not engaged in rendering legal, accounting, or other professional services. If legal advice or other expert assistance is required, the services of a competent professional person should be sought. Also, to confirm that the information has not been affected or changed by recent developments, traditional legal research techniques should be used, including checking primary sources where appropriate.

(Based on the Declaration of Principles jointly adopted by a Committee of the American Bar Association and a Committee of Publishers and Associations.)

You may order this or any other Oxford University Press publication by visiting the Oxford University Press website at www.oup.com

---

To My Husband Chris

Your love and support

are my motivation and inspiration

To My Sons, Michael, Nick and Chris

-and-

In memory of my son, Jimmy

Table of Contents

CHAPTER 2:
THE MORTGAGE LOAN PROCESS

CHAPTER 3:
HOME EQUITY FINANCING

CHAPTER 4:
THE REAL ESTATE CLOSING

CHAPTER 8:
FORECLOSURE

ABOUT THE AUTHOR

MARGARET C. JASPER is an attorney engaged in the general practice of law in South Salem, New York, concentrating in the areas of personal injury and entertainment law. Ms. Jasper holds a Juris Doctor degree from Pace University School of Law, White Plains, New York, is a member of the New York and Connecticut bars, and is certified to practice before the United States District Courts for the Southern and Eastern Districts of New York, the United States Court of Appeals for the Second Circuit, and the United States Supreme Court.

Ms. Jasper has been appointed to the law guardian panel for the Family Court of the State of New York, is a member of a number of professional organizations and associations, and is a New York State licensed real estate broker operating as Jasper Real Estate, in South Salem, New York.

Margaret Jasper maintains a web site at http://www.JasperLawOffice.com.

In 2004, Ms. Jasper successfully argued a case before the New York Court of Appeals, which gives mothers of babies who are stillborn due to medical negligence the right to bring a legal action and recover emotional distress damages. This successful appeal overturned a 26-year old New York case precedent, which previously prevented mothers of stillborn babies from suing their negligent medical providers.

Ms. Jasper is the author and general editor of the following legal Almanacs:

AIDS and the Law

The Americans with Disabilities Act

Animal Rights Law

Auto Leasing

Bankruptcy Law for the Individual Debtor

Banks and their Customers

Becoming a Citizen

Buying and Selling Your Home

Commercial Law

Consumer Rights and the Law

Co-ops and Condominiums: Your Rights and Obligations As Owner

Copyright Law

Credit Cards and the Law

Custodial Rights

Dealing with Debt

Dictionary of Selected Legal Terms

Drunk Driving Law

DWI, DUI and the Law

Education Law

Elder Law

Employee Rights in the Workplace

Employment Discrimination Under Title VII

Environmental Law

Estate Planning

Everyday Legal Forms

Executors and Personal Representatives: Rights and Responsibilities

Guardianship and the Law

Harassment in the Workplace

Health Care and Your Rights

Health Care Directives

Hiring Household Help and Contractors: Your Rights and Obligations Under the Law

Home Mortgage Law Primer

Hospital Liability Law

How To Change Your Name

How To Form an LLC

How To Protect Your Challenged Child

How To Start Your Own Business

Identity Theft and How To Protect Yourself

Individual Bankruptcy and Restructuring

Injured on the Job: Employee Rights, Worker's Compensation and Disability Insurance Law

International Adoption

Juvenile Justice and Children's Law

Labor Law

Landlord-Tenant Law

Law for the Small Business Owner

The Law of Adoption

The Law of Attachment and Garnishment

The Law of Buying and Selling

The Law of Capital Punishment

The Law of Child Custody

The Law of Contracts

The Law of Debt Collection

The Law of Dispute Resolution

The Law of Immigration

The Law of Libel and Slander

The Law of Medical Malpractice

The Law of No-Fault Insurance

The Law of Obscenity and Pornography

The Law of Personal Injury

The Law of Premises Liability

The Law of Product Liability

The Law of Speech and the First Amendment

Lemon Laws

Living Together: Practical Legal Issues

Marriage and Divorce

Missing and Exploited Children: How to Protect Your Child

Motor Vehicle Law

Nursing Home Negligence

Patent Law

Pet Law

Planes, Trains and Buses: Your Rights as a Passenger

Prescription Drugs

Privacy and the Internet: Your Rights and Expectations Under the Law

Probate Law

Protecting Your Business: Disaster Preparation and the Law

Real Estate Law for the Homeowner and Broker

Religion and the Law

Retirement Planning

The Right to Die

Rights of Single Parents

Small Claims Court

Social Security Law

Special Education Law

Teenagers and Substance Abuse

Trademark Law

Trouble Next Door: What to do With Your Neighbor

Veterans' Rights and Benefits

Victim's Rights Law

Violence Against Women

Welfare: Your Rights and the Law

What if It Happened to You: Violent Crimes and Victims' Rights

What if the Product Doesn't Work: Warranties & Guarantees

Workers' Compensation Law

Your Child's Legal Rights: An Overview

Your Rights in a Class Action Suit

Your Rights as a Tenant

Your Rights Under the Family and Medical Leave Act

You've Been Fired: Your Rights and Remedies

INTRODUCTION

Owning one's home is the American dream. Home ownership carries with it a multitude of benefits generally not available to those who lease or rent. For example, owning a home is often less expensive than renting property, and ownership affords tax deductions that are not available to the renter. There is also long-term security and flexibility in home ownership whereas a renter is subject to the landlord's requirements.

Nevertheless, most Americans do not have the financial means to purchase a home outright in a cash transaction. Thus one of the biggest obstacles one faces in realizing this dream is financing the purchase of a home. This is generally accomplished by obtaining a home mortgage from a bank or other real estate lender.

This Almanac discusses the history of real estate finance, the sources of real estate financing, the types of mortgage devices, and mortgage interest considerations, including fixed and adjustable rate mortgages. This Almanac also provides a basic guide to the mortgage loan process and the final closing of the real estate transaction. Illegal real estate finance practices are also discussed. In addition, foreclosure proceedings, and the legal options available to a homeowner facing foreclosure are also explored.

The Appendix provides resource directories, sample forms, applicable statutes, and other pertinent information and data. The Glossary contains definitions of many of the terms used throughout the Almanac.

CHAPTER 1:
MORTGAGE OVERVIEW

HISTORY OF THE MORTGAGE

English Common Law

Although the concept of mortgage can be traced back to the Roman Empire, American mortgage law developed in large part from early English common law, both in its substance and terminology. The common law mortgage that developed in England during the 14th and 15th centuries involved a deed of a "defeasible fee" from the borrower to the lender. Basically, this meant that the right of ownership was dependent on whether or not a certain event occurred. In this case, the event was the repayment of the debt on law day, as discussed below.

Law Day

The mortgage set forth a repayment date, known as "law day." If the borrower satisfied the debt on or before law day, the lender's estate ended and the borrower retained title to the land. If the borrower was unable to satisfy the debt on or before law day, the defeasible fee became a "fee simple absolute" for the lender—i.e., ownership that lasts forever and exists without any limitations or conditions—and the borrower forfeited all rights and title to the land to the lender. This was a harsh rule that was strictly applied even if the borrower could not locate and pay the lender.

The Equity of Redemption

Recognizing the severity of this law, particularly on the borrower, the courts of equity—known as the English Chancery—intervened to assist the borrower who failed to make payment on law day. If the borrower could establish certain equitable grounds for relief such as fraud, accident, misrepresentation, or duress, the equity courts would permit the borrower to redeem the land upon payment of the debt even though law day had passed.

Eventually, the granting of this equitable relief of late payment became so routine that the borrower no longer needed to establish the specific equitable grounds for relief. This right to late redemption was referred to as the borrower's "equity of redemption," and was recognized as an equitable estate or interest in the land.

Right of Strict Foreclosure

This permissive right of redemption distressed the lenders who feared that borrowers would now choose to delay satisfying their debt by law day, and instead sue in equity to redeem their property regardless of their late payment.

In order to address these concerns, the equity courts gave the lender a right to foreclose. Thus after the borrower either failed to pay the debt on law day, or bring a suit to redeem the property, the lender could request the equity court to order the borrower to pay the debt, interest, and costs within a fixed period. Failure to comply with the court decree meant that the borrower's right to redeem their property was forever barred.

This type of foreclosure, which is rarely used today, is known as strict foreclosure under which the land is not sold but forfeited to the lender regardless of its value in relation to the original mortgage debt. The lender is given a fee simple absolute—i.e., absolute ownership of the property without condition or limitation.

AMERICAN DEVELOPMENTS

The colonists came to America in pursuit of their dream of absolute ownership of a piece of the New World. The restrictiveness of land ownership under the English common law was not acceptable to them, and was a major cause of the colonial revolt.

The Allodial System

This dissatisfaction led to a form of land ownership in the United States known as the "allodial system." Under the allodial system, the titled owner of the property owns it absolutely, subject to the restrictions set forth by the established laws and regulations that govern real estate ownership in America.

Early Balloon Note Mortgages

Until the 1930s, most mortgages were of the "balloon-note" type. The periodic payments made under a balloon note mortgage are generally only applied to interest. Thus at the end of the loan term, the debtor must pay the entire principal in one "balloon" payment.

Typically, during the 1930s, balloon note mortgages were of short-term duration—e.g., three or five-year terms—which gave borrowers little time to save the entire principal that became due. Nevertheless, a borrower who was unable to pay the entire balloon payment on its due date was generally able to renew the note or refinance it with another lender.

Post-Depression Legislation

Following the depression, lenders were in desperate need for cash. For example, savings and loans associations (S&Ls) were receiving less in savings because of the high unemployment rate. Consequently, many lenders had to demand full payment and foreclose on properties when borrowers could not pay. As further discussed below, Congress responded to this disastrous financial situation with many sweeping legislative changes.

The Federal Home Loan Bank Act of 1932

Historically, the S&Ls provided a great deal of the financing for middle class urban homes prior to the depression. However, S&Ls experienced a liquidity crisis during the 1930s. In an effort to help save the S&Ls, Congress passed the Federal Home Loan Bank Act of 1932. Under the Act, the Federal Home Loan Bank System (FHLB) was created in order to provide funds to the S&Ls and make home mortgages more affordable.

The FHLB System provides low-cost funding to financial institutions for home mortgage loans, as well as other types of funding, and represents the largest collective source of home mortgage credit in the United States. The FHLB System banks do not provide loans directly to individuals, only to other banks. The FHLB System consists of twelve banks owned by over 8,100 financial institutions. The liabilities of each FHLB System bank are guaranteed by all of the other FHLB System banks.

The National Housing Act of 1934

The National Housing Act of 1934 created the Federal Housing Administration (FHA), which introduced mortgage insurance and popularized the amortized mortgage loan system under which borrowers were permitted to repay loans over many years. Today most mortgages are amortized or repaid over a substantial number of years.

Amortization is the periodic reduction of principal so that the borrower, when making his last regular payment, will have reduced his mortgage balance to zero. Each periodic payment of an amortized mortgage loan includes the interest as well as principal of the loan.

The Federal Savings and Loan Insurance Corporation (FSLIC)

In addition, in order to insure the safety of deposits in S&Ls, Congress authorized the creation of the Federal Savings and Loan Insurance Corporation (FSLIC) under the authority of Title IV of the National Housing Act of 1934.

The S&L Failures of the 1980s

Like the S&Ls during the depression, the S&Ls of the 1980s experienced numerous difficulties and consequently, many failed. One of the reasons for their failure during the 1980s is that they held low-yield, fixed-rate mortgages during periods of high inflation. Since that time, there have been many advances made to protect S&Ls from such risks.

The Financial Institutions Reform, Recovery and Enforcement Act (FIRREA)

One important step was the enactment of the Financial Institutions Reform, Recovery and Enforcement Act (FIRREA) in 1989, which completely changed how S&Ls were regulated. The FIRREA abolished the Federal Home Loan Bank Board and transferred oversight responsibilities to the Federal Housing Finance Board (FHFB).

The FHFB regulates the 12 FHLB System banks that were created in 1932 to improve the supply of funds to local lenders that, in turn, finance loans for home mortgages. The FHFB also ensures that the FHLB System banks, which are privately capitalized, government-sponsored enterprises, remain adequately capitalized and financially able to carry out their housing and community development finance mission.

WHAT IS A MORTGAGE?

A mortgage involves the transfer of a real estate interest by a borrower to a lender as security for payment of a debt. A borrower—also referred to as a "mortgagor"—is one who borrows money and, in return, gives a mortgage or deed of trust on real property as security to the lender—also known as a "mortgagee." In most instances, an individual is the borrower and a bank or mortgage company is the lender.

The mortgage represents the lender's security interest in the real estate. As further discussed below, the mortgage remains as a "real estate lien" on the property until the underlying debt is paid in full. The lender usually retains a "first mortgage" on the property, which generally gives the lender the first right to take the property if the borrower defaults.

The basic mortgage is a written two-party instrument between the borrower and lender that is similar to a deed. It contains words of a grant and a description of the mortgaged land. Like a contract, a mortgage has certain requirements that must be satisfied in order for it to be valid. The borrower must be competent and of legal age to enter into the mortgage.

The mortgage is executed by the borrower at the real estate closing, and delivered to the lender. The language in the mortgage document basically parallels that contained in the Mortgage Note, as more fully set forth below.

A sample Plain Language Mortgage can be found in Appendix 1 of this Almanac.

Since most lenders require that the mortgage be recorded to perfect their lien and to protect their interest from subsequent creditors and purchasers, it should also be acknowledged, i.e., signed before a notary public. The mortgage is then usually recorded expeditiously, following its execution, by filing it in the office of land records in the county where the property is located, along with the required filing fee.

When the mortgage debt has been paid in full, the lender executes a "release of lien," also generally known as a release deed, satisfaction or discharge of a mortgage debt, depending on the jurisdiction. The release of lien is filed in the office of land records so that the existing mortgage lien of record may be removed.

As discussed below, mortgages usually fall under the categories of conventional mortgages or government mortgages.

Conventional Mortgages

A conventional mortgage is one that is made directly by the lender to the buyer with very few regulations or restrictions. Following are commonly used conventional mortgage devices.

Purchase Money Mortgage

Where a lender finances a borrower's acquisition of mortgaged real estate, the mortgage is known as a purchase-money mortgage. Although traditionally, a purchase-money mortgage referred to a mortgage taken by the seller of the real estate as security for the loan, a mortgage given by a third party lending institution is now also generally considered to be a purchase-money mortgage.

Sellers often used purchase money mortgages to finance the sale without involving a financial institution in order to reduce federal income taxes. Thus if part of the purchase price is received in future years, the seller can treat the transaction as an installment sale and count as income only that portion of the profit represented by the year's payments. This device defers the tax due and may place the seller in a lower tax bracket by reducing income received in any one year.

During times of tight mortgage markets, sellers are often compelled to agree to finance the transaction in order to sell the property. If mortgage funds are not easily available or are only available at very high interest rates, buyers will seek alternate sources of funds. Sellers who are financially able to carry a purchase-money mortgage make their properties more attractive by providing this alternative source of financing.

When the transaction involves vacant, unimproved land—known as "raw" land—a purchase-money mortgage frequently contains a subordination clause to allow the purchaser to obtain a first mortgage loan to finance the building of improvements on the property. In that case, the purchase-money mortgage becomes a "junior" mortgage, which is more fully discussed below.

Non-Purchase Money Mortgage

If the lender lends money on real estate already owned by the borrower, the mortgage is known as a non-purchase money mortgage. A common example of a non-purchase-money mortgage is a second mortgage that a long-time homeowner gives to a lending institution on his or her home to secure a loan.

Deed of Trust

A deed of trust is generally defined as a mortgage with a "power of sale" provision. In some states, the deed of trust is considered a mortgage, and in other states it is considered to be "in the nature" of a mortgage. The deed of trust is a three-party instrument among a grantor (borrower); a trustee; and a beneficiary (lender). The appointed trustee is the individual or entity to whom the conveyance of real property is made as security for the loan. The trustee may be the lender's agent, although an impartial third party is preferable and often required.

The difference between a conventional mortgage and a deed of trust lies in the manner in which the lender can enforce the provisions of the deed should the borrower default in payment of the loan. The deed of trust permits the trustee, at the request of the beneficiary/lender, to foreclose on the property by power of sale—i.e., a sale which takes place generally without court supervision. Thus a deed of trust instrument must contain an appointed trustee, a trust clause, and a power of sale clause.

If the deed of trust is used as a mortgage, it normally contains a defeasance clause that renders the deed of trust void upon payment of the debt. However, because the title record still needs to be cleared of the lien, the beneficiary/lender usually executes a release of lien.

If the deed of trust is used "in the nature" of a mortgage, upon full payment of the note, the trustee generally executes a "deed of reconveyance," or "release deed," which reconveys whatever title the trustee may have had back to the grantor/borrower.

Junior Mortgage

Because a mortgage represents a security interest in land, a borrower is free to mortgage his property to as many lenders as are willing to make the loans. The placing of a second, third or even fourth mortgage on property is called "secondary financing." Such secondary and subsequent mortgages are categorized as junior mortgages.

Lenders enter into these junior mortgages only if the borrower has enough "equity" in the property. The borrower's equity is the difference between the current market value of the property and the total debt obligations against the property, including any prior mortgage loans.

A junior mortgage involves a relatively high risk because the secondary lender's security interest extends only to the value of the property in excess of prior liens. Therefore, lenders generally make junior mortgage loans for a shorter term and at a higher interest rate than first mortgage loans.

Home equity financing is discussed more fully in Chapter 3, "Home Equity Financing," of this Almanac.

Government Mortgages

Unlike conventional mortgages, government mortgages may contain strict restrictions on the mortgage terms and conditions. The most commonly sought government mortgages include the Federal Housing Administration (FHA) mortgages, which are insured, and the Veterans Administration (VA) mortgages, which are guaranteed.

FHA Mortgage

Under an FHA mortgage, the FHA insures the loan, which is actually made by a private lender. This is an incentive for the lender to make the loan, particularly since FHA mortgages call for much lower down payments, e.g., 95 to 97% loan to value financing. The FHA retains certain controls over approval of the mortgage. For example, the FHA makes its own appraisal of the property to make sure it meets their minimum standards. The FHA also places maximum limits on the mortgage amounts.

VA Mortgage

Under the VA mortgage program, lenders are refunded the full amount of the guaranteed portion of the loan if the veteran defaults. The VA also requires its own appraisal of the property prior to the loan being made.

Secondary Market Mortgage

The government has also created a secondary mortgage market in which they buy first mortgages from various lenders. This frees the lender's finances so that they can make additional loans, and serves the public interest, particularly when the economic climate is not good.

The most common secondary market purchasers are the Federal National Mortgage Association (FNMA), commonly known as "Fannie Mae;" the Government National Mortgage Association (GNMA), commonly known as "Ginnie Mae;" and the Federal Home Loan Mortgage Corporation (FHLMC), commonly known as "Freddie Mac." Each particular purchaser has their own rules and requirements concerning the mortgages they are willing to buy.

THE REAL ESTATE LIEN

As discussed above, the mortgage is represented as a "real estate lien" on the property in which the lender has a security interest. A lien is basically defined as a charge or encumbrance on property for the satisfaction of a debt or other obligation. In the case of real property, liens generally occur in one of the following ways:

1. A lien may arise by an agreement between the owner and other parties. Thus an owner may agree to place a lien on real property in order to obtain mortgage financing to purchase the property. This is typically the manner in which real property is purchased.

2. A lien may arise when a contractor does work on the property. This is known as a "mechanic's lien."

3. A lien may also result due to unpaid obligations of the property owner, as follows:

(a) The law usually permits a judgment creditor to file their judgment in the land records so that it becomes a lien on the debtor's real property, even though the debt is unrelated to the property. The judgment creditor may then collect the debt by either foreclosing on the lien, thus forcing a sale, or waiting until the debtor wishes to sell the property at which time all liens and encumbrances must be satisfied in order to give a clear title to the new owner.

(b) Unpaid property taxes may become a lien on the property.

(c) Unpaid federal and state taxes, such as income tax, sales taxes, and the like, may also become a lien on the taxpayer's real property if the taxing authorities undertake certain procedures.

(d) Depending upon state law, unpaid child support may be a lien on real property.

(e) The court in a matrimonial case may award one spouse ownership of the marital home, but grant the other spouse a lien on the property to the extent of the spouse's interest in the property at the time of the divorce.

If the debtor sells the property without satisfying a lien, the lien is not discharged and may still be satisfied by a sale of the property, even after it has been sold to a new owner. Thus in practice, a purchaser will generally not buy property that is encumbered by liens.

Further, a bank or other mortgage lender will generally not provide mortgage financing until all liens on the property have been removed.

THE MORTGAGE NOTE

The mortgage note—also known as a "real estate lien note" or "promissory note" depending on the jurisdiction—is the legal document that represents the borrower's actual "promise" to repay the loan at a specified interest rate over a stated time period.

The mortgage is the document that evidences a lien interest against the real estate. Thus both instruments serve entirely different functions, but are dependent on each other to: (1) effect a sufficient promise to pay; and (2) perfect a lien interest in real estate.

The borrower is required to execute a mortgage note in addition to the mortgage because the mortgage note, unlike the mortgage, is considered a "negotiable instrument"—i.e., a document that has cash value and can be sold. Thus the mortgage note, like a bank draft, can be endorsed on the back and sold to an investor.

In fact, it is a very common practice in the mortgage business for mortgage companies to sell millions of dollars in loans using the mortgage note as the primary instrument of transfer. The purchaser of the mortgage note (the "mortgage note holder") becomes what is known as a "holder in due course." This means the purchaser takes the mortgage note free and clear of all defenses that the maker of the mortgage note (the borrower) may have, except for fraud in the inducement of the mortgage note. This strengthens the guarantee that all payments will be made on the mortgage note.

Legally, because a mortgage note is a negotiable instrument, it is considered to be an unconditional promise to pay by the maker of the mortgage note (the borrower). Although a mortgage note holder may accept late payments, the general rule is that the mortgage note holder has the absolute right to accelerate all the payments—i.e., declare the total amount of the mortgage note due when a payment is late.

The mortgage note holder also has the right to foreclose on the property that secures the payment of the mortgage note. This is so even if the underlying mortgage was not assigned to the new mortgage note holder, because the right to foreclose under the underlying mortgage also passes to the new mortgage note holder upon purchase of the mortgage note.

Provisions

Every mortgage note will include the following provisions:

1. The borrower's promise to pay the mortgage payments;

2. The principal—i.e., the amount of the debt;

3. The interest rate charged on the outstanding principal;

4. The time and amount of principal and interest payments;

5. A reference to the mortgage note's security; and

6. The borrower's signature.

The following clauses are not essential to the creation of the mortgage note but may be inserted for business reasons:

1. A provision that overdue principal and interest shall also earn interest at a specified rate.

2. The penalty charge for prepayment of the debt, if applicable. The lender may seek a prepayment penalty to assure an acceptable rate of return on the loan.

3. Whether prepayments will be credited against the principal or against future interest or payments.

4. Default provisions, such as an acceleration clause. An acceleration clause permits the lender to initiate only one lawsuit to collect the entire debt rather than being forced to sue in separate lawsuits for the amount due under each successive delinquent mortgage payment.

5. A requirement that the borrower pay any legal fees necessitated by the borrower's default.

6. A provision waiving any legal requirement that a borrower must be given notice when each successive payment becomes due since this information is contained in the borrower's copy of the mortgage note.

A sample Mortgage Note can be found in Appendix 2 of this Almanac.

COMMON MORTGAGE CLAUSES

Late Payment Clause

To assist the lender in receiving timely payments and to avoid the problems of collecting payments after the agreed upon mortgage payment deadlines pass, late payment clauses are usually included in mortgage documents, promissory notes, or both. Late payment clauses enable the lender to charge a late fee for payments received a certain number of days after the due date.

The purpose of the late payment fee is to cover the bookkeeping expenses of having to post late payments. Late payment fees are legal in all types of loans. A typical late payment clause provides as follows:

If any payment due is received later than [#] days after the due date of the payment, a late charge of [xx%] percent of the amount then overdue may be charged by the lender for the purpose of defraying costs of collection and posting of the account.

Prepayment Penalty Clause

The lender has the right to earn the interest on the money invested and loaned to the borrower for the term of the mortgage. Thus unless the note or the mortgage specifically permits prepayment, the borrower has no right to prepay the amount due on the loan in advance of the mortgage term.

If the lender does not permit the borrower to make prepayments, the note or mortgage will generally contain a clause that requires the borrower to pay a penalty in order to prepay the amount due on the loan. Such a penalty is justified on the grounds that prepayment makes it necessary for the lender to find a new investment outlet and to incur the expenses associated with finding and making that reinvestment.

The prepayment penalty may apply to the entire period of the loan or may be applicable only during the first 5 to 10 years of the mortgage. A typical prepayment penalty clause provides as follows:

In the event of default hereunder, or in the event that said borrower desires by reason of sale or otherwise to prepay the total amount due and owing at the time of any of the above described prepayments, the lender shall have the right to assess and collect a premium of [xx%] percent of the then principal balance. The right of the lender to assess and collect such premium shall continue for a period of 10 years from the time the amortization of the above-described indebtedness begins.

The prepayment penalty clause is generally recognized as valid in all states. However, it should be noted that certain types of government insured loans prohibit prepayment penalties. Further, if loans are sold or transferred to certain government corporations, the loan arrangement cannot include a prepayment penalty. Interest is a charge paid by the borrower to the lender for the use of the lender's money. A lender will charge a borrower a certain percentage of the principal as interest for each year the debt is outstanding. The amount of interest due on any one installment payment date is generally calculated by computing the total yearly interest based on the unpaid balance and dividing that figure by the number of payments made each year.

Mortgage Interest

Mortgage interest is customarily due and charged at the end of each payment period, e.g., monthly or quarterly, etc. This is known as "payment in arrears." Since mortgage loan payments are generally made on a monthly basis, the interest portion of each payment covers the charge for using the borrowed money during the previous month. Some lenders specify in the mortgage note that interest is charged in advance, however, for practical purposes, the distinction only matters when and if the property is sold before the debt is repaid.

Due-On-Sale Clause

A "due-on-sale" clause, also known as a "call" clause, provides that the borrower may not convey the property to another party without first paying off the note or renegotiating the interest rate. The due-on-sale clause gives the lender the right to "call" the entire balance of an indebtedness due and payable if the borrower sells the mortgaged property.

Due-on-sale clauses may eliminate an important incentive for buyers to purchase mortgaged property, particularly when the interest rate on the current mortgage is substantially lower than that available on new mortgage loans.

On the other hand, due-on-sale clauses protect lenders by giving them an opportunity to make a new loan on terms that are more favorable to them. The following is a typical due-on-sale clause:

TRANSFER OF THE PROPERTY; ASSUMPTION: If all or any part of the property or an interest therein is sold or transferred by Borrower without Lender's prior consent, excluding: (a) the creation of a lien or encumbrance subordinate to this deed of trust; (b) the creation of a purchase money security interest for household appliances; (c) transfer by devise, descent, or by operation of law upon the death of a joint tenant; or (d) the grant of any leasehold interest of three years or less not containing an option to purchase, the Lender may, at the Lender's option, declare all sums secured by this Deed of Trust to be immediately due and payable. Lender shall have waived such option to accelerate if, prior to the sale or transfer, Lender and the person to whom the property is to be sold or transferred reach agreement in writing that the credit of such person is satisfactory to Lender and that the interest payable on the sums secured by this Deed of Trust shall be at such rate as the Lender shall request. If Lender has waived the option to accelerate provided in this paragraph, and if the Borrower's successor in interest has executed a written assumption agreement accepted by Lender, Lender shall release Borrower from all obligations under this Deed of Trust and Note. If Lender exercises the option to accelerate, Lender shall mail Borrower notice of such acceleration at least 30 days prior to the time Lender will declare such sums due and payable.

Due-on-sale clauses are viewed very differently by lenders and borrowers. In inflationary times, lenders view due-on-sale clauses as necessary for their economic security. At the same time, borrowers see due-on-sale clauses as unfair, as an unreasonable restraint on title transfer opportunities, and as an attempt to "gouge" the public for purely economic reasons.

This basic difference of opinion between lenders and borrowers has resulted in extensive litigation. Some states tend to favor automatic enforcement of the "due-on-sale" clause, while others tend not to approve this clause unless a mortgage assumption results in a material detriment to the security interest. However, all states tend to look for equitable and just results when the case merits it. There are so many exceptions and extreme fact situations that many of the due-on-sale litigations are determined on a case-by-case basis.

TRANSFER OF THE BORROWER'S INTEREST

The fact that the lender has a security interest in the property does not preclude the owner from selling the property. A mortgage provision attempting to prevent a sale is void as an illegal restraint on alienation.

Nevertheless, the mortgage amount must be satisfied as a condition of the sale. Thus the proceeds of the sale are used to satisfy the outstanding mortgage and any other liens against the property before the owner receives any money.

However, in the following situations, the owner may sell the property without satisfying the mortgage, unless the "due on sale" clause precludes such arrangements.

Sale Subject To Existing Mortgage

When property is sold "subject to" an existing mortgage, the buyer does not become personally obligated to pay off the mortgage but merely has the option of paying off the mortgage if he or she chooses to do so. The seller remains primarily liable on the note and the buyer has no obligation at all to the original lender. This represents a type of non-recourse financing because it does not personally obligate the buyer to pay the existing mortgage.

In the "subject to" transaction, there is some uncertainty as to whether the sale requires the approval of the lender before it can take place. This is because the lender's security is not impaired insofar as the seller remains primarily liable on the mortgage note.

Assumption of Mortgage Debt

In the above scenario, the buyer is not "personally" liable for the mortgage debt because the buyer was not a party to the original mortgage. However, the buyer can still lose the property in a foreclosure sale if the seller defaults on the mortgage payments.

However, if the buyer expressly "assumes" the existing mortgage debt, with the permission of the lender, the buyer also becomes liable for the debt. In this case, the lender may collect the outstanding mortgage debt from either the seller or the buyer.

Substitution

The seller is not relieved from its obligation under the mortgage unless the lender expressly agrees to "substitute" the buyer for the seller. However, because substitution lessens the lender's remedies should there be a default, it is not commonly done.

LENDER'S INTEREST: THEORIES OF TITLE AND POSSESSION

There has been much uncertainty regarding the nature of the lender's interest in the mortgaged property. As discussed below, three "theories" of mortgage law exist today in the United States that address the issue of possession.

Title Theory

The title theory has its roots in the English common law. Under this theory, legal "title" and the right to possession is always to the lender until the mortgage has been satisfied or foreclosed. However, those jurisdictions that still adhere to the common law "title" theory consider the lender's "title" as simply that of holding a security interest.

Intermediate Theory

According to the intermediate theory, the mortgage does not convey title to the lender but instead creates a security interest. The intermediate theory gives the right to possession to the borrower, at least until default, and, generally to the lender after default.

Lien Theory

The majority of states subscribe to the lien theory, which provides that the mortgage does not convey legal title to the lender, but gives the lender a lien on the property. The borrower generally retains the right to possession until a foreclosure.

CHAPTER 2:
THE MORTGAGE LOAN PROCESS

ACCEPTED OFFER

The process of purchasing a home and obtaining financing for that purchase begins when the buyer makes an offer on the property, and the seller accepts the offer. Following acceptance of the offer, a memorandum of agreement is usually prepared, which sets forth the basic details of the transaction, and identifies the brokers, the parties, and their respective attorneys.

In some jurisdictions, a binder—payment of a small sum of money that evidences the buyer's good faith—is made. However, the legal enforceability of the binder as a contract is questionable, thus it should not be depended upon in order to secure the deal.

THE REAL ESTATE CONTRACT

The next step in the real estate transaction involves drafting the real estate contract, which is generally done by the seller's attorney. The contracts are then sent to the buyer's attorney for review and signature, and returned to the seller's attorney with the buyer's down payment, which is held in escrow until closing.

The real estate contract, to be valid, must contain all of the essential terms of a legal contract, including an offer; acceptance of the offer; and consideration, i.e., an exchange of something of value by each of the parties. Further, the parties to the contract must be legally competent, must have voluntarily entered into the contract, and the contract must be for a legal purpose which is possible to perform.

The contract must also comply with the statute of frauds. The statute of frauds is a legal doctrine that provides, in part, that all contracts for the sale and purchase of real estate are required to be in writing. Further, the writing must be signed by the parties.

Although property can be legally conveyed without a real estate contract, it is the contract that creates the legal obligation between the parties to perform as agreed. For example, without the contract, one of the parties could simply renege on the deal, and the other party would not have any legal recourse. The contract provides specific remedies in case one of the parties defaults, such as forfeiture of the down payment to the seller, or money damages to the buyer.

Because land is considered unique, and money damages may not be a sufficient remedy to the buyer, the doctrine of specific performance may apply. If the buyer sues for specific performance—i.e., to force the seller to perform under the contract—the judge may compel the seller to turn the property over to the buyer as agreed.

The contract also sets forth the financing contingencies of the buyer, which basically permit the buyer to get out of the contract if he or she is unable to secure the type of financing set forth in the contract.

For example, the contract may specify a mortgage contingency of 90% financing of the purchase price. If the buyer is unable to qualify for a loan on those terms, but the lender agrees to finance 80%, the buyer has the option of going forward with the lesser financing, or of invoking the mortgage contingency clause to get out of the contract without losing the down payment.

However, if the buyer qualifies for the 90% loan, he or she must go forward with the purchase, or risk forfeiting the down payment to the seller for damages.

The contract may also provide remedies if a physical inspection of the property reveals any problems, such as termite infestation or structural damage. Such remedies may include a purchase price reduction, or a requirement that the necessary repairs be made as a condition to closing.

SELECTING A LENDER

Although you may purchase a home on an all cash basis, it is more likely you will need to obtain a mortgage to finance a large part of the purchase price through a real estate lender. Home loans are available from several types of lenders including, savings and loan institutions (thrift institutions); commercial banks, mortgage companies, and credit unions. In addition, anyone, including a private individual, may make a mortgage loan.

Compare Costs

Shopping around for a home loan or mortgage will help you to get the best financing deal. You should compare all of the costs involved in obtaining a mortgage. Different lenders may quote different prices, so it is advisable to contact several lenders to make sure you are getting the best price. You should take a checklist detailing the terms you want to compare.

A mortgage checklist can be found in Appendix 3 of this Almanac.

Prior to selecting a lender, you should check the real estate or business sections in the newspaper for information on current interest rates, and to undertake some comparative shopping. One should call several lenders for rates and terms based on the type of mortgage sought.

Mortgage Brokers

You can also obtain a home loan through a mortgage broker. Brokers arrange transactions rather than lending money directly, so they will find a lender for you. A broker's access to several lenders can mean a wider selection of loan products and terms from which you can choose.

Brokers are usually paid a fee for their services that may be separate from and in addition to the lender's origination or other fees. You should ask each broker you consult how he or she will be compensated so that you can compare the different fees.

Ask Questions

You must ask questions. Knowing just the amount of the monthly payment or the interest rate is not enough. Ask for information about the same loan amount, loan term, and type of loan so that you can compare the information among lenders.

For example, if you are looking for an adjustable rate mortgage (ARM), as discussed below, it is important to inquire about the maximum interest rate that can be charged during the life of the loan, how often the rate can change, and the index used to determine the rate change.

The following information is important to obtain from each lender:

Interest Rates

Ask each lender and broker for a list of its current mortgage interest rates and whether the rates being quoted are the lowest for that day or week. Also, ask whether the rate is fixed or adjustable, as discussed below. If the rate is adjustable, ask how the rate and loan payment will vary, including whether the loan payment will be reduced when the rates go down.

Ask about the loan's annual percentage rate (APR). The APR takes into account not only the interest rate but also points, broker fees, and certain other credit charges that you may be required to pay, expressed as a yearly rate.

Points

Points are fees paid to the lender or broker for the loan and are often linked to the interest rate—the more points you pay, the lower the interest rate. Ask for the points to be quoted as a dollar amount rather than just as the number of points so that you will actually know how much you will have to pay.

Fees

A home loan often involves many fees. Every lender or broker should be able to give you an estimate of its fees. Many of these fees are negotiable. Some fees are paid when you apply for a loan, such as application and appraisal fees, and other fees are paid at closing.

In some cases, you can borrow the money needed to pay these fees, but doing so will increase your loan amount and total costs. Ask for an explanation of any fee you do not understand.

Down Payments

Some lenders require 20% of the home's purchase price as a down payment. However, many lenders now offer loans that require less than 20% down—sometimes as little as 5% on conventional loans. Government-assisted programs such as FHA and VA, have substantially smaller down payment requirements.

Private Mortgage Insurance

If a 20% down payment is not made, lenders usually require the home buyer to purchase private mortgage insurance (PMI) to protect the lender in case the home buyer fails to pay.

If PMI is required for your loan: (1) Ask what the total cost of the insurance will be; (2) Ask how much your monthly payment will be when including the PMI premium; and (3) Ask how long you will be required to carry PMI.

Confirm Costs

Ask the lender or broker to write down all the costs associated with the loan. Then ask if the lender or broker will waive or reduce one or more of its fees or agree to a lower rate or fewer points. Make sure that the lender or broker is not agreeing to lower one fee while raising another.

Ask each lender for a complete list of closing costs and inquire as to which costs will be refunded to you if the loan application is not approved.

A list of the buyer's estimated closing costs can be found in Appendix 4 of this Almanac.

Some mortgage lenders may try to charge some borrowers more than others for the same loan product offered at the same time. This may include higher interest rates or origination fees or more points. Ask the lender if the rate you're being quoted is the lowest offered that day. The lender is probably basing the loan offer on the list of mortgage rates frequently issued by that institution to its loan officers. Ask to see this list.

If the lender refuses and you suspect you are not being offered the lowest rates or points available, you may want to negotiate for better terms or shop for another lender. Even if you decide to accept terms that are not the lowest available, ask the lender why you did not qualify for better terms. The answer may help you to correct errors and to become more creditworthy.

The Mortgage Buyer's Rights

According to the U.S. Department of Housing and Urban Development (HUD), you should be aware of the following rights you have when you apply for a home mortgage loan:

1. You have the RIGHT to shop for the best loan for you and compare the charges of different mortgage brokers and lenders.

2. You have the RIGHT to be informed about the total cost of your loan including the interest rate, points and other fees.

3. You have the RIGHT to ask for a Good Faith Estimate of all loan and settlement charges before you agree to the loan and pay any fees.

4. You have the RIGHT to know what fees are not refundable if you decide to cancel the loan agreement.

5. You have the RIGHT to ask your mortgage broker to explain exactly what the mortgage broker will do for you.

6. You have the RIGHT to know how much the mortgage broker is getting paid by you and the lender for your loan.

7. You have the RIGHT to ask questions about charges and loan terms that you do not understand.

8. You have the RIGHT to a credit decision that is not based on your race, color, religion, national origin, sex, marital status, age, or whether any income is from public assistance.

9. You have the RIGHT to know the reason if your loan was turned down.

PREDATORY LENDING

When shopping for a mortgage loan, be advised that all lenders are not trustworthy. For example, certain lenders target vulnerable homeowners, such as elderly homeowners and those who have low incomes or credit problems. These predatory lenders deceive their victims about the loan terms, and give them loans the lender knows they cannot repay. Their goal is to take your money and, ultimately, your home.

Be very wary of lenders who advise you to falsify the information on your loan application, or who pressure you to apply for a larger loan then needed. Never sign a blank form, and make sure that the terms you are promised are the same terms on the documents you are asked to sign.

If you are having financial problems and need to obtain a mortgage loan, before signing onto a bad loan, you should speak with someone who you trust, and who is knowledgeable about real estate and show them the loan terms that are being offered to you. If you absolutely need to obtain a mortgage loan, go to several lenders of different types, such as a bank, a savings and loan, and a credit union, and compare their terms.

False Advertising

According to the Federal Trade Commission, when you are shopping for a mortgage loan, you should be aware of the many false and deceptive ads, and the "buzz words" that should alert you to ask follow-up questions, as follows:

"Low Fixed Rate"

These ads do not tell you how long the rate will be "fixed." The rate may be fixed for an introductory period only, and that can be as short as 30 days. When you shop for a mortgage, you need to know when and how your rate, and payments, can change.

"Very Low Rates"

These ads do not tell you whether they are referring to the payment rate or the interest rate. The interest rate is the rate used to calculate the amount of interest you will owe the lender each month. The payment rate is the rate used to calculate the amount of the payment you are obligated to make each month. If the payment rate is less than the interest rate, you won't be covering the interest due. This is called "negative amortization."

Negative amortization means that your loan balance is actually increasing because you are not paying all of the interest that comes due, and the lender is adding the unpaid interest to the balance you owe. In addition, some offers advertise a low rate without telling you that it applies only during an introductory period, after which your rate may increase substantially.

"Very Low Payments"

These ads are deceiving because they don't explain how they can offer such low payments. For example, the offer might be for an "interest only" loan, where you pay only the amount of interest accrued each month. It does not tell you that you will eventually have to pay the principal. You may end up owing a large "balloon" payment—a lump sum due at the end of the loan. If you can't pay the balloon payment, and are unable to refinance with another lender, you could lose your home. In addition, some offers advertise a low payment without telling you that it applies only during an introductory period, after which your payment may increase substantially.

"Important Notice From Your Mortgage Company"

Watch out for notices that appear to be coming from your lender because they may be sent by other companies that want your business. Before you respond to any offer, review it carefully to make sure you know which company you are dealing with.

"Exclusive Rate Reduction Program"

Some businesses use official looking stamps, envelopes and forms that make you think they are an offer from a government agency or program. They make claims that are somehow "licensed" mortgages, and may even mention a government agency in the mailing. If you're concerned about a mailing you've received, contact the government agency mentioned in the letter.

Usury Violations

Usury refers to the maximum amount of interest a lender is legally entitled to receive under a state's statute. In general, the following three elements must be present for usury to exist: (1) a loan or forbearance; (2) excessive interest; and (3) wrongful intent.

State Exemptions

Because state usury statutes vary in their provisions, the reader is advised to check their own state's statute in this regard. Recent market increases in interest rates have caused many states to consider raising or even eliminating their usury rates, and many states have provided for statutory exemptions.

Exempt transactions are extremely important because, like interest rates, they impact directly on the flow of funds among the states. For example, if residential loans are exempt from usury penalties, and the major local demand for funds is for residential purchase and construction, a 6% usury rate would probably cause large amounts of funds to flow out of the community to other states.

Federal Exemption

In 1980, federal laws were passed which declared that the constitutional laws of any state expressly limiting the rate or amount of interest shall not apply to any loan which is: (1) secured by a first lien on residential property, or by a first lien on stock in residential cooperative housing corporations, or by a first lien on residential manufactured home; (2) made after March 31, 1980; and (3) described in Section 527(b) of the National Housing Act, where an owner finances the sale or exchange of residential real property which the owner has occupied as his principal residence.

Seller Exemption

Many states exempt a seller who takes back a purchase money mortgage from the buyer under the assumption that both parties to the transaction enter into the agreement from equal bargaining positions.

Penalties

Depending on the jurisdiction, a lender who charges usurious interest rates may have to forfeit all of the interest, or that part of the interest in excess of the legal rate. Some jurisdictions further penalize the lender by taking away the lender's right to recover all or a percentage of the principal on the loan.

THE MORTGAGE APPLICATION

Once you have selected your lender, your next step is to complete the loan application.

A sample Uniform Residential Loan Application can be found in Appendix 5 of this Almanac.

In order to process the loan application, the loan officer will generally require a copy of the memorandum of agreement or real estate contract. The loan officer may also request a personal financial statement and a request for verification of your employment and banking information. In general, you will be required to pay a loan application fee which may cover, among other things, the cost of an appraisal of the property, and the lender's cost in obtaining a copy of your credit report.

Under federal law, lenders are required to notify an applicant of the action taken on their loan application within thirty days. If the application is denied, the lender must inform the applicant of the reasons for the rejection.

Financial Statement

In reviewing the loan application, the lender will consider a number of factors in deciding whether to approve the loan. The most important criteria are your credit worthiness and financial ability to make the loan payments.

For example, the lender will review your past record of loan repayment, net worth and current earning capacity. This information is obtained partly from the financial statement you prepare, and partly from other sources such as credit bureaus, independent credit references, and additional sources you provide.

A sample Borrower's Financial Statement can be found in Appendix 6 of this Almanac.

In determining whether you are financially able to make the loan payments, the lender will also consider your housing expense ratio. The two elements that make up a housing expense ratio are: (1) the monthly out-of-pocket costs for continued ownership of a home; and (2) the monthly income generated by the prospective borrower. Many lenders require that the monthly housing payment be no greater than 25% to 35% of a borrower's monthly income.

Appraisal

The lender will also carefully review the property appraisal report to determine the value of the property. The appraised value of the property generally determines how much the lender will be willing to finance. Most conventional lenders will finance up to 80% of the appraised value of the property.

A sample Uniform Residential Appraisal Report can be found in Appendix 7 of this Almanac.

LOCK-IN RATES

"Locking in" one's rate or points at the time of application or during the processing of the loan will keep the rate and/or points from changing until settlement or closing of the escrow process. You should ask the lender if they charge a fee to lock-in the rate and, if so, whether the fee reduces the amount you must pay for points. In addition, it is important to find out how long the "lock-in" rate is effective, what happens if it expires, and whether the lock-in fee is refundable if the loan application is rejected.

LOAN COMMITMENT

A loan commitment is a promise by a lender to make a loan at some future date. The loan commitment's terms and conditions for a single family residential purchaser might be as brief as those contained in the following letter:

Dear Borrower:

We hereby commit to make you a mortgage loan on the property located at [address of property]. Said loan shall be in the amount of [$ amount of loan] amortized over a term of [#] years at an interest rate of [xx%] percent, subject to the terms of the interest adjustment provision in the mortgage note, and shall be closed on our Association's documents and governed by the provisions contained therein.

This commitment is also granted subject to satisfactory evidence of title and other related items required for the closing of this transaction and there being no substantial change in the collateral or in your credit status.

This commitment will expire if: (a) the loan to be granted under the terms of this commitment is not closed for any reason whatsoever, within [#] days of the date of this letter, or (b) the loan to be granted under this commitment is closed whereby the terms and conditions of the mortgage and the mortgage note will supersede this commitment.

Thank you for the opportunity of permitting us to be of service to you.

Signed, Lender.

Generally, a lender who does not provide a loan as promised in their commitment letter will be required to pay damages to the borrower to the extent of (1) the difference between the interest at the contract rate and the rate of interest the borrower must pay on the open market; (2) any of the costs of obtaining new financing; and (3) any other consequential damages contemplated by the parties at the time of the loan commitment.

In connection with the commitment letter, the lender will generally require you to pay a "commitment fee." The commitment fee is supposed to compensate the lender for the administrative costs of underwriting the loan and holding the funds available for your use. If you pay a commitment fee that is termed "non-refundable," and you obtain financing elsewhere, the lender may be entitled to keep the commitment fee as damages for breach of contract or compensation for holding the loan money for you.

TYPES OF MORTGAGE LOANS

Fixed Rate Amortized Mortgage

The most common mortgage loan is the fixed rate amortized mortgage. Under a fixed rate amortized mortgage, the loan amount generally bears interest at a fixed percentage rate per year. This means that the rate does not change and thus there is a set monthly payment over the entire term of the loan, e.g., 30 years. Each monthly payment consists of both principal and interest.

In the early years of the loan, the interest is usually the larger share of the payment. As the loan term comes to a close, the principal payment makes up the larger share of the payment. At the end of the loan period, the entire principal and interest debt is repaid.

A mortgage payment estimation chart can be found in Appendix 8 of this Almanac.

During the Great Depression, new programs such as FHA mortgage insurance led to widespread use of the long-term fixed interest rate mortgage, which has been the standard for more than six decades. Nevertheless, an extended maturity is not completely to the borrower's advantage. The longer a loan term is, the longer it takes for equity to build, which inevitably translates into larger total interest charges.

In fact, many state statutes have, until recently, limited the maximum loan amortization period to 30 years. Despite this, there is a trend to increase the maximum permissible term to 35 and even 40 years.

Adjustable Rate Mortgage

Many people seek to lock in low interest rates with a fixed rate mortgage. However, in years when inflation is high, a low interest fixed rate mortgage provides the lender with less of a yield than anticipated on the loan. Over the years, lenders became increasingly dissatisfied with the diminished returns on fixed rate mortgages. This led to the development of alternative mortgage instruments, such as the adjustable rate mortgage (ARM).

An adjustable rate mortgage, also known as a variable rate mortgage, does not have a fixed payment. The interest rate under an ARM is subject to periodic adjustment up or down at various intervals during the loan term—e.g., every 1, 3 or 5 years. The interest rate is gauged by the movement of a specified standard at the time of adjustment, such as the existing prime rate.

A variable rate mortgage may provide for balloon payments. This means that, although the loan is amortized over a longer period of time, e.g., thirty years, for the purpose of calculating a monthly payment, the loan actually becomes due and payable after a shorter period of time, such as five years, at which time the balloon payment—the entire indebtedness—must be paid.

If the ARM's interest rate increases are added to the principal of the loan, the principal balance of the loan may increase instead of decrease, depending on the rate of increase. This is known as negative amortization. More commonly, the interest rate increase extends the maturity of the loan, or is reflected in increased monthly payments.

Despite its common use in England, Canada and many other countries, the adjustable rate mortgage was not widely available in the United States until 1979, when the Federal Home Loan Bank Board (FHLBB) authorized federally chartered savings and loan associations to issue ARMs. Nevertheless, the FHLBB also required the Savings and Loan Institutions (S&Ls) to continue to offer fixed-rate mortgages, which consumers preferred.

In 1980, the FHLBB authorized the S&Ls to issue renegotiated-rate mortgages (RRM), also known as "rollover" mortgages, and allowed them to stop offering fixed interest rate loans. Under this plan, home loans could be made for a term of thirty years but would "roll over" every three to five years at a renegotiated interest rate.

Although the renegotiated rate mortgage has been used for some time in several jurisdictions—e.g., Wisconsin, Ohio, Florida, Washington and New England—the plan was strongly attacked by consumer groups, while vigorously defended by the savings and loan industry. Nevertheless, periods characterized by volatile shifts in interest rates are likely to see the use of a range of these variable-rate mortgages, such as the renegotiated-rate concept.

Graduated Payment Mortgage

The graduated payment mortgage uses the same interest rate as in a standard fixed rate mortgage, however, the monthly payments start out low and gradually increase until they rise above the level at which the standard mortgage would have been at the stage in the mortgage term. In effect, because the initial payments are not sufficient to amortize the loan, the borrower is borrowing the difference between the payments and the current interest, and paying off these amounts in later years.

The graduated payment mortgage concept is based upon the assumption that a family's income will increase over time and therefore the amount of income available to make payments on a home will also increase. It is particularly attractive to families who are just starting out who may have difficulty making the monthly payments required under a conventional fixed-rate mortgage during the first few years of the loan's life.

The graduated payment mortgage has three positive features:

1. It qualifies more potential homeowners for conventional loans;

2. It qualifies buyers to enter the housing market sooner; and

3. It qualifies buyers to purchase more house and amenities.

Graduated Payment Adjustable Mortgage

A variation of the graduated payment mortgage that includes the concept of variable interest rates is the graduated payment adjustable mortgage. As with the graduated payment mortgage, the initial payments are lower, however, they have the potential to increase substantially. The interest rate is generally adjustable up or down a maximum of one-half of one percentage point a year. Nevertheless, without a maximum on the "overall" increase in the interest rate, the monthly payments can rapidly increase.

For example, a thirty-year $50,000 loan at an initial rate of 13% can have an original payment of $428.09 a month. During the sixth year, with regular maximum interest rate increases, the monthly payment would be $657.46 whereas the payment would be $443.10 for a fixed rate mortgage at 13%.

Such rapid increases may create a difficult financial situation for a borrower whose income has not increased accordingly.

Split Rate Mortgage

The purpose of a split rate mortgage is to make the initial cash requirement to close more affordable for the borrower by financing the loan origination fee, i.e., the discount points. The points are financed by paying a higher rate of interest during the early months of the mortgage loan, e.g., the first 18 months. Thereafter, the principal and interest are adjusted to the initial commitment rate.

Basically, the borrower is paying the discount points on a monthly payment basis over the initial months of the loan rather than at the time of closing. This may be advantageous to a borrower who has little cash reserve insofar as the discount points can represent a significant portion of the closing costs, e.g., 1% to 3% of the amount of the loan.

A sample Split Rate Mortgage Clause can be found in Appendix 9 of this Almanac.

FLIP Mortgage

A FLIP mortgage is another graduated payment mortgage that is designed to reduce the borrower's monthly mortgage payments. The lower monthly payments are accomplished by using the borrower's down payment to fund a pledged savings account. Funds are drawn from the account each month to supplement the mortgage payment.

The pledged account also serves as additional collateral for the lender. The borrower's out-of-pocket monthly mortgage payment is less because the lender takes supplementary monthly payments from the interest-bearing pledged account funded from the borrower's down payment.

This pledged account is deposited with the lender at the time the mortgage is created. Each succeeding year, the monthly supplementary payments are reduced. In response to an individual borrower's requirements and capabilities, the FLIP mortgage takes into consideration the cost of the home, the cash available for down payment, the family income, mortgage terms and potential for income growth.

Shared Appreciation Mortgage

A Shared Appreciate Mortgage is designed to assist first—time home buyers. It has a fixed interest rate set below the prevailing market rate, along with contingent interest based on the appreciation of the property at maturity, or payment in full of the loan on sale or transfer of the property.

It is likely that the shared appreciation mortgage will be used more during periods of inflation or rising interest rates. Because the lower interest rates mean lower monthly payments, some borrowers may be more willing to purchase homes that otherwise would be beyond their reach.

The ability to buy a house that should appreciate in value may outweigh the potential appreciation given up in the form of contingent interest. The less pleasant alternative during tight money markets may be to forego the purchase because of a lack of affordable funds.

The price that must be paid for the reduced rate and payments is that the borrower will share the appreciation with the lender when the house is sold. If the borrower does not sell within ten years of obtaining a shared appreciation mortgage, then the house must either be sold or refinanced at the end of ten years. In either case, the lender collects a percentage, generally up to 40% of the increase in value of the home.

Buy-Down Mortgage

A buy-down mortgage is a loan whereby the borrower pays the lender a substantial amount of money up front in return for a loan at below the current interest rate. The upfront money is used to offset the lender's reduced rate of return on account of the lower interest rate.

Balloon Payment Mortgage

As discussed above, a mortgage is generally amortized over a certain number of years, so that the full amount of the mortgage loan and the interest are paid when the term of the mortgage has expired. For example, after 30 years of a typical residential 30-year mortgage, the borrower will have paid the full amount of the debt and interest due on the mortgage.

When the mortgage contains a "balloon payment" clause, the result will not be the same. Under a mortgage with a balloon payment clause, the borrower is still required to make periodic installment payments, but those payments do not fully amortize the loan. Thus the borrower will be required to pay the lump sum balance of the amount due at the end of the term of the mortgage. This lump sum is called a "balloon payment." Following is a typical balloon payment notice:

THIS IS A BALLOON MORTGAGE NOTE AND THE FINAL PAYMENT OR THE BALANCE DUE UPON MATURITY IS $_____ TOGETHER WITH ACCRUED INTEREST, IF ANY, AND ALL ADVANCEMENTS MADE BY THE MORTGAGEE UNDER THE TERMS OF THE MORTGAGE

Reverse Mortgage

A reverse mortgage loan pays a homeowner monthly cash advances or provides the homeowner with a line of credit by converting the home-owner's equity into cash. A reverse mortgage does not require repayment for as long as the borrower lives in the home. However, because the homeowner is drawing on the value of the home, there will be less equity available for the homeowner or his or her heirs in the future.

Interest rates on a reverse mortgage may be higher and are charged on a compound basis. Application fees, discount points and closing costs may also be higher than other types of loans. Further, interest rates are not tax deductible until the loan is repaid in full.

The three basic types of reverse mortgage are:

Single-Purpose Reverse Mortgages

Single-purpose reverse mortgages are offered by some state and local government agencies and nonprofit organizations. These mortgages generally have very low costs. In most cases, an applicant can qualify for these loans only if their income is low or moderate.

Single-purpose reverse mortgages can only be used for one purpose specified by the government or nonprofit lender. For example, the proceeds may be restricted to payments for home repairs, improvements, or property taxes.

Proprietary Reverse Mortgages

Proprietary reverse mortgages tend to be more costly than other home loans. The up-front costs can be high, so they are generally most expensive if the homeowner stays in the home for just a short time. They are widely available, have no income or medical requirements, and can be used for any purpose.

FHA Reverse Mortgage Program

The FHA Reverse Mortgage Program is available to senior homeowners to convert the equity in their home into a monthly income stream, or a line of credit to be repaid when they no longer occupy the home. The loan is known as Home Equity Conversion Mortgage (HECM). Homeowners who meet the eligibility criteria can complete a reverse mortgage application by contacting a FHA-approved lending institution such as a bank, mortgage company, or savings and loan association.

An FHA reverse mortgage does not require repayment as long as the home is the borrower's principal residence. Lenders recover their principal, plus interest, when the home is sold. If any home equity remains after sale, the remaining value of the home goes to the homeowner, estate or heirs. The owner can never owe more than the home's value.

If the sales proceeds are insufficient to pay the amount owed, HUD will pay the lender the amount of the shortfall. HUD's Federal Housing Administration (FHA) collects an insurance premium from all borrowers to provide this coverage.

Borrower Requirements

In order to qualify for an HECM, the applicant:

1. Must be age 62 years of age or older;

2. Must own the property;

3. Must live in the property as the primary residence; and

4. Must participate in a consumer information session given by a HUD-approved housing counseling agency.

Mortgage Amount

The mortgage amount is based on:

1. The age of the youngest borrower, if more than one;

2. The current interest rate; and

3. The lesser of the appraised value of the FHA insurance limit.

Financial Requirements

1. There are no income or credit qualifications required of the borrower;

2. There is no repayment as long as the property is the borrower's primary residence; and

3. The closing costs may be financed in the mortgage.

Property Requirements

1. The property must be a single family home or a 1–4 unit home with one unit occupied by the borrower; and

2. The property must meet FHA property standards and flood requirements.

Payment Plans

Homeowners can choose from five different payment plans offered by the FHA:

1. Tenure—Equal monthly payments as long as at least one borrower lives and continues to occupy the property as a principal residence.

2. Term—Equal monthly payments for a fixed period of months.

3. Line of Credit—Unscheduled payments or in installments, at times and amounts of borrower's choosing until the line of credit is exhausted;

4. Modified Tenure—Combination of line of credit with monthly payments for as long as the borrower remains in the home;

5. Modified Term—Combination of line of credit with monthly payments for a fixed period of months selected by the borrower.

LOAN SERVICING

Loan servicing refers to collecting your monthly loan payments, crediting your account, and handling your escrow account. Generally, your lender will also be responsible for servicing your mortgage loan. However, your lender may transfer the loan servicing responsibility to another company.

Under the Real Estate Settlement Procedures Act (RESPA), your lender is required to disclose to you, in writing, whether the servicing of your loan may be transferred, and the likelihood that this will occur. This is known as a "servicing transfer," under which the collection of principal, interest and escrow account payments are transferred to another party.

Mortgage loan servicing is discussed more fully in Chapter 7, "The Real Estate Settlement Procedures Act (RESPA)," of this Almanac.

CONSUMER INFORMATION

The following entities are able to provide consumers with more information about the various lenders and the mortgage loan process.

In addition, a Directory of State Banking Agencies can be found in Appendix 10 of this Almanac.

State Banks That Are Members of the Federal Reserve System:

Federal Reserve Consumer Help
PO Box 1200
Minneapolis, MN 55480
Tel: 888-851-1920/877-766-8533 (TTY)
Fax: 877-888-2520
E-mail: ConsumerHelp@FederalReserve.gov/
Website: www.FederalReserveConsumerHelp.gov/

Federally Insured State Non-Member Banks and Savings Banks:

Federal Deposit Insurance Corporation
Consumer Response Center
2345 Grand Boulevard, Suite 100
Kansas City, Missouri 64108
Tel: 877-275-3342
Website: www.fdic.gov/

National Banks and National Bank-Owned Mortgage Companies:

Office of the Comptroller of the Currency
Customer Assistance Group
1301 McKinney Street, Suite 3450

Houston, TX 77010
Tel: 800-613-6743
Website: www.occ.treas.gov/

Federally Insured Savings and Loan Institutions and Federally Chartered Savings Banks:

Office of Thrift Supervision
Consumer Programs
1700 G Street, N.W., 6th Floor
Washington, D.C. 20552
Tel: 800-842-6929
Website: www.ots.treas.gov/

Federal Credit Unions:

National Credit Union Administration
Office of Public and Congressional Affairs
1775 Duke Street
Alexandria, VA 22314
Tel: 703-518-6330
Website: www.ncua.gov/

State-Chartered Credit Unions:

Contact your state's regulatory agency.

Mortgage Companies and Other Lenders:

Federal Trade Commission
Consumer Response Center
600 Pennsylvania Avenue, N.W.
Washington, D.C. 20580
Tel: 877-382-4357 (877-FTC-HELP)
Website: www.ftc.gov/

Other Information Sources for Consumers:

U.S. Department of Justice
Civil Rights Division
950 Pennsylvania Ave., N.W.
Housing and Civil Enforcement Section, NWB
Washington, D.C. 20580
Tel: 202-514-4713
Website: www.usdoj.gov/crt/housing/index.html/

Federal Housing Finance Board
1777 F Street, N.W.
Washington, D.C. 20006
Tel: 202-408-2500
Website: www.fhfb.gov/

Department of Housing and Urban Development
451 7th Street, S.W.
Washington, D.C. 20410
Tel: 800-669-9777/800-927-9275 (TTY)
Website: www.hud.gov/

Office of Federal Housing Enterprise Oversight (OFHEO)
1700 G Street, N.W., 4th Floor
Washington, D.C. 20552
Tel: 202-414-6922
Website: www.ofheo.gov/

CHAPTER 3:
HOME EQUITY FINANCING

IN GENERAL

Many homeowners use the equity in their homes as a source of credit. Generally, the credit is in the form of a home equity loan or line of credit. Collateral is a term that refers to the property that a borrower pledges as security for a loan. With a home equity loan or line of credit, the home is the collateral for the loan. Therefore, if you do not repay the loan, the creditor can foreclose on the loan and you can lose your home.

Equity is the difference between how much your home is worth and the amount of any mortgages you may have on the home. For example, if you have no mortgages, then the equity in the house is equal to what the house is worth. On the other hand, if the home is worth $400,000, and there is an outstanding mortgage in the amount of $300,000, the equity in the home is $100,000.

A home equity loan or line of credit is basically a second mortgage on the home. The lender gives the homeowner a loan or line of credit based on the amount of equity in the home, which is secured by using the property as collateral, just like the first mortgage. If the homeowner sells the home, he or she is responsible for paying off the first mortgage and any outstanding home equity loans or lines of credit.

HOME EQUITY LOAN AND LINE OF CREDIT COMPARED

There are differences between a home equity loan and a home equity line of credit that should be considered before choosing between the two home equity plans.

Home Equity Loan

In general, a home equity loan is a lump sum of money given to the homeowner that he or she repays over a specific period of time. The loan usually has a fixed interest rate and requires set monthly payments, allowing you to budget accordingly. Generally, your payment will include both principal and interest; therefore, you will have paid off the loan completely at the end of the loan term.

A home equity loan is preferable if you need a lump sum of money for a particular purpose, such as a major home improvement or debt consolidation.

Home Equity Line of Credit

Unlike a home equity loan, a home equity line of credit, generally referred to as a HELOC, is a revolving credit line. Like a credit card account, the homeowner can borrow money up to a set credit limit. The homeowner generally accesses the line of credit using checks or credit cards that the lender provides. As the balance is repaid, the homeowner can access the money over and over again.

For example, if you have a $25,000 HELOC, and you borrow $15,000 to pay for a new roof, you will have $10,000 of credit left, which you can use, and you are obligated to repay the $15,000. If you repay $10,000 (in addition to any interest), you will still owe $5,000, and you will have $20,000 in credit available for you to borrow.

Generally, once your home equity line of credit is opened, if you pay as agreed, the lender may not terminate the line of credit, accelerate the payment of any outstanding balance, or change the terms of the account.

A home equity line of credit is preferable if you do not need a lump sum of money all at once, but you may need money periodically. A home equity plan is flexible because you only need to borrow what you need at the time you need it, and you are only incurring interest on the amount of money you use.

AMOUNT OF CREDIT

Depending on a review of your income and credit rating, a lender may allow you to borrow up to 80% of the appraised value of your home, less the amount of your first mortgage.

For example, if the appraised value of your house is $200,000, and you have a first mortgage in the amount of $100,000, a lender may allow you to borrow up to $60,000 (80% of $200,000 equals $160,000 less $100,000 equals $60,000).

INTEREST RATES

It is important to know the difference between the interest rate and the annual percentage rate (APR). The interest rate is the cost of borrowing money expressed as a percentage rate. The APR is often not the same as the interest rate.

You cannot compare the APR of a home equity loan with the APR of a home equity line of credit because they are not calculated the same. The APR for a fixed-term home equity loan takes into account the interest rate plus points and other finance charges, costs and fees, whereas the APR for a home equity line of credit is based on the periodic interest rate and does not include points and other costs and fees.

Variable Rates

Most home equity lines of credit come with variable interest rates, although if you shop around, you may be able to find a fixed rate. The interest rates on a variable rate loan, also referred to as an adjustable rate loan, are adjusted periodically based on changes in a pre-selected financial index. The interest rate on a fixed rate loan does not change during the entire term of the loan.

A variable rate line of credit may offer lower monthly payments at first, but during the rest of the repayment period the payments may change and go higher. A fixed interest rate, if available, may be slightly higher than the variable rate to start, but with a fixed rate loan, your payments do not fluctuate over the life of the credit line.

Therefore, if you are considering a variable rate line of credit, it is important to contact a number of lenders in order to compare the terms and choose the loan that works best for your situation. Inquire whether you will be able to convert the variable rate loan to a fixed rate loan at some point in the future.

Rate Caps

In addition, you should check both the "periodic cap" and the "lifetime cap." The periodic cap is the limit on interest rate changes at one time. The lifetime cap is the limit on interest rate changes throughout the term of the loan. For example, a loan may have a periodic cap that states the interest rate cannot jump more than 2 percentage points in any one year, and a lifetime cap that states the interest rate cannot jump more than 7 percentage points over the term of the loan.

Index and Margin

It is also important to find out the "index" and "margin" used by the lender. The index is the published rate used by lenders that serves as the basis for determining interest rate changes on variable rate loans. The "prime rate" is an example of an index. The margin is the specified percentage the lender adds to the index to determine the interest rate.

For example, if the prime rate is 4% and the margin is 2%, the initial rate is 6%. If the prime rate rises to 4.5%, the interest rate will rise to 6.5% (4.5% prime rate plus the 2% margin equals 6.5%).

It is also important to ask how much and how often the interest rate can change. Depending on the terms of your loan, the interest rate can adjust monthly, every three months, or yearly, etc.

Discounted Rates

You must also be aware of home equity financing that offers a temporarily "discounted" interest rate. This is a rate that is unusually low, and lasts only for an introductory time period, e.g., 3 or 6 months. The payments during the introductory period are low, however, once introductory period ends, the rate and the payments increase, often significantly.

It is important to find out how your rate will be determined at the end of the introductory period, and how much your payments will be at that time, to avoid getting into a loan that appears attractive but turns out to be unaffordable.

FEES AND COSTS

Some lenders charge various upfront fees and costs on home equity financing. These fees and costs are similar to the types of expenses you pay when you finance your first mortgage. These items may include an application fee, attorney fees, and the costs of the title search and appraisal. You may also have to pay a fee—known as "points"—based on a percentage of the amount you borrow. Some lenders will pay for certain expenses, therefore, it is wise to shop around and negotiate with the lender to reduce your up-front costs.

In addition to the upfront closing costs, some lenders require you to pay continuing fees throughout the life of the loan. These may include an annual membership or participation fee, which is due whether or not you use the account, and/or a transaction fee, which is charged each time you borrow money.

In addition, some home equity financing plans have a prepayment penalty that is charged if you pay off the loan before the end of the loan term, or before a specified period of time, e.g., in the first year of the loan term. If you have any intention of moving, you should make sure your home equity financing plan does not contain a prepayment penalty clause.

DRAW AND REPAYMENT PERIODS

Some home equity lines of credit have a "draw period" and a "repayment period." The draw period is a fixed period of time during which you can make withdrawals from the account. You must make minimum monthly payments that generally cover the interest, although you can make additional payments towards the principal balance. The draw period is typically five or ten years, although the lender can set any draw period.

Once the draw period expires, you will not be able to borrow any more money unless you are allowed to renew your credit line. If you are not allowed to renew your credit line, you will enter the "repayment period." During the repayment period, you will not be allowed to make any more withdrawals from the account. Depending on the terms of your loan, at that time, you will either be required to pay the full outstanding balance, or start repaying the balance in payments over a fixed period of time. The repayment period is typically ten or fifteen years, although again, the lender can set any repayment period.

It is important to find out whether the payments you make during the repayment period will satisfy both the interest and principal owed on your line of credit. If not, there will be a large payment owed at the end of the loan term, known as a balloon payment.

You should find out whether you will be able to renegotiate your payment terms if you are unable to afford the balloon payment when it becomes due. If so, you should make sure that contingencies for refinancing any balance owed at the end of the loan term, or extending the time for repayment, are included, in writing, in the loan documents.

RIGHT OF RESCISSION

You have three days to cancel the home equity transaction for any reason whatsoever, without incurring a penalty. This is generally known as the borrower's "right of rescission." In order to cancel the transaction, you must advise the lender, in writing, that you are exercising the right to cancel.

The lender is required to give you a "right to cancel" form that contains instructions on how to cancel the loan and the deadline within which the cancellation notice must be received by the lender. The lender is required to cancel the credit line and return any fees that have been paid.

TAX DEDUCTIBILITY

One important advantage of home equity financing is that you may get a tax deduction on the interest you pay on the loan. This is particularly helpful if you are using the money to consolidate your debts, such as credit card debt. The interest you pay on your credit cards is not tax deductible. However, once you take out a home equity loan to consolidate your credit card debt, the interest becomes tax deductible.

There is a limit on the interest you can deduct. Generally, you can deduct the interest you pay on the first $100,000 of the home equity loan or line of credit. Beyond $100,000, deductibility depends on whether the proceeds were used to improve your first or second home, or to purchase a second home. It is advisable to check IRS regulations to determine whether you are entitled to deduct the interest on any amounts above $100,000.

SHOPPING AROUND

As set forth above, you should shop around for the best terms before you agree to a home equity financing plan. Compare interest rates, costs and fees, and repayment terms among various lenders. According to the Federal Trade Commission (FTC), you should ask for answers and consider the following factors when shopping around for a home equity plan.

1. Will the interest rate change?

2. If so, when, how often, and by how much will the interest rate change?

3. How much will you have to pay in points, if any?

4. The amount you will have to pay in fees, if any, including the following items:

   (a) Application or loan processing fee

   (b) Origination or underwriting fee

   (c) Lender or funding fee

   (d) Appraisal fee

(e) Document preparation and recording fees

(f) Broker fees

(g) Other fees

5. Are any of the fees refundable if you don't get the loan?

6. How many years will you have to repay the loan?

7. Is the plan an installment loan or a line of credit?

8. Is there a balloon payment?

9. What are the total closing costs?

10. If you use a broker, how will he or she be paid?

11. Does the loan include optional credit insurance?

12. If you want optional credit insurance, can you pay for it monthly instead of financing the premiums as part of your loan?

Finally, the most important thing to consider is whether you can actually afford the loan.

APPLICATION PROCESS

Applying for a home equity loan or line of credit is not quite as complicated as applying for your first mortgage.

Creditworthiness

In making its decision, the lender will consider your creditworthiness. The lender will obtain a copy of your credit report to determine how much outstanding debt you have, and whether you pay your bills on time, and whether there are any judgments, bankruptcies, or foreclosures in your credit history.

Income

In addition, the lender will want to know how much income you have, and how long you have been employed. You will be asked to provide proof of your income, such as your tax returns, pay stubs, and W-2 forms, etc. The lender will consider how much debt you have—including mortgage payments, car notes, credit card balances, and other financial obligations—in relation to your income and assets.

Loan to Value Ratio

The lender will also consider the loan to value (LTV) ratio of your home, which is the ratio between the amount you owe on your home and the appraised value of your home. In order to calculate the LTV, divide the total loan amount by the value of your home. For example, if your home is worth $300,000, and your mortgage balance is $150,000, your LTV is 50% ($150,000 is 50% of $300,000).

The lender will then calculate the new LTV ratio, taking into consideration the amount of home equity financing you are seeking. Using the above example, if you are asking for $75,000 in home equity financing, that amount will be added to your mortgage balance for a total financing debt of $225,000, thus your new LTV will be approximately 75% ($225,000 is 75% of $300,000).

In general, for home equity financing, a lender wlll not approve a loan that will cause the LTV ratio to exceed 80%, although there are lenders who will approve a higher loan to value ration loan, which generally carries a higher interest rate.

CASH-OUT REFINANCING ALTERNATIVE

An alternative way of accessing the equity in your home is to refinance your first mortgage for more than the outstanding balance. Of course, it is only advisable to refinance if the current interest rates are lower than the rate on your existing mortgage, and your home has increased in value.

For example, you bought your home five years ago for $200,000 and the balance on your first mortgage is $100,000. Since that time, your house has increased in value to $300,000. With the increased equity, you could do a cash-out refinance for $175,000, pay off your existing mortgage of $100,000 and take $75,000 in cash, less any fees and costs associated with the refinance.

It is important to make sure you can afford the mortgage payment on the higher mortgage, and compare rates to determine whether a cash-out refinance is a more affordable alternative to available home equity financing plans.

THE HOME OWNERSHIP AND EQUITY PROTECTION ACT

The Home Ownership and Equity Protection Act of 1994 (HOEPA) was enacted to protect borrowers from certain deceptive and unfair practices in home equity financing. The Act amended the Truth in Lending Act by establishing requirements for refinances and home equity loans that carry high rates and/or fees. The rules do not cover home equity lines of credit, or loans to purchase a home. These loans are referred to as "Section 32 Mortgages," because the rules are set forth in Section 32 of Regulation Z, which implements the Truth in Lending Act.

Qualified Loans

The following loans are covered under the HOEPA:

1. First Mortgage—If the annual percentage rate (APR) exceeds the rates on Treasury securities of comparable maturity by more than eight percentage points; or

2. Second Mortgage—If the annual percentage rate (APR) exceeds the rates on Treasury securities of comparable maturity by more than ten percentage points; or

3. The total fees and points payable by the borrower at or prior to closing exceed the larger of 8% of the total loan amount or $561, which is the amount set by the Federal Reserve for 2008. This amount will be adjusted annually based on the Consumer Price Index.

Required Disclosures

For qualified loans, the lender must give the borrower several written Section 32 disclosures, at least three days before the loan closes, as follows:

1. You are not required to complete this agreement merely because you have received these disclosures or have signed a loan application.

2. If you obtain this loan, the lender will have a mortgage on your home. You could lose your home, and any money you have put into it, if you do not meet your obligations under the loan.

3. In the case of a credit transaction with a fixed rate of interest, the disclosure must set forth the annual percentage rate and the amount of the regular monthly payment.

4. In the case of any other credit transaction, the disclosure must set forth the annual percentage rate of the loan; the amount of the regular monthly payment; a statement that the interest rate and monthly payment may increase; and the amount of the maximum monthly payment based on the maximum interest rate allowed.

These Section 32 disclosures must be given in addition to any other applicable disclosures required under the Truth in Lending Act.

Prohibited Practices

The Homeowner and Equity Protection Act specifies certain prohibited practices, such as negative amortization; balloon payments for loans with less than five-year terms; and most prepayment penalties. Therefore, the reader is advised to check that statute for specific rules.

In addition, when making the loan, the lender must consider the borrower's ability to repay the loan, and cannot rely solely on the basis of the value of the borrower's home. In addition, the loan cannot be refinanced within the first 12 months of closing unless refinancing is in the borrower's best interest.

Under the HOEPA, the borrower has the right to sue if the lender violates any of the prohibitions set forth in the Act. If successful, the borrower may be able to recover actual and statutory damages, court costs, and legal fees.

The text of the Home Ownership and Equity Protection Act can be found in Appendix 11 of this Almanac.

ABUSIVE LENDING PRACTICES

Predatory lending is discussed more fully in Chapter 2, "The Mortgage Loan Process," of this Almanac, however, there are certain practices aimed specifically at home equity financing plans that borrowers should know. In particular, elderly, minority and low-income applicants have been targeted by unscrupulous lenders who employ abusive and exploitative tactics targeting borrowers in these categories.

Equity Stripping

If you have limited income, and have built up equity in your home, some lenders will attempt to steal the equity you have built up in your home. These lenders will approve a loan even though they are aware that you do not have enough income to make the monthly payments. Some lenders will even advise you to inflate your income on the application in order to ensure that the loan is approved.

In such cases, the lender does not care if you are unable to make your monthly payments because it is the lender's intention to foreclose on your home as soon as you miss a payment. Therefore, if you can't afford the monthly payments, do not take out the loan, or you could end up losing your home.

Hidden Balloon Payment

As discussed above, beware of the hidden balloon payment provision. If you are offered low payments on a loan that requires interest only payments each month, it is likely that the amount you borrow—the principal—will become due in one lump sum at the end of the loan term. If you are unable to make the balloon payment, or refinance the loan, the lender may foreclose on your home and you could end up losing your home.

Home Improvement Loan Scam

Certain contractors work with lenders to lure unsuspecting homeowners into home equity lines of credit. The contractor will offer to provide the financing for a costly home improvement project through a lender the contractor knows. At some point after the work has begun, the contractor or lender will give you loan papers, and ask you to sign them, without giving you a chance to read the paperwork. In some cases, the papers may contain blank spaces.

The contractor will pressure you to sign the paperwork or threaten to stop work on the project. After you sign the paperwork, you discover that you have signed a home equity agreement that contains a very high interest rate, with exorbitant costs and fees. You have put your home at risk if you are unable to make the payments. To make matters worse, you may be left with shoddy workmanship by a contractor who has been paid by the unscrupulous lender and is now on to his next victim.

Therefore, do not sign any document you haven't read or any document that has blank spaces to be filled in after you sign. In addition, do not let anyone pressure you into signing any document. Take the time to read it and, if you don't understand any of the terms, have a lawyer review the document.

CHAPTER 4:
THE REAL ESTATE CLOSING

IN GENERAL

The real estate "closing," also referred to as the "settlement," is the finalization of the real estate transaction that takes place soon after the mortgage has been approved. The closing is usually held at the office of the attorney for one of the participants, e.g., the buyer, seller or lender.

At the closing, each of the parties finalizes their part of the agreement. The buyer pays the purchase price of the property to the seller, less any deposits already made. There are also adjustments based on items such as property taxes and utility bills incurred during the time the seller held title to the property, which may have been paid by the seller, or which are payable by the seller. If the buyer is financing part of the purchase price, the lender will pay the loan proceeds to the seller on the buyer's behalf.

CLOSING COSTS

"Closing Costs" are those additional costs the buyer or seller must pay in connection with closing the real estate transaction. Common closing costs include the following:

Title Insurance

Title insurance is an insurance policy which protects the lender and buyer against loss due to disputes over ownership of a property which may arise after the real estate transaction closes. In some states, attorneys offer title insurance as part of their services in examining title and providing a title opinion. The attorney's fee may include the title insurance premium. In other states, a title insurance company or title agent directly provides the title insurance.

In order to insure the title, prior to the closing, the title examiner undertakes an investigation of municipal records to ensure that the seller is the legal owner of a property and can convey marketable title. This examination is known as a "title search." The title search also reveals any liens or encumbrances that may exist against the property, which must be satisfied at or before closing.

Lenders or title insurance agents often also require a survey to mark the boundaries of the property. A survey is a drawing of the property showing the perimeter boundaries and marking the location of the house and other improvements. The buyer may be able to avoid the cost of a complete survey if they can locate the person who previously surveyed the property and request that the survey be updated.

Prior to the closing or settlement of the escrow, the title insurance company will issue a document containing a summary of any defects in title which have been identified by the title search, as well as any exceptions from the title insurance policy's coverage. This is generally known as the "binder," "commitment to insure," or "preliminary report."

The binder is usually sent to the lender for use until the title insurance policy is issued at or after the closing. The buyer can request a copy of the binder, or have a copy sent to their attorney, so that they can object if there are matters affecting the title that the buyer did not agree to accept when he or she signed the agreement of sale.

If the buyer is financing the purchase, the lender will require that, at the very least, the lender's interest in the property—to the extent of the amount of the mortgage—is covered by title insurance. Nevertheless, a lender's title insurance policy does not protect the buyer. Similarly, the prior owner's policy does not protect the new buyer.

If the buyer wants to be protected from claims by others against the new home, they will need an "owner's policy." When a claim does occur, it can be financially devastating to an owner who is uninsured. If you buy an owner's policy, it is usually much less expensive if you buy it at the same time and with the same insurer as the lender's policy.

The buyer also has the option to pay an additional premium to cover the difference between the mortgage amount and the purchase price. It is also wise to purchase—for a small additional fee—a market value rider. A market value rider provides that the property is covered up to the fair market value at the time the claim is made.

For example, if the purchase price of the property is $300,000, and the mortgage amount is $200,000, the lender will require that a title insurance policy be purchased indemnifying the lender up to $200,000.

The buyer may pay an additional premium to have the property covered for the full purchase price of $300,000. However, if a claim is made ten years after the purchase, when the fair market value of the property is $500,000, the insured is only covered up to $300,000. Purchase of the market value rider would indemnify the insured up to the full market value at the time of the loss, which in this case is $500,000.

As set forth in Chapter 7, "The Real Estate Settlement Procedures Act (RESPA)," of this Almanac, under RESPA, the seller may not require the buyer, as a condition of the sale, to purchase title insurance from any particular title company. Generally, the lender will require title insurance from a company that is acceptable to it. A violation of this provision makes the seller liable in an amount equal to three times all charges associated with the title insurance.

In most cases, the buyer can shop for and choose a company that meets the lender's standards. One may also compare rates among various title insurance companies. If the property being purchased has changed hands within the last several years, the title company may offer a "reissue rate," which may be less costly. The buyer should inquire as to what services and limitations on coverage are provided under each policy so that they can decide whether coverage purchased at a higher rate may be better for their needs.

Nevertheless, in many states, title insurance premium rates are established by the state and may not be negotiable. The reader is advised to check the law of his or her jurisdiction in this regard.

Escrow Account for Homeowner's Insurance and Real Estate Tax Payments

The borrower will generally have to contribute funds into an escrow account at closing for payment of homeowner insurance premiums and real estate tax payments. The lender generally collects 3 to 6 month's of payments at closing. Escrow accounts are widely used to protect lenders, as further discussed below.

The escrow account is an account held by the lender to which the borrower pays monthly installments, collected as part of the monthly mortgage payment, for homeowner insurance premiums and real estate tax payments. The lender disburses escrow account funds on behalf of the borrower when payments become due.

At the settlement or within the next 45 days, the person servicing the loan must give the borrower an initial escrow account statement. That form will show all of the payments that are expected to be deposited into the escrow account and all of the disbursements that are expected to be made from the escrow account during the year ahead.

The lender or servicer will review the escrow account annually and send the borrower a disclosure each year, which shows the prior year's activity and any adjustments necessary in the escrow payments that will be made in the forthcoming year.

Escrow accounts are more fully discussed in Chapter 7, "The Real Estate Settlement Procedures Act (RESPA)," of this Almanac.

Homeowner's Insurance

Both borrower and lender have insurable interests regarding the mortgaged premises. The insurable interest of the borrower is the value of the mortgaged premises and the lender's interest is the amount of the mortgage debt. Neither party normally would have an interest in the proceeds of the other's policy, since courts traditionally have looked upon insurance as a purely personal contract of indemnity. On the other hand, a lender is not allowed to collect both the proceeds of its own policy and the debt because the insurer becomes subrogated to the mortgage debt.

The normal practice today is for the lender to require that the borrower carry casualty insurance insuring the interests of both parties. Two types of such policy provisions are the open mortgage clause—known as the loss payable policy—and the standard mortgage clause.

Under a loss payable policy, the policy is issued to the borrower with a clause providing that the loss be payable to the borrower and to the lender as its interest may appear.

The standard mortgage clause is more commonly used today and generally provides as follows:

> Loss or damage, if any, under this policy shall be payable to the lender as his interest may appear, and this insurance, as to the lender only therein, shall not be invalidated by any act or neglect of the borrower or owner of the within described property, nor by any change in the title or ownership of the property, nor by the occupation of the premises for purposes more hazardous than are permitted by this policy, provided, that in case the borrower or owner shall neglect to pay any premium under this policy, the lender shall on demand pay the same.

Most lenders will not lend money to buy a home in a flood hazard area unless the borrower pays for flood insurance. Some government loan programs will not allow a borrower to purchase a home that is located in a flood hazard area. The lender may charge a fee to check for flood hazards.

The borrower should be notified if flood insurance is required. If a change in flood insurance maps brings the home within a flood hazard area after the loan is made, the lender or servicer may require the borrower to buy flood insurance at that time.

Real Estate Tax Payments

Lenders are adamant that the borrower promptly pays real estate taxes and special assessments. Lenders are understandably vigilant about this because if the taxes on the land or special assessments for local improvements are not paid, both the lender and borrower may lose their interests.

The state generally has the right to foreclose on property to collect back taxes. Further, the state's claim will override all prior interests. In other words, a "first" mortgage on real estate can be wiped out by a sale under a subsequently arising real estate tax lien. This is why lenders generally include mortgage clauses specifically imposing the duty to pay taxes on the borrower which make failure to do so a cause for acceleration of the mortgage debt.

The Loan Origination Fee

The loan origination fee—also known as "discount points"—is the service charge made by the lender for the granting of the loan. It is commonly referred to in terms of "points"—i.e., a percentage point of the loan amount. For example, on a $100,000 loan, a two-point loan origination fee would be $2,000.

Private Mortgage Insurance

Private Mortgage Insurance (PMI) is an insurance policy that protects the lender in case the borrower defaults on the mortgage loan. PMI is generally not required with conventional loans if the down payment is at least 20%. If the equity in the property is less than 80%, the borrower will have to pay PMI premiums.

Private mortgage insurance enables the lender to make a loan that the lender considers a higher risk. The borrower may be billed monthly, annually, by an initial lump sum, or some combination of these practices for the mortgage insurance premium.

Mortgage insurance should not be confused with mortgage life, credit life or disability insurance, which are insurance policies designed to pay off a mortgage in the event of the borrower's death or disability.

The borrower may also be offered "lender paid" mortgage insurance ("LPMI"). Under LPMI plans, the lender purchases the mortgage insurance and pays the premiums to the insurer. The lender will increase the interest rate to pay for the premiums, but LPMI may reduce the settlement costs.

The borrower cannot cancel LPMI or government mortgage insurance during the life of the loan. However, it may be possible to cancel private mortgage insurance at some point, such as when the borrower's equity in the property increases to 80%, as discussed below.

The Homeowner's Protection Act of 1998 (The PMI Act)

On July 29, 1999, the new Homeowner's Protection Act of 1998, also known as the PMI Act, regarding the cancellation of PMI took effect. The PMI Act provides two situations in which borrower paid PMI may be canceled: (1) Automatic; and (2) By Request. The law excludes lender-paid PMI, but requires an up front disclosure to the borrower about lender-paid PMI.

Automatic Cancellation

In general, when the homeowner's equity position reaches 22% of the original value of the property, the mortgage servicer must automatically cancel the PMI. The borrower must be current in making payments for automatic cancellation to apply.

Cancellation By Request

Homeowners can request cancellation of the PMI when their equity position reaches 20% of the original value of the property, if they meet certain criteria set forth by the lender.

To complain about a lender who does not comply with the PMI Act, the borrower should contact the appropriate federal regulator.

A Directory of PMI Enforcement Authorities can be found in Appendix 12 of this Almanac.

Prepaid Interest

Prepaid interest refers to interest on the real estate loan that is paid in advance of when it is due. Prepaid interest is typically charged to the borrower at closing to cover the interest on the loan between the closing date until the end of the month.

CLOSING DOCUMENTS

The legal documents that finalize the real estate transaction are executed at the closing. Of primary importance, the borrower is required to sign the Mortgage and Promissory Note, among many other financing documents; and the seller is required to execute the Deed.

The Mortgage

As discussed in Chapter 2, the mortgage is a written instrument, duly executed by the Borrower at the real estate closing, and delivered to the Lender.

The Mortgage Note

As discussed in Chapter 2, "The Mortgage Loan Process," of this Almanac, the mortgage note is the legal document that represents the borrower's actual "promise" to repay the loan at a specified interest rate over a stated time period. At the real estate closing, the borrower is required to execute a mortgage note in addition to the mortgage because the mortgage note, unlike the mortgage, is considered a "negotiable instrument."

The Deed

The Deed is the most common method of transferring ownership in real estate. At the real estate closing, the Deed is executed and turned over to the party who is responsible for its recording. This is usually the title examiner.

Requirements

In order for the deed to be valid, it must meet certain requirements, as set forth below:

1. The seller of the property, also known as the grantor, must have the legal right to transfer the property and must sign the deed over to the buyer. The grantor may be an individual, a partnership, a corporation, a governmental authority, or someone in a fiduciary capacity who has authority to transfer ownership of the property, such as a court order or a written and recorded agreement. Examples of fiduciaries are trustees, executors, and administrators.

2. The buyer of the property, also known as the grantee, must be accurately identified, and the addresses for both the grantor and grantee must be stated.

3. The deed must also specify the form of ownership that is being transferred, and the language of conveyance that expresses the intent to transfer the property.

4. Another requirement for any valid contract is the recital of consideration, i.e., the exchange of something of value by each party. In this case, consideration refers to the payment of a sum of money by the buyer, and the surrender of the deed to the property by

the seller. The usual recital of consideration in a deed reads as follows:

Witnesseth, that the party of the first part, in consideration of ten dollars and other valuable consideration paid by the party of the second part, does hereby grant and release unto the party of the second part . . . all that certain plot, piece or parcel of land . . .

The exact purchase price is generally not stated in the Deed for confidentiality reasons. The fact that there is a recital of consideration suffices to satisfy the requirement.

5. The deed must be delivered to, and accepted by, the grantee. This is evidenced by the payment of the purchase price in exchange for the deed.

6. The signatures on the deed must be acknowledged by a notary public in order for the deed to be accepted for recording.

7. The deed must also contain a legal description of the property that is the subject of the transaction. The legal description is based on a detailed survey of the property. It is important that the description be as accurate as possible so that the parties understand exactly what is being conveyed. There are three common types of legal descriptions used:

(a) Metes and Bounds—"Metes" refers to the actual measurement of the property, and "Bounds" refers to the physical boundaries of the property. The property description details the direction of, and the distance between, physical points of reference.

(b) Record Plat Descriptions—Record plat descriptions refers to the method of describing the property by lot and block, also incorporating the existing method of legal description into the detailed record plat.

(c) The Rectangular System—The rectangular system is the method used by the majority of states. The rectangular system uses a grid with lines running north and south—known as meridians—and lines running east and west—known as parallels. These lines create squares, each of which represents a certain distance within the town. The squares are divided and subdivided until the land within each section is identified.

Types of Deeds

The most common types of deeds used to convey property include those listed below.

The Full Covenant and Warranty Deed

The full covenant and warranty deed is one in which the grantor fully warrants, or guarantees, that there is good title to the property. This guarantee dates back through the chain of title, and each prior grantor of a warranty deed may be liable to the buyer if a claim is made which is traced back to the date of conveyance by a particular prior grantor.

The Bargain and Sale Deed With Covenant

The bargain and sale deed with covenant is the simplest and most commonly used deed. It conveys all of the rights and interests that the grantor of the property holds. It also contains a covenant warranting good title to the property. However, unlike the full covenant and warranty deed, the bargain and sale covenant only relates to claims arising out of the period of ownership of the grantor who is conveying the deed.

The Bargain and Sale Deed Without Covenant

The bargain and sale deed without covenant does not contain the statement of warranty of title. It is similar to the quitclaim deed in that it does not protect the buyer from liens or other third party claims on the property should they arise. The difference between the quitclaim deed and the bargain and sale deed without covenant is that the latter contains language that, at the very least, implies that the grantor actually owns the property being conveyed.

The Quitclaim Deed

The quitclaim deed, like the bargain and sale deed without covenant, conveys all of the rights and interest that the grantor of the property holds, however, it does not contain language which implies that the grantor actually owns the property. Thus if the grantor has no rights to the property, the grantee, in reality, receives nothing by way of the deed.

The Referee's Deed

The referee's deed is used to convey property by the referee following a foreclosure sale. Like the quitclaim deed, the referee's deed does not contain covenants warranting title.

The Executor's Deed

The executor's deed is used by the executor of a will to convey property of a decedent's estate. The executor's deed usually contains a covenant against the executor's acts, similar to the covenant against grantor's acts contained in the bargain and sale deed.

Recording the Deed

Following the real estate closing, the person responsible for recording the deed—usually the title company representative—files the deed, along with the required fee, with the appropriate authority.

It is important that the deed be recorded as soon thereafter as practicable so as to give the public constructive notice of the transaction, and make the transfer part of the chain of title for that property. Because laws may vary, the reader is cautioned to check the recording requirements of their own jurisdiction to make sure that their rights are preserved.

TAKING POSSESSION

Following the closing, the buyers are generally entitled to take immediate possession of the house, unless some other arrangement has been made. The contract usually requires the seller to turn over the property in a "broom-swept" condition. This generally means that the seller removes all personal property and debris from the premises.

If the seller is unable to immediately vacate the house, the contract usually provides for certain payments to be made to the buyers for each day the seller occupies the property after the closing.

CHAPTER 5:
MORTGAGE LOAN DISCRIMINATION

IN GENERAL

In evaluating the credit worthiness of mortgage loan applicants, lenders have traditionally engaged in practices that could be considered discriminatory against certain borrowers. For example, a working wife's income was usually not given as much weight as the husband's income because of the fear that the wife would stop working. Single women were sometimes required to have additional cosigners to their notes where single males would not be so required. These are clear examples of gender discrimination.

Federal law prohibits discrimination in the provision of credit, including mortgage loans, on the basis of race, color, national origin, religion, sex, marital status, age, receipt of public assistance funds, familial status, or the exercise of rights under the consumer credit protection laws.

These rights are guaranteed under the Fair Housing Act (FHA) and the Equal Credit Opportunity Act (ECOA). In cases involving discrimination in mortgage loans or home improvement loans, the Department of Justice may file suit under both the FHA and the ECOA, as more fully discussed below.

THE FAIR HOUSING ACT

The Fair Housing Act (FHA) (42 U.S.C. 3601 et seq.) prohibits discrimination by direct providers of housing, such as landlords and real estate companies as well as other entities, such as municipalities, banks or other lending institutions and homeowners insurance companies.

The FHA prohibits discrimination in all aspects of residential real estate related transactions based on: (1) race or color; (2) religion; (3) sex;

(4) national origin; (5) familial status; and (6) disability. Thus based on any of the foregoing factors, the mortgage lender may not:

1. Discourage an applicant from applying for a mortgage or refuse to make a mortgage loan;

2. Refuse to provide information regarding loans;

3. Impose different terms or conditions on a loan, e.g., interest rates, points, or fees;

4. Discriminate in appraising the property;

5. Consider the racial composition of the neighborhood where the applicant wants to live. This also applies when the property is being appraised;

6. Refuse to purchase a loan;

7. Set different terms or conditions for purchasing a loan;

8. Refuse to provide homeowners insurance coverage;

9. Discriminate in the terms or conditions of homeowners insurance coverage;

10. Impose less favorable terms or conditions of homeowners insurance coverage;

11. Refuse to provide available information on the full range of homeowners insurance coverage options available; or

12. Make, print, or publish any statement, in connection with the provision of homeowners insurance coverage, that indicates a preference, limitation or discrimination based on these factors.

13. Ask about the applicant's plans for having a family, although questions about expenses related to the applicant's dependents are permissible;

14. Require a co-signer if the applicant meets the lender's standards.

In addition, under the FHA, the lender must:

1. Consider reliable public assistance income in the same way as any other income;

2. Consider reliable income from part-time employment, Social Security, pensions, and annuities;

3. Consider reliable alimony, child support, or separate maintenance payments, if you choose to provide this information, although the

lender may ask you for proof that this income is received consistently; and

4. Accept someone other than the applicant's spouse, if a co-signer is needed.

Selected provisions of the Fair Housing Act can be found in Appendix 13 of this Almanac.

THE EQUAL CREDIT OPPORTUNITY ACT

The Equal Credit Opportunity Act (ECOA) prohibits discrimination in any aspect of a credit transaction. These prohibitions apply to all mortgage lenders. Initially, when this legislation went into effect in 1975, it prohibited the use of sex or marital status as factors in credit-granting decisions. Since 1977, when the Act was amended, seven other factors were outlawed as causes for discrimination in lending.

Thus there are nine illegal factors which may not be used in the decision to grant credit, including:

1. Sex;

2. Marital status;

3. Race;

4. Color;

5. Religion;

6. Country of origin;

7. Age;

8. Receipt of public assistance benefits; and

9. The good faith exercise of rights held under the Consumer Credit Protection Act.

In short, the ECOA is an attempt to assure that credit granting decisions are based solely on business judgment and repayment capacity. In addition, some states and regulators have added additional prohibitions against discriminating against applicants based upon their sexual orientation.

The ECOA requires lenders to notify the credit applicant of the decision made on their application. In the case of a credit denial, applicants must be notified of the reasons the credit was denied. The explanation must be in writing and made within 30 days if "adverse action" is taken on a credit application. Offering different terms or a lesser amount is not considered adverse action, but rather is interpreted as a counter offer. In addition, action taken as a result of a borrower's default is not considered adverse action.

The notice required under the ECOA must contain a statement that discrimination is illegal, and include the list of factors considered discriminatory. The notice must also include the name of the federal agency responsible for enforcing the ECOA, which may vary, depending on the type of lender involved.

Credit is often denied for a combination of factors rather than for one specific factor. In the past, some creditors used a score sheet containing certain factors, and denied credit when a certain aggregate score was not obtained. Under the ECOA, failure to attain the required score is not a sufficient reason in and of itself for denying credit. Rather, the specific reasons must be listed.

REDLINING

Redlining is the practice by lending institutions of refusing to grant home mortgages or home-improvement loans for properties in certain designated urban neighborhoods. Redlining may consist of more subtle practices than a blunt refusal to lend in those designated areas. Such practices might include:

1. Higher down payments and earlier loan-maturity dates;

2. Charging higher interest rates or special discount points for mortgages in redlined areas;

3. Establishing "minimum loan amounts" that exclude lower-priced, older urban housing; and

4. Under-appraising properties in redlined areas.

Whether redlining actually exists is a hotly debated topic. Some studies have used deed records to indicate that commercial banks, mutual savings banks and savings and loan associations have put more of their money into suburbs than into the central cities. Other studies conclude that redlining is largely a myth. They contend that the relative small number of loans in the central or inner city is more a product of lower demand there, in response to general urban decay. Some even claim that central or inner city borrowers receive preferential treatment because of the greater risk and cost of administration of loans in those areas.

The question of how to evaluate risk is at the heart of the redlining controversy. Community groups opposing redlining practices feel that mortgage lenders are discriminating against older urban properties and the people who live in those neighborhoods. They contend that redlining is a self-fulfilling prophecy. If lenders deny mortgage funds to an area because they feel it is declining, then the neighborhood will decline because homeowners cannot improve their properties and prospective homeowners cannot finance their purchases.

Many financial institutions take an opposite view. They point out that they have the responsibility to invest funds in a sound and prudent manner, and that this requirement dictates that they follow sound business practices in evaluating risk. In fact, many contend that they are now subsidizing inner-city neighborhoods by making loans on properties with greater potential for loss at terms similar to those found in the suburbs.

Opponents charge that redlining is a direct cause of and principal contributor to urban decline, and they seek additional legislation to force financial institutions to make more loans in older urban neighborhoods. They argue that the increased flow of funds would revitalize the inner city and halt urban decay.

The financial institutions and their supporters assert that redlining is an effect and not a cause. Neighborhoods first deteriorate, thus lenders are then more cautious about making loans in those areas. Their policy prescription is for the community to examine the real causes of urban decay and to establish programs and strategies to deal with those problems. If this is done, they contend, the mortgage funds will definitely follow.

The Home Mortgage Disclosure Act

The Home Mortgage Disclosure Act (HMDA) is an attempt to eliminate the practice of "redlining" or refusing to make loans in certain geographical areas. It requires certain lenders to disclose the magnitude of mortgage loans made in each census tract or zip code area in the Standard Metropolitan Statistical Area (SMSA) that they serve.

The HMDA applies to lending institutions whose net worth exceeds $10 million and who make "federally related mortgages." With respect to the latter, the HDMA applies to any lender who is federally insured or regulated. In this way, the HMDA reporting requirements may serve to encourage lenders to make loans in all areas.

The Community Reinvestment Act of 1977

The Community Reinvestment Act of 1977 specifically prohibits discrimination in lending on the basis of the age of the dwelling or its neighborhood.

The Act also requires lending institutions to keep records on applicant characteristics such as race, sex, age and neighborhood, and to make them available for inspection.

THE "EFFECTS TEST"

In determining whether illegal discrimination has occurred, the Courts generally use what was first termed an "effects test" in *Griggs v. Duke Power Company*, 401 U.S. 424 (1971), a case decided by the U.S. Supreme Court. The *Griggs* case appears to eliminate the requirement of proving "intent" to find that there has been discrimination. Thereafter, in a Senate Report issued in 1976, Congress specifically directed the judiciary to follow the reasoning in *Griggs*.

A companion U.S. Supreme Court case included in the Congressional directive, *Albermarle Paper Company v. Moody*, 422 U.S. 405 (1977), further suggested that showing a disproportionate racial impact created a "prima facie" discrimination case and shifted the burden of proof to the defendant to prove nondiscrimination.

In any event, the "effects test" has been undergoing continual judicial interpretation, which may have some impact on the way the ECOA is applied in the future.

FILING A DISCRIMINATION COMPLAINT

If you suspect that you have been discriminated against, you must take action. You should first complain to the lender, and request that the lender reconsider your application.

If the lender refuses to reconsider your application, you should pursue your rights under the federal anti-discrimination laws. A number of federal agencies share enforcement responsibility for the ECOA and the FHA. Determining which agency to contact depends, in part, on the type of financial institution you dealt with, as set forth below.

For ECOA violations involving mortgage lenders, contact:

Federal Trade Commission
Consumer Response Center
Washington, D.C. 20580
Tel: 202-326-2222/TDD: 1-866-653-4261
Website: http://ftc.gov/

While the Federal Trade Commission (FTC) generally does not intervene in individual disputes, the information you provide may indicate a pattern of violations requiring action by the FTC.

For FHA violations, contact:

Office of Fair Housing and Equal Opportunity
U.S. Department of Housing and Urban
Development (HUD), Room 5204
Washington, D.C. 20410-2000
Tel: 1-800-424-8590/TDD: 1-800-543-8294

You have one year to file an FHA discrimination complaint with HUD, but you should file as soon as possible. Your complaint to HUD should include the following information:

1. Your name and address;
2. The name and address of the person or company who is the subject of the complaint;
3. The address or other identification of the housing involved;
4. A short description of the facts that caused you to believe your rights were violated; and
5. The dates of the alleged violation.

You should send your letter to the HUD Regional Office nearest you.

A directory of HUD Fair Housing Regional Offices can be found in Appendix 14 of this Almanac, and a HUD Housing Discrimination Complaint Form can be found in Appendix 15 of this Almanac.

HUD will notify you when it receives your complaint. Generally, HUD will also:

1. Notify the alleged violator of your complaint and permit the person to submit an answer;
2. Investigate your complaint and determine whether there is a reasonable cause to believe the Fair Housing Act has been violated; and
3. Notify you if it cannot complete an investigation within 100 days of receiving your complaint.

In addition to pursuing your rights under applicable federal laws, you should check with your state Attorney General's office to find out whether the lender violated any state laws. Consumers who believe they have suffered illegal discrimination by a bank may also make a complaint to the appropriate governing agency.

All states have banking agencies that regulate and supervise state-chartered banks. Many of them handle or refer problems and complaints about other types of financial institutions as well. Some also answer general questions about banking and consumer credit. When dealing with a federally chartered bank, the consumer is advised to check with the appropriate Federal Banking Agency.

FILING A PRIVATE CIVIL LAWSUIT

Even if HUD dismisses your complaint, the Fair Housing Act gives you the right to file a private civil lawsuit in Federal District Court. You must file your lawsuit at your own expense; however, if you cannot afford an attorney, the Court may appoint one for you.

You must file your lawsuit within two (2) years of the most recent date of the alleged discrimination. The time during which HUD was processing your complaint is not counted in the 2-year filing period. Even if HUD is still processing your complaint, you may file a private civil lawsuit unless:

1. You have already signed a HUD Conciliation Agreement to resolve your HUD complaint; or

2. A HUD Administrative Law Judge has commenced an Administrative Hearing for your complaint.

If your lawsuit is successful, you may be able to recover your actual damages, legal fees, and court costs. If the Court finds that the lender's conduct was willful, you may also be able to recover punitive damages. If you find that the lender's conduct is pervasive, you may be able to join other victims and file a class action lawsuit against the lender.

PATTERN OR PRACTICE DISCRIMINATION

Under the FHA, the U.S. Department of Justice (DOJ) may bring a lawsuit where there is reason to believe that a person or entity is engaged in a "pattern or practice" of discrimination or where a denial of rights to a group of persons raises an issue of general public importance. The DOJ may also bring a lawsuit under the ECOA where a creditor has engaged in a "pattern or practice" of discrimination in credit transactions.

The courts have found a "pattern or practice" when the evidence establishes that the discriminatory actions were the defendant's regular practice, rather than an isolated instance. This does not mean that the DOJ has to prove that a defendant always discriminates or that a large number of people have been affected. A "pattern or practice" means that the defendant has a policy of discriminating, even if the policy is not always followed.

The courts have held that the Attorney General has discretion to decide what constitutes an issue of "general public importance," and the courts will not second-guess that decision. Thus the DOJ can bring suit even when a discriminatory act has occurred only once, if it affects a group of persons and the DOJ believes that the discrimination raises an issue of general public importance.

CHAPTER 6:
THE TRUTH-IN-LENDING ACT

IN GENERAL

The Truth-in-Lending Act was passed by Congress in 1968 as part of the Federal Consumer Protection Act. In order to carry out the basic provisions of the Act, the Federal Reserve Board promulgated specific regulations on compliance, which are referred to in their entirety as "Regulation Z," an exhaustive publication dealing with almost every imaginable area of extension of credit. This chapter addresses the provisions of the Truth-in-Lending Act that impact mortgage law.

The purpose of the Truth-in-Lending Act is to assure that everyone being extended commercial credit by a creditor covered by the Act is given meaningful disclosures regarding the cost of the credit being extended. The disclosures must be clear and according to the statutory forms published pursuant to the Act and Regulation Z.

APPLICABILITY

Regulation Z applies to all businesses and individuals who are:

1. Offering or extending credit to consumers;

2. Offering or extending such credit on a regular basis;

3. Offering or extending credit either:

    (a) subject to a finance charge, or

    (b) payable by written agreement in more than four installments; and

4. Offering or extending credit primarily for personal, family, or household purposes.

The types of real estate transactions that are excluded from Regulation Z coverage are as follows:

1. Business transactions;

2. Commercial transactions;

3. Agricultural transactions;

4. Organizational credit transactions; and

5. Credit transactions that involve more than $25,000 but which are not secured by real estate or a dwelling.

DISCLOSURE

If Regulation Z is applicable to a lender in connection with a real estate transaction, then the lender is required to make certain disclosures. Generally, these disclosures are made on a statement separate from the promissory note and mortgage documents.

Under Regulation Z, Section 226.4(a), the following information must be furnished to the borrower:

1. Annual percentage rate;

2. Finance charge;

3. Amount financed;

4. Total payment amount;

5. Number of payments;

6. Amount per payment;

7. Payments due date; and

8. Late payment charge.

Finance Charge

Regulation Z defines the finance charge as follows:

> ". . . [T]he sum of all charges, payable directly or indirectly by the creditor as an incident to or as a condition of the extension of credit, whether paid or payable by the customer, the seller, or any other person on behalf of the customer to the creditor or a third party."

It should be noted that the regulations do not place a ceiling on the finance charges. The requirements only specify that the charges be disclosed.

Variable Rate Interest Loans

If the note has a variable interest rate, the following disclosure statement is also required under Regulation Z:

"The annual percentage rate may increase during the term of this transaction if the primary rate of the lender increases. The rate may not increase more often than once a year, and may not increase by more than 1% annually. The interest rate will not increase above ___%. Any increase will take the form of higher payment amounts. If the interest rate increases by ___ % in 1 year, your regular payment would increase to $_____."

Advertisements and Triggering Language

Regulation Z also restricts the manner in which lenders advertise their credit terms. Under Regulation Z, an advertisement is defined as "[A] commercial message in any media that promotes, directly or indirectly, a credit transaction."

Advertisements must be accurate and state only those terms that are actually available. Advertisements that address finance charges must also state those charges in terms of the annual percentage rate (APR)—i.e., an expression of the cost of credit according to its yearly rate. Formulas for computing the APR are set forth in the regulations, along with a table that can be used in such computation.

Triggering Language

Regulation Z also provides that if certain "triggering language" is used in advertisements, then additional disclosures must also be included. Triggering language includes:

1. Amount or percentage of any down payment;

2. Number of payments or period of repayment;

3. Amount of any payment; and

4. Amount of any finance charge.

The additional disclosures that must be made in advertisements using triggering language include:

1. Terms of repayment;

2. Annual percentage rate; and

3. Disclosures of any increases in payments or rates that may occur.

For example, the phrase "30-year loan" is an example of a triggering term because it indicates the repayment period. The phrase "payable in monthly installments of $550" is also triggering language because it relates to the amount of the payments. Use of any of these types of "triggering" phrases requires the advertising lender to include the additional disclosures.

Nevertheless, general phrases such as "no down payment," "years to repay," and "monthly installments to suit your budget," may be used without triggering the additional disclosure requirements.

Miscellaneous Disclosures

In addition to the preceding disclosures required for real estate credit transactions, the following items must be included on the disclosure statement regardless of the type of loan or note involved:

1. Identity of the creditor;

2. Demand feature of the note, if one exists;

3. Prepayment penalties, if any;

4. Whether the loan is assignable or transferable; and

5. Separate identification of credit insurance premiums.

RIGHT OF RESCISSION

Although Regulation Z provides for a 3-day rescission period for security interests and second mortgages, the rescission period does not apply to residential mortgage transactions that are defined in Section 226.2(a) (24) as follows:

> "[T]ransactions in which a mortgage, deed of trust, purchase money security interest arising under an installment sales contract, or equivalent consensual security interest is created or retained in the consumer's principal dwelling to finance the acquisition or initial construction of that dwelling."

Thus the exception to the 3-day rescission period and notice of that period is for first notes and mortgages on property being purchased by a consumer for use as a residence. However, the consumer who executes a second note and mortgage on a property is permitted to cancel that transaction within the 3-day period. In that case, the lender must disclose the right of cancellation and must also provide, in written form, the procedures for exercising the right of cancellation.

A sample Notice of Right to Cancel can be found in Appendix 16 of this Almanac.

THE TRUTH-IN-LENDING SIMPLIFICATION AND REFORM ACT OF 1980

The Federal Truth-in-Lending Act and Regulation Z were both changed in 1980 by The Truth-in-Lending Simplification and Reform Act. This new statute became effective in 1982 and was further amended in 1983 to comply with the Depository Institutions Act of 1982. The most significant changes in the Act affecting real estate are the definitions of "creditor" and "arrangers of credit."

Under the amendments, a "creditor" is basically defined as "a person who extends credit more than five times in a preceding calendar year or in a current calendar year for a transaction secured by a dwelling (Reg. Z, Section 226.2(a)(I))." An "arranger of credit" would include real estate brokers who arrange for sellers to take secondary loans.

CHAPTER 7:
THE REAL ESTATE SETTLEMENT
PROCEDURES ACT (RESPA)

IN GENERAL

The Real Estate Settlement Procedures Act (RESPA) is a federal disclosure statute enacted to help consumers become better shoppers for settlement services. RESPA requires that borrowers receive disclosures at various times. Some disclosures spell out the costs associated with the settlement; outline lender servicing and escrow account practices; and describe business relationships between settlement service providers.

The RESPA statute was also designed to eliminate kickbacks and unearned fees. Congress concluded that consumers need protection from "unnecessarily high settlement charges caused by certain abusive practices that have developed in some areas of the country."

APPLICABILITY

The RESPA statute relates to all federally related mortgage loans. In order to be covered under the statute, a mortgage loan must meet the following three criteria:

1. The loan must be for the purchase of a one to four family residential dwelling;

2. The loan must constitute a first lien on the property; and

3. The loan must be made by or for a lender supervised by a federal agency.

In practice, the majority of residential real estate loans are subject to this statute.

DISCLOSURES

Under the RESPA statute, when a lender receives an application for a federally related mortgage loan, the lender is required to provide the prospective borrower with disclosures at various times. As discussed below, some disclosures spell out the costs associated with the settlement, outline lender servicing and escrow account practices, and describe business relationships between settlement service providers.

If the borrowers don't get these documents at the time of application, the lender must mail them within three business days of receiving the loan application. If the lender turns down the loan within three days, however, then the statute does not require the lender to provide these documents.

The RESPA statute does not provide an explicit penalty for the failure to provide the required documents, however, bank regulators may choose to impose penalties on lenders who fail to comply with federal law.

Disclosures Required at the Time of Loan Application

When the borrowers apply for a mortgage loan, lenders and mortgage brokers are required to provide the borrowers with the following:

HUD Information Booklet

The information booklet, published by HUD, contains consumer information regarding various real estate settlement services.

Good Faith Estimate

The RESPA statute requires that, when someone applies for a loan, the lender or mortgage broker must give the applicant a Good Faith Estimate (GFE) of settlement costs that he or she will likely have to pay on or before closing. If a lender requires the borrower to use a particular settlement provider, then the lender must disclose this requirement on the Good Faith Estimate.

It should be noted that the amounts listed on the Good Faith Estimate are only estimates. Actual costs may vary and changing market conditions can affect prices. The lender's estimate is not a guarantee. The applicant should keep the Good Faith Estimate so that they can compare it with the final settlement costs.

A sample Good Faith Estimate Chart can be found in Appendix 17 of this Almanac.

Loan Servicing Transfers

Under The RESPA statute, the lender is further required to disclose to the loan applicant, in writing, whether their mortgage loan payments may be transferred to another party, and the likelihood that such an event will occur. This is known as a "servicing transfer," under which the collection of principal, interest and escrow account payments are transferred to another party.

Disclosures Required Before Settlement

Under The RESPA statute, the following disclosures must be given to the borrower at some point prior to settlement. The reader should be aware that the term "settlement" refers to the closing of the loan, and the terms are often used interchangeably.

Affiliated Business Arrangement Disclosure

An Affiliated Business Arrangement Disclosure is required whenever a settlement service provider involved in a RESPA covered transaction refers the consumer to a provider with whom the referring party has an ownership or other beneficial interest.

For example, several businesses that offer settlement services may be owned or controlled by a common corporate parent. These businesses are known as "affiliates." When a lender, real estate broker, or other participant in the settlement refers the borrower to an affiliate for a settlement service, the statute requires the referring party to give the borrower an Affiliated Business Arrangement Disclosure. This disclosure form is intended remind the borrower that he or she is not required, with certain exceptions, to use the affiliate, and is free to shop for other providers.

The referring party must give this disclosure to the consumer at or prior to the time of referral. The disclosure must describe the business arrangement that exists between the two providers and give the borrower an estimate of the second provider's charges.

Except in cases where a lender refers a borrower to an attorney, credit reporting agency or real estate appraiser to represent the lender's interest in the transaction, the referring party may not require the consumer to use the particular provider being referred.

For example, the statute prohibits a seller from requiring the home buyer to use a particular title insurance company, either directly or indirectly, as a condition of sale. Buyers may sue a seller who violates this provision for an amount equal to three times all charges made for the title insurance.

A sample Affiliated Business Arrangement Disclosure Statement can be found in Appendix 18 of this Almanac.

HUD-1 Settlement Statement

At or before the closing, the lender is required to provide both the borrower and the seller with a completed Uniform Settlement Statement Form, commonly referred to as a "HUD-1" Form. The HUD-1 Settlement Statement is a standard form that clearly shows all charges imposed on borrowers and sellers in connection with the settlement. This form is filled out by the settlement agent who conducts the settlement.

Generally, the fully completed HUD-1 Settlement Statement must be delivered or mailed to the borrower at or before the settlement meeting. In cases where there is no settlement meeting, the escrow agent will mail the HUD-1 after settlement.

Nevertheless, the statute allows the borrower to request to see the HUD-1 Settlement Statement one day before the actual settlement. The settlement agent must then provide the borrowers with a completed HUD-1 Settlement Statement based on information known to the settlement agent at that time.

A sample HUD-1 Form can be found in Appendix 19 of this Almanac.

Disclosures Required at the Settlement

HUD-1 Settlement Statement

As set forth above, the HUD-1 Settlement Statement is required to be given at or before the closing. If provided to the borrower prior to the settlement, it contains the information known to the settlement agent at that time.

At the settlement, the HUD-1 Settlement Statement shows the actual settlement costs of the loan transaction. Separate forms may be prepared for the borrower and the seller. Where it is not the practice that the borrower and the seller both attend the settlement, the HUD-1 will be mailed or delivered as soon as practicable after settlement.

Initial Escrow Account Statement

The Initial Escrow Statement itemizes the estimated taxes, insurance premiums and other charges that will be paid from the borrower's Escrow Account during the first twelve months of the loan. It lists the escrow payment amount and any required cushion.

Although the statement is usually given at settlement, the lender has 45 days from settlement to deliver it.

Disclosures Required After the Settlement

Annual Escrow Account Statement

Loan servicers must deliver an Annual Escrow Statement to the borrower once a year. The annual escrow account statement summarizes all escrow account deposits and payments during the servicer's twelve-month computation year. It also notifies the borrower of any shortages or surpluses in the account and advises the borrower about the course of action being taken.

Under Section 10 of the RESPA statute, HUD has the authority to impose a civil penalty on loan servicers who do not submit initial or annual escrow account statements to borrowers. Borrowers are advised to contact HUD's Office of RESPA to report servicers who fail to provide the required escrow account statements.

Servicing Transfer Statement

A Servicing Transfer Statement is required if the loan servicer sells or assigns the servicing rights to a borrower's loan to another loan servicer. Generally, the loan servicer must notify the borrower 15 days before the effective date of the loan transfer. As long as the borrower makes a timely payment to the old servicer within 60 days of the loan transfer, the borrower cannot be penalized.

The notice must include the following information:

1. The effective date of the transfer;

2. The date your current servicer will stop accepting payments and the date the new servicer will begin accepting payments;

3. The name, address, and toll-free or collect call telephone number for the new servicer;

4. Information that tells whether you can continue any optional insurance, such as mortgage life or disability insurance, and what action, if any, you must take to maintain coverage; and

5. A statement that the transfer of servicing does not affect any term or condition of your mortgage documents other than the terms directly related to the servicing of the loan.

Section 6 of the RESPA statute provides borrowers with important consumer protections relating to the servicing of their loans. Under Section 6 of the statute, borrowers who have a problem with the servicing of their loan should contact their loan servicer, in writing, outlining the nature of their complaint.

The servicer must acknowledge the complaint in writing within 20 business days of receipt of the complaint. Within 60 business days, the servicer must resolve the complaint by correcting the account or giving a statement of the reasons for its position. Until the complaint is resolved, borrowers should continue to make the servicer's required payment.

Borrowers who believe a settlement service provider has violated the statute may wish to file a complaint. The complaint should provide the borrower's contact information, outline the violation, and identify the violators by name, address and phone number. Complaints should be sent to:

> Director, Office of RESPA and Interstate Land Sales
> U.S. Department of Housing and Urban Development
> Room 9154
> 451 7th Street, SW
> Washington, D.C. 20410

In addition, a borrower may bring a private law suit, or a group of borrowers may bring a class action suit, within three years, against a servicer who fails to comply with the provisions of Section 6. Borrowers may obtain actual damages, as well as additional damages, if there is a pattern of noncompliance.

AFFILIATED BUSINESSES AND ILLEGAL REFERRALS

In addition to the disclosures required under the RESPA statute, Section 8 of the statute prohibits certain practices that increase the cost of settlement services. For example, the statute prohibits anyone from giving or taking a fee, kickback, or anything of value under an agreement that business will be referred to a specific person or organization. In addition, the statute prohibits home sellers from requiring home buyers to purchase title insurance from a particular company.

The statute also prohibits a person from giving or accepting any part of a charge for services that are not performed, as follows:

> "It is illegal under RESPA for anyone to pay or receive a fee, kickback or anything of value because they agree to refer settlement service business to a particular person or organization. For example, your mortgage lender may not pay your real estate broker $250 for referring you to the lender. It is also illegal for anyone to accept a fee or part of a fee for services if that person has not actually performed settlement services for the fee. For example, a lender may not add to a third party's fee, such as an appraisal fee, and keep the difference."

Nevertheless, the statute does not prevent title companies, mortgage brokers, appraisers, attorneys, settlement/closing agents and others, who actually perform a service in connection with the mortgage loan or the settlement, from being paid for the reasonable value of their work.

The RESPA statute is primarily aimed at eliminating arrangements whereby one party agrees to return part of their fee in order to obtain business from a referring party. One of the negative results of such an arrangement is that fees are unnecessarily raised to cover the hidden "referral fee," thus harming the prospective borrower.

Penalties

There are criminal and civil penalties that include both fines and imprisonment for violations of the anti-kickback, referral fees and unearned fees provisions of the RESPA statute. In a criminal case, a person who violates Section 8 may be fined up to $10,000 and imprisoned up to one year.

There are also provisions whereby the victim of such an arrangement may recover three times the amount of the kickback, rebate, or referral fee involved, through a private lawsuit. In addition, if the action is successful, the court may award attorney's fees and costs.

LIMITS ON ESCROW ACCOUNTS

As set forth below, Section 10 of the RESPA statute sets limits on the amounts that a lender may require a borrower to put into an escrow account for purposes of paying taxes, insurance premiums, and other charges related to the property. During the course of the loan, the statute prohibits a lender from charging excessive amounts for the escrow account.

The RESPA statute does not require lenders to impose an escrow account on borrowers, although certain government loan programs or lenders may require escrow accounts as a condition of the loan.

Required Escrow

Each month the lender may require a borrower to pay into the escrow account no more than 1/12 of the total of all disbursements payable during the year, plus an amount necessary to pay for any shortage in the account. The lender must perform an escrow account analysis once during the year and notify borrowers of any shortage. Any excess of $50 or more must be returned to the borrower.

Escrow Cushion

In addition to the regular escrow payment, the lender may require an escrow "cushion." The term cushion refers to the excess balance a lender may require a borrower to pay into their escrow account to cover unanticipated increases in the following year's tax and insurance bills.

The RESPA statute and regulations do not require the lender to maintain a cushion. However, since 1976, the statute has allowed lenders to maintain a cushion equal to one-sixth of the total amount of items paid out of the account, or approximately two months of escrow payments.

Nevertheless, if state law or mortgage documents allow for a lesser amount, the lesser amount prevails. Many lenders have recently increased the escrow account cushion to the maximum allowed by law.

Late Payments

The RESPA statute requires that the servicer pay escrow items by the dates due to avoid a penalty or late charge, provided the borrower is up-to-date with his or her mortgage payments. Some servicers who are late in paying such items pass the late fees on to the borrowers instead of absorbing the costs of their own mistakes.

Thus it is important to review the Escrow Account Statement to determine whether the servicer paid any of the escrow items late, and determine whether any late fees were charged to the escrow account as a result. If so, the borrower should complain directly to the loan servicer and request a refund of the late fees. The complaint letter should be labeled as a "qualified written request under Section 6 of RESPA."

If the lender pays the tax bill late and the homeowner is current in making the mortgage payment, HUD would consider the lender responsible for any penalty or late charge, barring any justifiable excuse. The borrower should send a copy of his or her "qualified written request" to HUD so that they can monitor compliance with the statute.

The letter should not be included with the mortgage payment, but should be sent separately to the customer service address. In addition, the required mortgage and escrow payment should be made until the request is resolved.

A sample Qualified Written Request under Section 6 of RESPA can be found in Appendix 20 of this Almanac.

CHAPTER 8:
FORECLOSURE

IN GENERAL

The term foreclosure generally refers to the legal process by which a mortgaged property may be sold to pay off a mortgage loan that is in default. If the borrower defaults on the mortgage payments, the lender has the right to foreclose on the property and sell it. The proceeds of the foreclosure sale are applied against the debt.

Mortgages made after the first mortgage, such as a second mortgage, are considered subordinate mortgages. The lender who holds a subordinate mortgage must wait until the first lender is paid before recovering the debt owed on the subordinate mortgage. This is a precarious position to be in because if the sale does not result in enough money to cover both mortgages, the subordinate lender is not paid in full, if at all.

If there is still an amount owing after the sale, the lender and any subordinate lenders have the right to seek a deficiency judgment against the borrower for any additional amounts owed. Alternatively, if the sale yields a profit, any amounts received above the outstanding debts are returned to the borrower.

LENDER'S RIGHT OF ACCELERATION

When a mortgage loan goes into default, the lender usually has the right to "accelerate" the mortgage—i.e., to accelerate the maturity date of the note and render the entire debt due and payable. The acceleration clause is recognized as valid in all states and is also permitted in connection with government insured real estate loans. The typical acceleration clause is exercisable at the option of the holder of the note.

The reason almost all mortgage notes contain an acceleration clause is that in their absence, the lender does not have a powerful remedy upon the borrower's default. Without an acceleration clause, the lender's only possible means of recourse for default would be a suit to collect the amount of payments missed or a partial foreclosure for the amount of the borrower's default. The lender would thereby be required to bring suit each time there was a default and would not be permitted to have one dispositive and final suit.

The acceleration clause permits the lender to initiate only one lawsuit to collect the entire debt rather than being forced to sue in separate lawsuits for the amount due under each successive delinquent mortgage payment. The lender can then proceed with foreclosure on the mortgage.

The interest increase provision of the acceleration clause allows the interest being paid on the debt to increase to either the maximum amount permitted by law or some other amount established in the clause when the borrower has defaulted on the loan payments. A sample provision is set forth below.

> Should default occur and acceleration of the full amount of the entire indebtedness is called for, interest on the entire amount of the indebtedness shall accrue thereafter at the maximum rate of interest then permitted under the laws of the State of [state name], or continue at the rate provided herein, whichever of said rates is greater.

FORECLOSURE BY SALE

The primary method of foreclosure in the United States involves a public sale of the property. Generally, the borrower cannot lose his "equity of redemption" unless there has been a valid foreclosure of the mortgage. This is so even if the mortgage is in substantial default. Thus no agreement of the parties to the mortgage, or contemporaneous with it, can cut off a recalcitrant borrower's rights in the mortgaged property without the lender resorting to foreclosure. This concept has been referred to as "the prohibition against clogging the borrower's equity of redemption."

There are two methods by which a property may be sold in foreclosure: (1) judicial foreclosure; and (2) power of sale foreclosure.

Judicial Foreclosure

A "judicial foreclosure" refers to a public sale that is held after a judicial proceeding takes place. All of the persons interested in the property must be named as parties to the proceeding. In many states this is the sole method of foreclosure because its court supervision provision provides the utmost protection to the borrower.

Foreclosure proceedings under a regular mortgage require judicial due process, similar to any breach of contract. Therefore, all of the procedures and defenses of any proceeding in litigation must be followed, which can be time-consuming and costly. The signatory borrowers are necessary parties, as well as the lender. Everyone must be served with notice of the pending litigation as provided by state law for all judicial proceedings.

Upon final judgment, the court will order a public foreclosure sale. There is seldom any competitive bidding, particularly if the borrower has a right of redemption, because the real estate purchased does not usually lend itself to quick, speculative profits.

After the sale has taken place, the borrower's interest and all those interests acquired after the date of the initial recording of the mortgage are extinguished. When the sale price is accepted and confirmed by the court, a deed is issued. Although variations exist in state laws, it is usually difficult to have the sale set aside once the deed has been issued.

All foreclosure judgments may be collaterally attacked or appealed. When coupled with the statutory redemption rights existing in many states, the foreclosure procedures can be quite complicated and lengthy. Statutory redemption rights generally set out specific time periods following the foreclosure sale during which the borrower can "redeem" the real estate by reimbursing the foreclosure sale purchaser for all expenses.

Power of Sale Foreclosure Under a Deed of Trust

A "power of sale foreclosure" refers to a public sale that takes place after there has been some form of notice to the parties without the requirement of a judicial proceeding. A power of sale foreclosure is generally available only where the mortgage instrument—generally known as a "deed of trust"—contains a provision that gives the lender the "power" to sell the property without judicial supervision.

The foreclosure provision in a deed of trust is important. Typically, it provides that upon default, the lender (beneficiary) may request that the trustee sell the property at a foreclosure sale. There is usually a provision requiring notification to the borrower/owner of the impending sale.

The foreclosure sale procedure is usually set out in the power of sale clause and is enforced as a contractual agreement between the parties. Thus a deed of trust foreclosure sale is less expensive and less time-consuming than a judicial foreclosure sale.

Any party can bid at the foreclosure sale, although the lender is typically the only bidder. When the nonjudicial foreclosure sale is properly conducted, it has the same effect as a judicial foreclosure. As a result, all persons claiming an interest under or through the borrower lose their interest when the foreclosure sale is completed. Title acquired by a foreclosure sale relates back to the date the deed of trust was recorded, extinguishing all subsequent liens and ownership interests, subject to the various rights of redemption.

Since the foreclosure sale under a deed of trust is usually a nonjudicial proceeding, the borrower cannot appeal it directly. On the other hand, he can initiate a lawsuit to enjoin the sale prior to its taking place, or to set aside the sale after it has taken place upon proof of irregularities, e.g., violations of the borrower's contractual rights.

Nevertheless, if the borrower was properly notified and the foreclosure sale was properly executed, it will rarely be set aside. While this may seem somewhat harsh to the borrower, he still may be able to regain title under the statutory right of redemption existing in some states.

DEFICIENCY JUDGMENT

The foreclosure sale proceeds are used to pay off the mortgage debt. However, the lender is never entitled to more money than the principal and interest due, plus expenses. If the foreclosure sale proceeds exceed the sum of the existing mortgage debt and the foreclosure sale expenses, the surplus, if any, goes to any subordinate lien-holders, and finally the borrower.

In most states, if the sale does not yield enough to cover the borrower's indebtedness, the lender and any subordinate lienholder may obtain a "deficiency judgment" against the borrower. This means that the borrower still has the legal obligation to pay the unpaid balance of the loan.

However, as a practical matter, this debt may be difficult to collect, since the lender has lost its security—i.e., the real estate sold at foreclosure—and no longer has a "lien" on any of the borrower's specific assets. This places the lender in a similar position to the borrower's other "general" or "unsecured" creditors.

EQUITABLE AND STATUTORY REDEMPTION

As discussed in Chapter 1, "Mortgage Overview," of this Almanac, at one time in history, any failure to timely make a mortgage payment automatically caused the borrower to lose his entire interest in the land.

Because of the severity of this provision, the law gradually moved toward other approaches that were less financially devastating to borrowers. These solutions included an equitable redemption and a statutory redemption for the borrower.

Equitable Redemption

The equitable redemption is available in all states to prevent foreclosure. It permits a borrower to prevent foreclosure from occurring by paying the lender the principal and interest due, plus any expenses the lender has incurred in attempting to collect the debt, and in initiating foreclosure proceedings. Equitable redemption may be exercised by borrowers, junior lenders, the borrower's heir and devisees, any other party potentially adversely affected by foreclosure, and by anyone who buys the equity of redemption—i.e., "the right to redeem"—from the borrower.

Most courts have generally ruled that an equitable right of redemption may not be waived, and that waiver clauses in a mortgage are null and void, although this is not always the case. Legally, these courts hold that an equitable right of redemption is automatically a part of every mortgage and cannot be contractually modified by the parties. To decide otherwise would be unfair to borrowers, as some lenders might otherwise refuse to lend unless the equity of redemption was waived.

Statutory Redemption

Statutory redemption rights generally permit a borrower to redeem mortgaged property after the foreclosure sale. Not all states permit statutory redemption, and in those that do permit it, the maximum permissible redemption time period varies from approximately six months to two years.

Statutory redemption was designed to encourage high bidding at the original sale. Thus to implement this objective, the redemption amount is usually the sale price and not the mortgage debt.

The reader is advised to check the law of his or her own jurisdiction to determine the availability of statutory redemption.

PRIORITY OF LIENS

Where more than one mortgage exists on the same property, questions of priority are significant when it comes to a foreclosure sale. One of the basic functions of foreclosure is to put the foreclosure sale purchaser in the shoes of the borrower at the time he executed the mortgage being foreclosed. As a result, the purchaser will obtain a title that is free and clear of all mortgages or other liens junior or subordinate to the mortgage being foreclosed.

Thus a sale purchaser will generally get title free of the second mortgage. This means that any junior liens are wiped out. If, however, the sale brings more than the first mortgage debt, the second lender should normally have a claim to the surplus that is superior to that of the borrower.

Because the foreclosure sale generally extinguishes all inferior lien interests, the holders of inferior liens often bid on or buy property at foreclosure sales to make sure the sale price is sufficient to cover the outstanding loan balance owed them. Also, as previously discussed, inferior lien holders may exercise the equity of redemption to protect their lien interest.

If it is the second mortgage that is in default instead of the first mortgage, the second lender forecloses. In this case as well, the sale should put the purchaser in the shoes of the borrower as of the time the mortgage being foreclosed was executed. As a result, a purchaser will obtain a fee title subject to the first mortgage because the foreclosure of a junior mortgage normally does not affect the status of a senior mortgage on the property. The property is sold "subject to" the superior security interest(s). The purchaser must make payments on the prior existing indebtedness, and is considered to be "subrogated," or placed in the position of the original borrower on the inferior lien.

Thus in the foreclosure process the purchaser at a foreclosure sale is said to have acquired the right to "redeem up," and the trustee or court "foreclosures down." This simply means that foreclosure dissolves all inferior interests, and the foreclosure sale purchaser acquires the right to pay off the superior interests.

Lien priorities generally follow the so-called "barber-shop rule," meaning that the first in time gets priority. Priority is established by compliance with recording acts, so (i) the lack of knowledge of previous mortgages, and (ii) the date that competing mortgages are recorded, are both important factors in determining priority of mortgage payment in case of foreclosure.

Thus in calculating what a purchaser should bid at a foreclosure sale, he or she should at least subtract the amount of the first mortgage, free and clear of liens, from the market value of the property. Although the sale purchaser is generally not personally liable on the first mortgage debt, he or she runs the risk that the first mortgage will be foreclosed and that he will lose his title to the property if he does not satisfy it.

AVOIDING FORECLOSURE

If you are facing a financial crisis, and are having difficulty making your mortgage payments, you should not ignore the problem because it will not go away. Make sure you open any letters you receive from your lender and respond promptly. The letter may contain valuable advice on options available to you. On the other hand, the letter may be a notice of impending legal action. You must address the problem directly and take the steps that are necessary to protect your investment.

Prioritize Your Debts

If at all possible, you should try to keep your mortgage payments current. You must prioritize your bills and pay them in order of importance. Obviously, the necessities should top the list, such as food and utilities. Although your credit rating will suffer if you don't pay your credit card debt, if you don't make your mortgage payments, you are in danger of losing your home.

Dedicate all available income after paying for necessities to your mortgage payments. You may have to forego other non-necessities for a while until your financial situation improves, but at least you will be able to keep your home. If you still do not have enough money to pay your mortgage payments, consider cashing out any other financial resources you have, such as bank accounts, stocks and bonds, and valuable personal property.

Contact Your Lender

If you are still unable to make your mortgage payments despite your attempt to budget, you should contact your lender and discuss your financial situation. You might qualify for a loan workout option, particularly if you have an FHA mortgage.

Do not be afraid that your lender will immediately foreclose on your home because the lender discovers you are having money problems. Generally, lenders do not like to foreclose on homes because it is an expensive process and the lender does not want to get stuck with an inventory of homes.

If you avoid speaking with your lender, then it is inevitable that you will lose your home in a foreclosure sale. If you contact your lender when you first start falling behind in your payments, it is easier to work out a solution. However, the longer you wait, the fewer options remain available.

It is important to prepare before you speak with your lender. You should familiarize yourself with your loan documents and understand the loan terms. Be prepared to explain why you missed any mortgage payments, and provide documentation to support your explanation. In addition, you should be able to tell your lender how you plan on resolving your financial problems.

In addition, in order to decide the best route you should take to avoid foreclosure, you should determine whether your financial situation is temporary, long-term, or permanent. The workout options available to you depend largely on your future ability to handle your mortgage payments.

It is important to keep a journal detailing your conversations with the lender, including the name of the representative, and the date, time, and nature of each conversation. It is advisable to send a follow-up letter confirming the conversation and any important points that were discussed.

Workout Options

If your financial problems are temporary, the following options may be available:

1. Reinstatement—Your lender may be willing to reinstate your mortgage if you promise to pay the total amount owed by a certain date. This is a good option if you are expecting a lump sum of money in the near future, e.g., an insurance settlement, a bonus, a tax refund, etc.

2. Forbearance—Your lender may be willing to reduce or suspend your mortgage payments temporarily until you are able to bring the account current. A forbearance may be combined with a reinstatement, as discussed above.

3. Repayment Plan—Your lender may agree to allow you to start making your full monthly payments along with an additional payment towards the past due amount, until you bring your account current.

If your financial problems are expected to be long-term, your lender may agree to modify your mortgage and change the terms so that you are able to bring your account current. There are a number of ways this can be accomplished. For example, your lender may be able to lower your interest rate or extend the number of years you have to pay, thus lowering your monthly payments; or add the past due payments on to your existing loan balance.

If you decide that your best course of action given your financial situation is to sell your home, the following options may be available in lieu of foreclosure:

1. Sell Your House—Your lender may agree to give you a certain amount of time to sell your house and pay off your mortgage.

2. Assumption—Your lender may allow you to find a qualified buyer to assume—i.e., take over—your mortgage.

3. Deed-in-lieu of Foreclosure—Your lender may allow you to surrender your home and, in return, your debt is forgiven.

4. Short Sale—Your lender may allow you to sell your home and agree to forgive any deficiency between the sale price and the balance owed on the mortgage. However, you may have to include the cancelled amount in income for tax purposes, depending on the circumstances.

Partial Claim—FHA Loans

If you have an FHA guaranteed loan, you may qualify for a one-time interest-free loan from your mortgage guarantor in order to bring your account current. In addition, to give you some time to get your finances in order, the payments on the loan may not be due for several years. However, the loan must be paid if you sell your home or pay off your first mortgage.

In order to obtain this loan, your lender will file what is known as a "partial claim," and the guarantor will pay the lender the amount necessary to bring the mortgage current. You will be required to sign a promissory note for this amount, and a lien will be placed on your home until the note is paid in full.

In order to qualify for an FHA partial claim:

1. Your loan must be between four and twelve months delinquent; and

2. You must be able to resume making your full mortgage payments.

Foreclosure Workout Scams

If you are facing foreclosure, you may be targeted by scam artists who prey on the desperation of homeowners at risk of losing their homes. Following are some of the most common schemes that have been reported:

1. Foreclosure Prevention Specialist—The scam artist, posing as a specialist in preventing foreclosure, charges exorbitant fees in return for making phone calls or completing paperwork that the homeowner

could do on his or her own. The efforts of the so-called "specialist" do nothing to prevent the foreclosure. This is a waste of money and valuable time.

2. Lease/Buyback Proposal—The scam artist deceives the homeowner into signing over the deed to their home by telling the homeowner that they can remain in the house as a renter and eventually buy the home back once their financial problems are resolved. However, the terms for buyback are generally so demanding that the homeowner cannot buy back their home and instead end up being evicted by the scam artist who now owns the home, including all of the equity in the property.

3. Bait and Switch—The scam artist gives the homeowner documents to sign, telling the homeowner that the documents will bring the mortgage current. In reality, the homeowner is unwittingly signing over the deed to their home to the scam artist.

To avoid being victimized by a scam artist, be wary of any business that claims it can stop the foreclosure process, particularly if the representative instructs you not to contact your lender or lawyer. In addition, be skeptical if you are pressured into signing documents you have not had the time to read, or if you are told to send your mortgage payments to the representative.

If you think you have been the victim of foreclosure fraud, you should contact the Federal Trade Commission (FTC). The FTC works for the consumer to prevent fraudulent, deceptive and unfair business practices in the marketplace and to provide information to help consumers spot, stop, and avoid them. You can file a complaint at the FTC website (ftc.gov), or by telephone (1-877-FTC-HELP).

THE MORTGAGE FORGIVENESS DEBT RELIEF ACT OF 2007

The Mortgage Forgiveness Debt Relief Act of 2007 generally allows taxpayers to exclude income from the discharge of debt on their principal residence. Debt reduced through mortgage restructuring, as well as mortgage debt forgiven in connection with a foreclosure, qualify for this relief. The Act applies to debt forgiven in 2007, 2008 or 2009.

Not all mortgage loans qualify for this tax relief. For example, home equity loans where the proceeds were not used to buy, build, or improve the residence, and mortgages on second houses and rental properties, do not qualify for the exclusion.

In addition, the exclusion does not apply if the discharge is due to services performed for the lender or any other reason not directly related to a decline in the home's value or the taxpayer's financial condition. Prior to enactment of the Act, if a lender canceled the borrower's debt, the borrower generally had to include the canceled amount in their income for tax purposes. The lender was required to report the amount of the canceled debt to both the borrower and the Internal Revenue Service.

Up to two million dollars of forgiven debt is eligible for this exclusion, or one million dollars if the taxpayers are married filing separately. The borrower must claim this tax relief on the Internal Revenue Form entitled Reduction of Tax Attributes Due to Discharge of Indebtedness (IRS Form 982).

FILING FOR BANKRUPTCY PROTECTION

If you are facing foreclosure, and your lender refuses to voluntarily work with you on resolving the problem, as a last resort, you may find some temporary relief in the Bankruptcy Court. However, it is recommended that you obtain competent legal advice before proceeding.

Bankruptcy is a serious step that may have certain relatively long-term consequences, thus you must carefully assess your financial situation and determine whether bankruptcy is the right course to take given all of the advantages and disadvantages.

The Bankruptcy Code

The Bankruptcy Code is part of the collection of federal statutes known as the United States Code. The United States Code is broken down into sections known as "Titles." The Bankruptcy Code is Title 11 of the United States Code. Title 11 is further broken down into sections known as "chapters."

The debtor generally chooses which chapter of the Bankruptcy Code provides the desired relief, and determines whether he or she is eligible to file under that chapter considering his or her financial circumstances. There are four chapters of the Bankruptcy Code available to individual consumer debtors: Chapters 7, 13, 11 and 12.

This Almanac discusses bankruptcy protection under Chapter 13 of the Bankruptcy Code, the section of law that protects homeowners who are facing foreclosure on their home by their home mortgage lender because they fall behind in their payments.

Chapter 13 is designed for individuals with regular income who would like to pay all or part of their debts in installments over a period of time. A Chapter 13 bankruptcy case is also referred to as a "wage earner's plan."

Under Chapter 13, an individual debtor who has a regular source of income pays his or her creditors using future earnings pursuant to a court-approved repayment plan ("the chapter 13 plan") for a certain duration, e.g., 3 to 5 years. This enables the debtor to maintain possession of certain valuable assets, such as a house or car.

Advantages

The Automatic Stay

When a Chapter 13 bankruptcy petition is filed, the debtor receives an "automatic stay" that stops most collection actions against the debtor or the debtor's property. The stay is called "automatic" because it does not require a court order, but is simply triggered by the filing of the Chapter 13 petition.

The automatic stay prevents all creditors from taking any legal action against you, including foreclosure proceedings, once the bankruptcy petition has been filed. The purpose of the automatic stay is to take some of the pressure off of the debtor by allowing him or her to work within the bankruptcy system to manage their financial debt, without having to simultaneously deal with creditors.

Thus filing bankruptcy will give you some time to rethink your financial situation without worrying about an immediate foreclosure sale of your home due to mortgage arrears. In order to fully take advantage of the automatic stay, you should immediately notify all of your creditors instead of waiting for the court to make the notification.

If your lender continues to pursue a foreclosure action against you in violation of the automatic stay, you may be entitled to take legal action against the lender and obtain a court order prohibiting the lender from taking further collection action. In addition, a creditor that willfully violates the automatic stay by continuing to pursue legal action may be held in contempt of court and suffer penalties as a result.

Discharge

In addition, bankruptcy gives you a new start if you are also saddled with consumer debt that you are unable to repay. Credit card debt is particularly difficult to resolve. Bankruptcy provides a legal method to wipe out a significant amount—if not all—of consumer debts. This is known as a "discharge." In order to receive the discharge, however, you must complete an instructional course on personal financial management.

If you filed bankruptcy under Chapter 13, and complete all of the payments required under your Chapter 13 reorganization plan, you will receive a discharge of any remaining debts. Once you receive the discharge, your creditors can no longer take any collection action against you for those debts that are discharged. You are no longer legally responsible for those debts.

Certain debts, however, are not dischargeable, including support obligations; most student loans; certain taxes; most criminal fines and restitution obligations; certain debts which are not properly listed in your bankruptcy papers; certain debts for acts that caused death or personal injury; and certain long term secured obligations.

Nevertheless, as discussed below, if there is a valid lien upon specific property that secured the debt, the secured creditor can still enforce the lien to recover the property secured by the lien. Thus although bankruptcy will temporarily stop foreclosure proceedings and give you extra time to work out your mortgage problem, you will ultimately have to pay the debt if you want to keep your home.

Disadvantages

Damage to Credit Rating

The most apparent disadvantage of filing for bankruptcy protection is the serious damage inflicted on your credit rating. A bankruptcy filing can remain on your credit report for 10 years under the provisions of the Fair Credit Reporting Act. This negative credit information generally impedes any efforts to obtain credit, e.g., for a home or automobile purchase, for a considerable period of time.

Public Record

Another disadvantage to filing bankruptcy is that the bankruptcy petition, schedules and other filings are a matter of public record. You must disclose all of your personal financial information for at least the previous two years, and all of this information is available for public scrutiny. In Chapter 13 cases, your employer may also be involved because this chapter may require deductions from the debtor's paycheck as part of the plan to repay debt.

Initiating the Bankruptcy Case

If you decide that bankruptcy is the right course of action for you, it is advisable to consult with an attorney. While there is no requirement for you to be represented by an attorney in bankruptcy matters, it is strongly encouraged to seek legal counsel if possible. The bankruptcy process can be very confusing and complex. In addition, an attorney can advise as to whether bankruptcy or some alternative is the best solution for your financial problems. An attorney will prepare the necessary paperwork and be present during bankruptcy proceedings.

There are businesses that offer to prepare bankruptcy petitions for those seeking to file bankruptcy without an attorney. You should be aware, however, that the services of bankruptcy petition preparers are limited to the typing of forms. They are not permitted to advise individuals on the law, and their services are subject to various statutory requirements and limitations.

Although bankruptcy petition preparers are required to sign all documents they prepare for filing, they are not authorized to sign any documents on your behalf. The bankruptcy petition includes declarations that you must sign attesting to the accuracy of the information contained in the petition. Therefore, it is important that you review the information set forth in the bankruptcy petition to make sure it is accurate or you may jeopardize your case.

The bankruptcy case begins when you file the bankruptcy petition with the bankruptcy court serving the area where you live. In order to file your bankruptcy petition, you are generally required to undergo credit counseling before you file the petition, unless there is an emergency.

After the petition is filed, the bankruptcy court will send you a notice that contains important information concerning your bankruptcy case, including a statement regarding the automatic stay provision. At this point, creditors may no longer try to collect their debts outside of the proceeding. In addition, you are not allowed to transfer property that has been declared part of the "bankruptcy estate" without permission of the Bankruptcy Court. The bankruptcy estate basically includes your home, your assets, and your income.

Exemptions

The law permits you to protect certain property from creditors even if the value of your assets is greater than his or her debts. These items are known as "exempt property" and they are not available for distribution to your creditors. You are required to file a schedule of your "exempt property" in order to protect that property from your creditors.

Typically, exempt property includes but is not limited to vehicles up to a certain dollar amount; the equity in your home up to a certain amount; certain personal property; jewelry up to a certain amount; and your tools of trade, if applicable. If no one objects to the exemptions listed on your schedule within the time frame specified by the bankruptcy court, these assets will not be a part of your bankruptcy estate and will not be used to pay your creditors.

There are exemptions available under both federal and state laws. Section 522(d) of the Bankruptcy Code specifies the items of personal and real property that a creditor cannot take to satisfy a claim. These items are known as the federal bankruptcy exemptions. In addition, the law permits each state to adopt its own exemption law in place of the federal exemptions.

In some states, the debtor may choose between the federal exemptions and the exemptions allowed under the laws of his or her home state. However, the debtor cannot pick and choose exemptions from amongst the two categories. Thus you are advised to compare your state bankruptcy exemption statute with the federal statute to see which statute—federal or state—affords you the greatest protection.

Reinstating Your Mortgage

A home mortgage is the most common type of "secured debt." A secured debt is a debt that is backed by property, known as collateral. In this case, the collateral is your home. The creditor—your lender—has a contractual right to take your home to satisfy the debt. Thus your mortgage must be paid in full if you wish to keep your home. You also have the option of surrendering your home and giving the lender an unsecured claim for any deficiency remaining for the difference between the amount of the secured debt and the value of your surrendered home.

If you file a chapter 13 bankruptcy plan, which is intended to reorganize your debt, the lender still retains a lien on your home. If you want to keep your home, the original loan must be reinstated by paying the mortgage arrears, and maintaining the payments under the original loan terms during the life of the plan and thereafter.

MORTGAGE LENDER OR SERVICER BANKRUPTCY

Today's mortgage market is unstable and many mortgage lenders and servicers are facing their own financial difficulties. It is possible that your mortgage lender or servicer will be the one who files for bankruptcy or closes its doors, and you are left wondering where and how to make your payments, and how this will impact your mortgage loan.

As discussed in Chapter 2, "The Mortgage Loan Process," of this Almanac, the mortgage servicer is the entity that collects your monthly loan payments, credits your account, and handles your escrow account.

Your mortgage servicer and lender may be one and the same, or may be different entities entirely.

If Your Lender Files Bankruptcy Before Loan Closing

If you've been pre-approved for a mortgage and find out that the lender has filed for bankruptcy, call to find out if or when the company intends to make good on your loan. If the lender cannot proceed with the loan, or has gone out of business altogether, you should start shopping around for another mortgage immediately.

If Your Lender Files Bankruptcy After Loan Closing

If your lender files for bankruptcy after your loan closes, the loan and the loan servicing rights are generally bought and sold. If your mortgage servicer is different from your original lender—and your original lender goes out of business—you should continue to make timely payments to your mortgage servicer.

If Your Mortgage Servicer Files Bankruptcy

If your mortgage servicer files for bankruptcy or goes out of business, it will likely transfer the servicing of your loan to another company. In the meantime, if you have an escrow account, even if your servicer files for bankruptcy or goes out of business, it is responsible for making the escrow payments in a timely manner.

You will be notified if your loan has been transferred to another company by both the current servicer and the new servicer. The current servicer must notify you at least 15 days before the effective date of the transfer. The new servicer must notify you within 15 days of the transfer. The effective date is when the first payment is due at the new servicer's address. However, it is advisable to contact the new loan servicer before you begin sending payments, to confirm that they are, in fact, taking over the servicing of your loan.

You have a 60-day grace period after your loan servicing is transferred, during which you cannot be charged a late fee if you accidentally send your mortgage payment to the old servicer. In addition, the new servicer cannot report that payment to a credit bureau as a late payment.

Make sure you keep records of your payments, including billing statements; canceled checks; bank account statements; and online account histories, if applicable. If you have a dispute, continue to make your mortgage payments, but challenge the servicing in writing and keep a copy of your letter and any enclosures for your records. Send your letter by certified mail, and request a return receipt to confirm that the servicer received your letter.

APPENDIX 1:
PLAIN LANGUAGE MORTGAGE

WORDS USED OFTEN IN THIS DOCUMENT

(A) "Mortgage." This document, which is dated _____, 20__, will be called the "Mortgage."

(B) "Borrower." _____ will sometimes be called "Borrower" and sometimes simply "I."

(C) "Lender." _____ will be called "Lender." Lender is a corporation or association which was formed and which exists under the laws of _____. Lender's address is _____.

(D) "Mortgage Note." The mortgage note signed by Borrower and dated _____ will be called the "Mortgage Note." The Mortgage Note shows that I owe Lender _____ Dollars plus interest, which I have promised to pay in monthly payments of principal and interest and to pay in full by _____.

(E) "Property." The property that is described below in the section titled "Description of the Property" will be called the "Property."

BORROWER'S TRANSFER TO LENDER OF
RIGHTS IN THE PROPERTY

I mortgage, grant and convey the Property to Lender subject to the terms of this Mortgage. This means that, by signing this Mortgage, I am giving Lender those rights that are stated in this Mortgage and also that those rights that the law gives to lenders who hold mortgages on real property. I am giving Lender these rights to protect Lender from possible losses that might result if I fail to:

(A) Pay all the amounts that I owe Lender as stated in the Mortgage Note;

(B) Pay, with interest, any amounts that Lender spends under this Mortgage, to protect the value of the Property and Lender's rights in the Property;

(C) Keep all of my other promises and agreements under this Mortgage

DESCRIPTION OF PROPERTY

I give Lender rights in the Property described in (A) through (J) below:

(A) The property which is located at (Street), (City), (State and Zip Code). This property is in (County) in the State of New York. It has the following legal description:

[Provide exact legal description of property]

(B) All buildings and other improvements that are located on the Property described in subsection (A) of this section;

(C) All rights in other property that I have as owner of the Property described in subsection (A) of this section. These rights are known as "easements and appurtenances attached to the Property;"

(D) All rights that I have in the land which lies in the streets or roads in front of, or next to, the Property described in subsection (A) of this section;

(E) All fixtures that are now or in the future will be on the Property described in subsections (A) and (B) of this section;

(F) All of the rights and property described in subsections (B) through (E) of this section that I acquire in the future; and

(G) All replacements of or additions to the Property described in subsections (B) through (F) of this section and all Insurance Proceeds for loss or damage to, and all Miscellaneous Proceeds of the Property described in subsections (A) through (F) of this section.

BORROWER'S RIGHT TO MORTGAGE THE PROPERTY AND BORROWER'S OBLIGATION TO DEFEND OWNERSHIP OF THE PROPERTY

I promise that except for the "exceptions" listed in any title insurance policy which insures Lender's rights in the Property: (A) I lawfully own the Property: (B) I have the right to mortgage, grant and convey the Property to Lender; and (C) there are no outstanding claims or charges against the Property.

I give a general warranty of title to Lender. This means that I will be fully responsible for any losses which Lender suffers because someone other than myself has some of the rights in the Property which I promise that I have. I promise that I will defend my ownership of the Property against any claims of such rights.

UNIFORM PROMISES

I promise and I agree with Lender as follows;

1. BORROWER'S PROMISE TO PAY PRINCIPAL AND INTEREST UNDER THE MORTGAGE NOTE AND TO FULFILL OTHER PAYMENT OBLIGATIONS

I will promptly pay to Lender when due; principal and interest under the Mortgage Note; late charges and prepayment charges as stated in the Mortgage Note; and principal and interest on Future Advances that I may receive under Paragraph 23 below.

2. AGREEMENT ABOUT MONTHLY PAYMENT FOR TAXES AND INSURANCE

(A) Borrower's Obligation to Make Monthly Payments to Lender for Taxes and Insurance

I will pay to Lender all amounts necessary to pay for taxes, assessments, ground rents (if any), and hazard insurance on the Property and mortgage insurance (if any), I will pay those amounts to Lender unless Lender tells me, in writing that I do not have to do so, or unless the law requires otherwise. I will make those payments on the same day that my monthly payments of principal and interest are due under the Mortgage Note.

The amount of each of my payments under this paragraph 2 will be the sum of the following:

(i) One-twelfth of the estimated yearly taxes, assessments and ground rents (if any) on the Property which under the law may be superior to this Property; plus

(ii) One-twelfth of the estimated yearly premium for hazard insurance covering the Property; plus

(iii) One-twelfth of the estimated yearly Premium for mortgage insurance (if any).

Lender will determine from time to time my estimated yearly taxes, assessments, ground rents and insurance premiums based upon existing assessments and bills, and estimates of future assessments and bills. (Taxes, assessments, ground rents and insurance premiums will be called "taxes and insurance.") The amounts that I pay to Lender for taxes and insurance under this Paragraph 2 will called the "Funds."

(B) Lender's Obligations Concerning Borrower's Monthly Payments for Taxes and Insurance

Lender will keep the Funds in a savings or banking institution which has its deposits or accounts insured or guaranteed by a Federal or state agency. If Lender is such an institution then lender may hold the Funds. Except as described in this Paragraph 2, Lender will use the Funds to pay taxes and insurance. Lender will give to me, without charge, an annual accounting of the Funds. That accounting must show all additions to and deductions from the Funds and the reason for each deduction. Lender may not charge me for holding or keeping the Funds on deposit, for using the Funds to pay taxes and insurance, for analyzing my payments of Funds, or for receiving, verifying and totaling assessments and bills. However, Lender may charge me for these services if Lender pays me interest on the Funds and if the law permits Lender to make such a charge. Lender will not be required to pay me any interest or earnings on the Funds unless either (i) Lender and I agree in writing, at the time I sign this Mortgage, that Lender will pay interest on the Funds; or (ii) the law requires Lender to pay interest on the Funds. If Lender's estimates are too high or if taxes and insurance rates go down, the amounts that I pay under this Paragraph 2 will be too large. If this happens at a time when I am keeping all of my promises and agreements made in this Mortgage, I will have the right to have the excess amount either promptly repaid to me as a direct refund or credited to my future monthly pay the taxes and insurance when they are due.

If, when payments of taxes and insurance are due, Lender has not received enough Funds from me to make those payments, I will pay to Lender whatever additional amount is necessary to pay the taxes and insurance in full. I must pay that additional amount in one or more payments as Lender may require. When I have paid all of the amounts due under the Mortgage Note and under this Mortgage, Lender will promptly refund to me any Funds that are then being held or kept on deposit by Lender under Paragraph 20 below either Lender acquire the Property or the Property is sold, then immediately before the acquisition or sale, Lender will use any Funds which Lender is holding or has on deposit at that time to reduce the amount that I owe to Lender under the Mortgage Note and under this Mortgage.

3. LENDER'S APPLICATION OF BORROWER'S PAYMENTS

Unless the law requires otherwise, Lender will apply each of my payments under the Mortgage Note and under Paragraphs I and 2 above in the following order and for the following purposes:

(A) First, to pay the amounts then due to Lender under Paragraph 2 above;

(B) Next, to pay interest then due under the Mortgage Note;

(C) Next, to pay principal then due under the Mortgage Note: and

(D) Next, to pay interest and principal on any Future Advances that I may have received from Lender under Paragraph 23 below.

4. BORROWER'S OBLIGATION TO PAY CHARGES AND ASSESSMENTS AND TO SATISFY CLAIMS AGAINST THE PROPERTY

I will pay all taxes, assessments, and any other chargers and fines that may be imposed on the Property and that may be superior to this Mortgage. I will also make payments due under my lease of I am a tenant on the Property and I will pay ground rents (if any) due on the Property. I will do this either by making the payments to Lender that are described in Paragraph 2 above or, if I am not required to make payments under Paragraph 2. By making payments, when they are due, directly to the persons entitled to them. (In this Mortgage, the word "person" means any person, organization, governmental authority, or other party.) If I make direct payments, then promptly after making any of those payments I will give Lender a receipt which shows that I have done so. If I make payment to Lender under Paragraph 2, 1 will give Lender all notices or bills that I receive for the amounts due under this Paragraph 4.

Any claim, demand or charge that is made against property because an obligation has not been fulfilled is known as a "lien." I will promptly pay or satisfy all liens against the property that may be superior to this Mortgage. However, this Mortgage does not require me to satisfy a superior lien if: (A) I agree, in writing, to pay the obligation which gave rise to the superior lien and Lender approves the way in which I agree to pay that obligation; or (B) 1, in good faith, argue or defend against the superior lien in a lawsuit so that, during the lawsuit, the superior lien may not be enforced and no part of the Property must be given up.

5. BORROWER'S OBLIGATION TO OBTAIN AND TO KEEP HAZARD INSURANCE ON THE PROPERTY

I will obtain hazard insurance to cover all buildings and other improvements that now are or in the future will be located on the Property. The insurance must cover loss or damage caused by fire, hazards normally covered by "extended coverage" hazard insurance policies, and other hazards for which Lender requires coverage. The insurance must be in the amounts and for the periods of time required by Lender. It is possible that the insurance policy will have provisions that may limit the insurance company's obligation to pay claims if the amount of coverage is too low. Those provisions are known as "co-insurance requirements. Lender may not require me to obtain an amount of coverage that is more than the larger" larger of the following two amounts: either (1) the amount that I owe to Lender under the Mortgage Note and under this Mortgage; or (ii) the amount necessary to satisfy the co-insurance requirements.

I may choose the insurance company, but my choice is subject to Lender's approval. Lender may not refuse to approve my choice unless the refusal is reasonable. All of the insurance policies and renewals of those policies must include what is known as a "standard mortgage clause" to protect Lender. The form of all policies and the form of all renewals must be acceptable to Lender. Lender will have the right to hold the policies and renewals.

I will pay the premiums on the insurance policies either by making payments to Lender, as described in Paragraph 2 above, or by paying the insurance company directly when the premium payments are due. If Lender requires, I will promptly give Lender all receipts of paid premiums and all renewal notices that I receive.

If there is a loss or damage to the Property, I will promptly notify the insurance company and Lender. If I do not promptly prove to the insurance company that the loss or damage occurred, then Lender may do so. The amount paid by the insurance company is called proceeds will be used to repair or to restore the damage Property unless: (a) it is not economically possible to make the repairs or restoration; or (b) the use of the proceeds for that purpose would lessen the protection given to Lender by this Mortgage; or (c) Lender and I have agreed in writing not to use the proceeds for that purpose. If the repair or restoration is not economically possible or if it would lessen Lender's protection under this Mortgage, then the proceeds will be used to reduce the amount that I owe to Lender under the Mortgage Note and under this Mortgage. If any of the proceeds will be paid to me. The use of proceeds to reduce the amount that I owe to Lender will not be a prepayment that is subject to the prepayment that is subject to the prepayment charge provisions, if any, under the Mortgage Note.

If I abandon the Property, or if I do not answer, within 30 days, a notice from Lender stating that the insurance company has offered to settle a claim for insurance benefits, then Lender has the authority to collect the proceeds. Lender may then use the proceeds to repair or restore the Property or to reduce the amount that I owe to Lender under the Mortgage Note and under this Mortgage. The 30-day period will begin on the date the notice is mailed or, if it is not mailed, on the date the notice is delivered.

If any proceeds are used to reduce the amount of principal which I owe to Lender under the Mortgage Note, that use will not delay the due date or change the amount of any of my monthly payments under the Mortgage Note and under Paragraphs 1 and 2 above. However, Lender and I may agree in writing to those delays or changes.

If Lender acquires the Property under Paragraph 20 below, all of my rights in the insurance policies will belong to Lender. Also, all of my rights in any proceeds which are paid because of damage that occurred before the Property is acquired by Lender or sold will belong to Lender. However, Lender's rights in those proceeds will not be greater than the amount that I owe to Lender under the Mortgage Note and under this Mortgage immediately before the Property is acquired by Lender or Sold.

6. BORROWER'S OBLIGATION TO MAINTAIN THE PROPERTY

(A) Agreements about Maintaining the Property and Keeping Promises in Lease I will keep the Property in good repair. I will not destroy, damage or substantially change the Property, and I will not allow the Property to deteriorate.

7. LENDER'S RIGHT TO TAKE ACTION TO PROTECT THE PROPERTY

If: (a) I do not keep my promises and agreements made in this Security Instrument; (b) someone, including me, begins a legal proceeding that may significantly affect Lender's interest in the Property; or (c) I have abandoned the Property, then Lender may do whatever is reasonable or appropriate to protect Lender's interest in the Property.

8. LENDER'S RIGHT TO INSPECT THE PROPERTY

Lender, and others authorized by Lender, may enter on and inspect the Property. They must do so in a reasonable manner and at reasonable times. Before one of those inspections is made, Lender must give me notice stating a reasonable purpose for the inspection. That purpose must be related to Lender's rights in the Property.

9. AGREEMENTS ABOUT CONDEMNATION OF THE PROPERTY

A taking of property by any governmental authority by eminent domain is known as "condemnation." I give to Lender my right: (A) to proceeds of all awards or claims for damages resulting from condemnation or other governmental taking of the Property; and (B) to proceeds from a sale of the Property that is made to avoid condemnation. All of those proceeds will be paid to Lender.

If all of the Property is taken, the proceeds will be used to reduce the amount that I owe to Lender under the Mortgage Note and under this Mortgage. If any of the proceeds remain after the amount that I owe to Lender has been paid in full, the remaining proceeds will be paid to me. Unless Lender and I agree otherwise in writing, if only a part of the Property is taken, the amount that I owe to Lender will only be reduced by the amount of proceeds multiplied by the following amount: (1) the total amount that I owe to Lender under the Mortgage Note and under this Mortgage immediately before the taking, divided by (ii) the fair market value of the Property immediately before the taking, divided by (ii) the fair market value of the Property immediately before the taking. The remainder of the proceeds will be paid to me. The use of proceeds to reduce the amount that I owe to Lender will not be a prepayment that is subject to the prepayment charge provisions, if any, under the Mortgage Note. If I abandon the Property, or if I do not answer, within 30 days, a notice from Lender stating that a governmental authority has offered to make a payment or to settle a claim for damages, then Lender has the authority to collect the proceeds. Lender may then use the proceeds to repair or restore the Property or to reduce the amount that I owe to Lender under the Mortgage Note and under this Mortgage. The 30-day period will begin on the date the notice is mailed or, if it is not mailed, on the date the notice is delivered. If any proceeds are used to reduce the amount of principal which I owe to Lender under the Mortgage Note, that use will not delay the due date or change the amount of any of my monthly payments under the Mortgage Note and under Paragraphs 1 and 2 above. However, Lender and I may agree in writing to those delays or changes.

10. CONTINUATION OF BORROWER'S OBLIGATIONS

Lender may allow a person who takes over my rights and obligations to delay or to change the amount of the monthly payments of principal and interest due under the Mortgage Note or under this Mortgage. Even if Lender does this, however, that person and I will both still be fully obligated under the Mortgage Note and under this Mortgage unless the conditions stated in Paragraph 19 below have been met.

Lender may allow those delays or changes for a person who takes over my rights and obligations, even if Lender is requested not to do so. Lender will not be required to bring a lawsuit against such a person for not fulfilling obligations under the Mortgage Note or under this Mortgage, even if Lender is requested to do so.

11. CONTINUATION OF LENDER'S RIGHTS

Even if Lender does not exercise or enforce any right of Lender under this Mortgage or under the law, Lender will still have all of those rights and may exercise and enforce them in the future. Even if Lender obtains insurance, pays taxes, or pays other claims, charges or liens against the Property, Lender will still have the right, under Paragraph 20 below, to demand that I make Immediate Payment In Full (see Paragraph 20 for a definition of this phrase) of the amount that I owe to Lender under the Mortgage Note and under this Mortgage.

12. LENDER'S ABILITY TO ENFORCE MORE THAN ONE OF LENDER'S RIGHTS

Each of Lender's rights under this Mortgage is separate. Lender may exercise and enforce one or more of those rights, as well as any of Lender's other rights under the law, one at a time or all at once.

13. OBLIGATIONS OF BORROWERS AND OF PERSONS TAKING OVER BORROWER'S RIGHTS OR OBLIGATIONS; AGREEMENTS CONCERNING CAPTIONS

Subject to the terms of Paragraph 19 below, any person who takes over my rights or obligations under this Mortgage will have all of my rights and will be obligated to keep all of my promises and agreements made in this Mortgage. Similarly, any person who takes over Lender's rights or obligations under this Mortgage will have all of Lender's rights and will be obligated to keep all of Lender's agreements made in this Mortgage.

If more than one person signs this Mortgage as Borrower, each of us is fully obligated to keep all of Borrower's promises and obligations contained in this Mortgage. Lender may enforce Lender's rights under this Mortgage against each of us individually or against all of us together.

This means that any one of us may be required to pay all of the amounts owed under the Mortgage Note and under this Mortgage. However, if one of us does not sign the Mortgage Note, then:

(A) that person is signing this Mortgage only to give that person's rights in the Property to Lender under the terms of this Mortgage; and

(B) that person is not personally obligated to make payments or to act under the Mortgage Note or under this Mortgage.

The captions and titles of this Mortgage are for convenience only. They may not be used to interpret or to define the terms of this Mortgage.

14. AGREEMENTS ABOUT GIVING NOTICES REQUIRED UNDER THIS MORTGAGE

Unless the law requires otherwise, any notice that must be given to me under, this Mortgage will be given by delivering it or by mailing it addressed to me at the address stated in the section above titled "Description Of The Property." A notice will be delivered or mailed to me at a different address if I give Lender a notice of my different address. Any notice that must be given to Lender under this Mortgage will be given by mailing it to Lender's address stated in paragraph (C) of the section above titled "Words Used Often In This Document." A notice will be mailed to Lender at a different address if Lender gives me a notice of the different address. A notice required by this Mortgage is given when it is mailed or when it is delivered according to the requirements of this Paragraph 14.

15. AGREEMENTS ABOUT UNIFORM MORTGAGE AND LAW THAT GOVERNS THIS MORTGAGE

This is a "Uniform Mortgage." It contains "uniform promises" that are in mortgages used all over the country and also "non-uniform promises" that vary, to a limited extent, in different parts of the country.

The law that applies in the place that the Property is located will govern this Mortgage. If any term of this Mortgage or of the Mortgage Note conflicts with the law, all other terms of this Mortgage and of the Mortgage Note will still remain in effect if they can be given effect without the conflicting term. This means than any terms of this Mortgage and of the Mortgage Note which conflict with the law can be separated from the remaining terms, and the remaining terms will still be enforced.

16. BORROWER'S COPY OF THE MORTGAGE NOTE AND OF THIS MORTGAGE

I will be given a copy of the Mortgage Note and of this Mortgage. Those copies must show that the original Mortgage Note and this Mortgage have been signed. I will be given those copies either when I sign the Mortgage Note and this Mortgage or after this Mortgage has been recorded in the proper official records.

17. AGREEMENTS THAT APPLY TO VA LOANS

A loan that is guaranteed or insured by the United States Veterans Administration is known as a "VA loan." If the loan that I promise to pay in the Mortgage Note is a VA loan, then my rights and obligations, as well as those of Lender, are governed by that law which is known as Title 38 of the United States Code and the Regulations made under that Title (called the "VA Requirements"). One or more terms of this Mortgage, or of other documents that are signed in connection with my VA loan, might conflict with the VA Requirements. For example, the prepayment terms in the Mortgage Note or Paragraph 19 of this Mortgage might conflict with the VA Requirements. Lender and I agree that if there is a conflict, the conflicting terms of this Mortgage or other documents are modified or eliminated as much as is necessary to make all of the conflicting terms agree with the VA Requirements.

18. BORROWER'S OBLIGATION TO PAY MORTGAGE INSURANCE PREMIUMS

If Lender required mortgage insurance as a condition of making the loan that I promise to pay under the Mortgage Note, I will pay the premiums for that mortgage insurance. I will pay the premiums until the requirement for mortgage insurance ends according to my written agreement with Lender or according to law. Lender may require me to pay the premiums in the manner described in Paragraph 2 above.

NON-UNIFORM PROMISES

I also promise and agree with Lender as follows:

19. AGREEMENTS ABOUT ASSUMPTION OF THIS MORTGAGE AND ABOUT LENDER'S RIGHTS IF BORROWER TRANSFERS THE PROPERTY WITHOUT MEETING CERTAIN CONDITIONS

If I sell or transfer all or part of the Property or any rights in the Property, any person to whom I sell or transfer the Property may take over all of my rights and obligations under this Mortgage (known as an "assumption of the Mortgage") if certain conditions are met. Those conditions are: (A) I give Lender notice of the sale or transfer; (B) Lender agrees that the person's credit is satisfactory; (C) the person agrees to pay interest on the amount owed to Lender under the Mortgage Note and under this Mortgage at whatever rate Lender requires; and (D) the person signs an assumption agreement that is acceptable to Lender and that obligates the person to keep all of the promises and agreements made in the Mortgage Note and in this Mortgage. If I sell or transfer the Property and each of the conditions in (A), (B), (C) and (D) of this Paragraph 19 is satisfied, Lender will release me from all of my obligations under the Mortgage Note and under this Mortgage.

If I sell or transfer the Property and the conditions in (A), (B), (C) and (D) of this Paragraph 19 are not satisfied, I will still be fully obligated under the Mortgage Note and under this Mortgage and Lender may require Immediate Payment in Full, as that phrase is defined in Paragraph 20 below. However, Lender will not have the right to require Immediate Payment in Full as a result of certain transfers. Those transfers are: (i) the creation of liens or other claims against the Property that are inferior to this Mortgage; (ii) a transfer of rights in household appliances, to a person who provides me with the money to buy those appliances, in order to protect that person against possible losses; (iii) a transfer of the Property to surviving co-owners, following the death of a co-owner, when the transfer is automatic according to law; (iv) leasing the Property for a term of three years or less, as long as the lease does not include an option to buy.

If Lender requires Immediate Payment in Full under this Paragraph 19, Lender will send me, in the manner described in Paragraph 14 above, a notice which states this requirement. The notice will give me at least 30 days to make the required payment. The 30-day period will begin on the date the notice is mailed or, if it is not mailed, on the date the notice is delivered. If I do not make the required payment during that period, Lender may bring a lawsuit for "foreclosure and sale" under Paragraph 20 below without giving me any further notice or demand for payment. (See Paragraph 20 for a definition of "foreclosure and sale.")

20. LENDER'S RIGHTS IF BORROWER FAILS TO KEEP PROMISES AND AGREEMENTS

If all of the conditions stated in subparagraphs (A), (B), and (C) of this Paragraph 20 are met, Lender may require that I pay immediately the entire amount then remaining unpaid under the Mortgage Note and under this Mortgage. Lender may do this without making any further demand for payment. This requirement will be called "Immediate Payment in Full."

If Lender requires Immediate Payment in Full, Lender may bring a lawsuit to take away all of my remaining rights in the Property and to have the Property sold. At this sale Lender or another person may acquire the Property. This is known as "foreclosure and sale." In any lawsuit for foreclosure and sale, Lender will have the right to collect all costs allowed by law.

Lender may require Immediate Payment In Full under this Paragraph 20 only if all of the following conditions are met:

(A) I fail to keep any promise or agreement made in this Mortgage, including the promises to pay when due the amounts that I owe to Lender under the Mortgage Note and under this Mortgage; and

(B) Lender sends to me, in the manner described in Paragraph 14 above, a notice that states:

(i) The promise or agreement that I failed to keep;

(ii) The action that I must take to correct that failure;

(iii) A date by which I must correct the failure. That date must be at least 30 days from the date on which the notice is mailed to me, or, if it is not mailed, from the date on which it is delivered to me;

(iv) That if I do not correct the failure by the date stated in the notice, I will be in default and Lender may require Immediate Payment in Full, and Lender or another person may acquire the Property by means of foreclosure and sale;

(v) That I may speak with a named representative of Lender to discuss any questions which I have about the things stated in the notice;

(vi) That if I meet the conditions stated in Paragraph 21 below, I will have the right to have any lawsuit for foreclosure and sale discontinued and to have the Mortgage Note and this Mortgage remain in full effect as if Immediate Payment In Full had never been required; and

(vii) That I have the right in any lawsuit for foreclosure and sale to argue that I did keep my promises and agreements under the Mortgage Note and under this Mortgage, and to present any other defenses that I may have; and

(C) I do not correct the failure stated in the notice from Lender by the date stated in that notice.

21. BORROWER'S RIGHT TO HAVE LENDER'S LAWSUIT FOR FORECLOSURE AND SALE DISCONTINUED

Even if Lender has required Immediate Payment in Full, I may have the right to have discontinued any lawsuit brought by Lender for foreclosure and sale or for other enforcement of this Mortgage. I will have this right at any time before a judgment has been entered enforcing this Mortgage if I meet the following conditions:

(A) I pay to Lender the full amount that would have been due under this Mortgage, the Mortgage Note, and any notes for Future Advances under Paragraph 23 below if Lender had not required Immediate Payment in Full; and

(B) I correct my failure to keep any of my other promises or agreements made in this Mortgage; and

(C) I pay all of Lender's reasonable expenses in enforcing this Mortgage including, for example, reasonable attorney's fees; and

(D) I do whatever Lender reasonably requires to assure that Lender's rights in the Property, Lender's rights under this Mortgage, and my obligations under the Mortgage Note and under this Mortgage continue unchanged.

If I fulfill all of the conditions in this Paragraph 21, then the Mortgage Note and this Mortgage will remain in full effect as if Immediate Payment in Full had never been required.

22. LENDER'S RIGHTS TO RENTAL PAYMENTS FROM THE PROPERTY AND TO TAKE POSSESSION OF THE PROPERTY

As additional protection for Lender, I give to Lender all of my rights to any rental payments from the Property. However, until Lender requires Immediate Payment in Full under Paragraphs 19 or 20 above, or until I abandon the Property, I have the right to collect and keep those rental payments as they become due. I have not given any of my rights to rental payments from the Property to anyone else, and I will not do so without Lender's consent in writing.

If Lender requires Immediate Payment in Full under Paragraph 19 or 20 above, or if I abandon the Property, then Lender, persons authorized by Lender, or a receiver appointed by a court at Lender's request may: (A) collect the rental payments, including overdue rental payments, directly from the tenants; (B) enter on and take possession of the Property; (C) manage the Property; and (D) sign, cancel and change leases. I agree that if Lender notifies the tenants that Lender has the right to collect rental payments directly from them under this Paragraph 22, the tenants may make those rental payments to Lender without having to ask whether I have failed to keep my promises and agreements under this Mortgage.

If there is a judgment for Lender in a lawsuit for foreclosure and sale, I will pay to Lender reasonable rent from the date the judgment is entered for as long as I occupy the Property. However, this does not give me the right to occupy the Property.

All rental payments collected by Lender or by a receiver, other than the rent paid by me under this Paragraph 22, will be used first to pay the costs of collecting rental payments and of managing the Property. If any part of the rental payments remains after those costs have been paid in full, the remaining part will be used to reduce the amount that I owe to Lender under the Mortgage Note and under this Mortgage. The costs of managing the Property may include the receiver's fees reasonable attorney's fees, and the cost of any necessary bonds. Lender and the receiver will be obligated to account only for those rental payments that they actually receive.

23. AGREEMENTS ABOUT FUTURE ADVANCES

I may ask Lender to make one or more loans to me in addition to the loan that I promise to pay under the Mortgage Note. Lender may, before this Mortgage is discharged, make those additional loans to me. This Mortgage will protect Lender from possible losses that might result from any failure to pay the amounts of any of those additional loans plus interest, only if the notes which contain my promises to pay those additional loans state that this Mortgage will give Lender such protection. Additional loans made by Lender that are protected by this Mortgage will be called "Future Advances." The principal amount that I owe to Lender under the Mortgage Note and under all notes for Future Advances, not including the amounts spent by Lender to protect the value of the Property and Lender's rights in the Property, may not be greater than the original amount of the Mortgage Note plus $_____.

24. LENDER'S OBLIGATION TO DISCHARGE THIS MORTGAGE WHEN THE MORTGAGE NOTE AND THIS MORTGAGE ARE PAID IN FULL

When Lender has been paid all amounts due under the Mortgage Note, under this Mortgage and under any notes for Future Advances, Lender will discharge this Mortgage by delivering a certificate stating that this Mortgage has been satisfied. I will not be required to pay Lender for the discharge, but I will pay all costs of recording the discharge in the proper official records.

25. AGREEMENTS ABOUT NEW YORK LIEN LAW

I will receive all amounts lent to me by Lender subject to the trust fund provisions of Section 13 of the New York Lien Law. This means that if, on the date this Mortgage is recorded in the proper official records, construction or other work on any building or other improvement located on the Property has not been completed for at least four months, I will: (A) hold all amounts, which I receive and which I have a right to receive from Lender under the Mortgage Note and as Future Advances, as a "trust fund"; and (B) use those amounts to pay for that construction or work before I use them for any other purpose. The fact that I am holding those amounts as a "trust fund" means that I have a special responsibility under the law to use the amounts in the manner described in this paragraph 25.

By signing this mortgage, I agree to all of the above.

Witnesses:

Borrower:

Borrower:

State of New York

County of [Name]

On this ___ day of _____ 20__, before me personally came [Borrower Name(s)] to me known and known to me to be the individual(s) described in and who executed the foregoing instrument, and he/she/they duly acknowledged to me that he/she/they executed the same.

Notary Public Signature/Seal

APPENDIX 2:
MORTGAGE NOTE

1. BORROWER'S PROMISE TO PAY

Borrower promises to pay to the Lender the principal sum of $_____ ("principal"), plus interest, to the order of Lender.

Borrower understands that the Lender may transfer this Mortgage Note. The Lender or anyone who takes this Mortgage Note by transfer and who is entitled to receive payments under this Mortgage Note is called the "Mortgage Note Holder."

2. INTEREST

Interest under this Mortgage Note will be charged on unpaid principal until the full amount of principal has been paid. Borrower will pay interest at a yearly rate of _____ percent.

3. PAYMENTS

(A) Time and Place of Payments

Borrower will pay principal and interest by making payments every month on the _____ day of each month beginning on _____, 20__.

Borrower will make these payments until I have paid all of the principal and interest and any other charges described below that I may owe under this Mortgage Note.

Borrower's monthly payments will be applied to interest before principal.

A final payment of unpaid principal balance and accrued interest due, if any, will be paid on the final payment date ("maturity date")

Borrower will send monthly payments to Lender located at [Lender's Address] or at any different location required by the Mortgage Note Holder.

(B) Amount of Monthly Payments

Borrower's initial monthly payment will be in the amount of $_____ plus any other monies payable monthly as described in the mortgage instrument.

4. BORROWER'S RIGHT TO PREPAY

Borrower has the right to make payments of principal at any time before they are due. A payment of principal only is known as a "prepayment." When Borrower makes a prepayment, Borrower will so notify the Mortgage Note Holder, in writing.

Borrower may make a full prepayment or partial prepayments without paying any prepayment charge. The Mortgage Note Holder will use all of Borrower's prepayments to reduce the amount of principal that Borrower owes under this Mortgage Note. If Borrower makes a partial prepayment, there will be no changes in the due date or in the amount of my monthly payment unless the Mortgage Note Holder agrees in writing to those changes.

5. LOAN CHARGES

If a law, which applies to this loan and which sets maximum loan charges, is finally interpreted so that the interest or other loan charges collected or to be collected in connection with this loan exceed the permitted limits, then the following shall apply:

(A) Such loan charge shall be reduced by the amount necessary to reduce the charge to the permitted limit; and

(B) Any sums already collected from Borrower which exceeded permitted limits will be refunded. The Mortgage Note Holder may choose to make this refund by reducing the principal Borrower owes under this Mortgage Note or by making a direct payment to Borrower. If a refund reduces principal, the reduction will be treated as a partial prepayment.

6. BORROWER'S FAILURE TO PAY

(A) Late Charges

If the Mortgage Note Holder has not received the full amount of any monthly payment within _____ days after the due date, Borrower will promptly pay a late charge to the Mortgage Note Holder to compensate the Mortgage Note Holder for their inconvenience. The late charge is not to be considered additional interest.

The amount of the late charge will be _____ percent of the overdue payment of principal and interest.

(B) Default

If Borrower does not pay the full amount of each monthly payment within _____ days of the date it is due, Borrower will be in default.

(C) Notice of Default

If Borrower is in default, the Mortgage Note Holder may, but is not required to, send Borrower a written notice advising Borrower that if Borrower does not pay the overdue amount by a certain date, the Mortgage Note Holder may require Borrower to pay immediately the full amount of principal which has not been paid and all the interest that is owed on that amount.

(D) No Waiver

If at the time Borrower is in default, the Mortgage Note Holder does not require Borrower to pay immediately in full as described above, the Mortgage Note Holder will still have the right to do so if Borrower is in default at a later time.

(E) Payment of Costs and Expenses

If the Mortgage Note Holder has required Borrower to pay immediately in full as described above, the Mortgage Note Holder will have the right to be reimbursed by Borrower for all of its costs and expenses in enforcing this Mortgage Note to the extent permitted by applicable law, including reasonable legal fees.

7. NOTICES

Unless applicable law requires a different method, any notice that must be given to Borrower under this Mortgage Note will be given by delivering it or by mailing it by first class mail to Borrower at the Property Address listed above, or at a different address if Borrower gives the Mortgage Note Holder a notice of a different address.

Any notice that must be given to the Mortgage Note Holder under this Mortgage Note will be given by mailing it by first class mail to the Mortgage Note Holder at the address listed in Section 3(A) above, or at a different address if Borrower is given a notice of a different address.

8. OBLIGATIONS OF PERSONS UNDER THIS NOTE

If more than one person signs this Mortgage Note, each person is fully and personally obligated to keep all of the promises made in this Mortgage Note, including the promise to pay the full amount owed. Any person who takes over these obligations, including the obligations of a guarantor, surety or endorser of this Mortgage Note, is also obligated to keep all of the promises made in this Mortgage Note. The Mortgage Note Holder may enforce its rights under this Mortgage Note against each person individually or against all persons jointly.

9. WAIVERS

Any person who has obligations under this Mortgage Note waives the rights of presentment and notice of dishonor. "Presentment" means the right to require the Mortgage Note Holder to demand payment of amounts due. "Notice of dishonor" means the right to require the Mortgage Note Holder to give notice to other persons that amounts due have not been paid.

10. SECURED NOTE

In addition to the protections given to the Mortgage Note Holder under this Mortgage Note, a Mortgage, dated the same date as this Mortgage Note, protects the Mortgage Note Holder from possible losses which might result if Borrower does not keep the promises made in this Mortgage Note. The Mortgage describes how and under what conditions Borrower may be required to make immediate payment in full of all amounts owed under this Mortgage Note.

Borrower acknowledges receipt of an exact copy of this Mortgage Note.

[Borrower Signature Line]

APPENDIX 3:
MORTGAGE CHECKLIST

1. Lender Name:

2. Name of Contact:

3. Date of Contact:

4. Mortgage Amount:

5. Type of Mortgage:

   (a) Fixed rate:

   (b) Adjustable rate:

   (c) FHA:

   (d) Conventional:

   (e) Other:

6. Minimum down payment required:

7. Loan term:

8. Contract interest rate:

9. Annual percentage rate (APR):

10. Points:

11. Private Mortgage Insurance (PMI) Premiums

    (a) How long must you keep PMI?

12. Estimated monthly escrow for taxes and hazard insurance:

13. Estimated monthly payment (Principal, Interest, Taxes, Insurance, PMI):

14. Fees:

(a) Application fee or Loan processing fee:

(b) Origination fee or Underwriting fee:

(c) Lender fee or Funding fee:

(d) Appraisal fee:

(e) Attorney fees:

(f) Document preparation and recording fees:

(g) Broker fees:

(h) Credit report fee:

(i) Other fees:

15. Other Costs at Closing/Settlement:

16. Title search

(a) Lender cost:

(b) Borrower cost:

17. Title Insurance

(a) Lender cost:

(b) Borrower cost:

18. Estimate prepaid amounts for interest, taxes, hazard insurance, payments to escrow:

19. State and local taxes, stamp taxes, transfer taxes:

20. Flood determination:

21. Prepaid Private Mortgage Insurance (PMI):

22. Surveys and home inspections:

23. Total Fees and Other Closing/Settlement Cost Estimates:

24. Are any of the fees or costs waivable?

25. Prepayment penalties:

(a) Is there a prepayment penalty?

(b) If so, how much is it?

(c) How long does the penalty period last? (for example, 3 years? 5 years?)

(d) Are extra principal payments allowed?

26. Lock-ins:

(a) Is the lock-in agreement in writing?

(b) Is there a fee to lock-in?

(c) When does the lock-in occur—at application, approval or another time?

(d) How long will the lock-in last?

(e) If the rate drops before closing, can you lock-in at a lower rate?

27. If the loan is an adjustable rate mortgage:

(a) What is the initial rate?

(b) What is the maximum the rate could be next year?

(c) What are the rate and payment caps each year and over the life of the loan?

(d) What is the frequency of rate change and of any changes to the monthly payment?

(e) What is the index that the lender will use?

(f) What margin will the lender add to the index?

28. Credit life insurance:

(a) Does the monthly amount quoted to you include a charge for credit life insurance?

(b) If so, does the lender required credit life insurance as a condition of the loan?

(c) How much does the credit life insurance cost?

(d) How much lower would your monthly payment be without the credit life insurance?

(e) If the lender does not require credit life insurance, and you still want to buy it, what rates can you get from other insurance providers?

Source: The Federal Trade Commission.

APPENDIX 4:
BUYER'S ESTIMATED CLOSING COSTS

ITEM	ESTIMATED AMOUNT	ACTUAL AMOUNT
(1) Application Fee	Charged by Lender, May range from $100–$300	$_____
(2) Appraisal Fee	Approximately $250	$_____
(3) Credit Report	Approximately $50	$_____
(4) Escrow Fees (Insurance)	Amounts paid to lender for insurance, generally, includes advance payments of homeowner's insurance (2 months); and flood and PMI insurance, when required (2 months)	$_____
(5) Escrow Fees (Taxes)	Amounts paid to lender for property and school taxes, generally, includes advance (3 months)	$_____
(6) Flood Certification Fee	Required by lender to verify flood zone status of property, approximately $15	$_____
(7) Flood Insurance	Varies depending on flood zone, generally, $500–$1000 per year	$_____
(8) Funding Fee	A percentage of the loan amount charged on VA loans instead of PMI	$_____
(9) Home Inspection	Approximately $300–$500	$_____
(10) Homeowner's Insurance	Varies, generally .0025 of purchase price per year	$_____

ITEM	ESTIMATED AMOUNT	ACTUAL AMOUNT
(11) Buyer's Legal Fees	Legal fees vary depending on attorney and location, but, generally, range from $750–$1,000	$_____
(12) Lender's Legal Fee	For review of documents, ranges from $150–$250, where applicable	$_____
(13) Mortgage Tax	Generally, 0.75% of mortgage amount, where applicable	$_____
(14) Points	Amount paid to lender to "buydown" interest rate on mortgage, usually ranges from 0 to 3 points	$_____
(15) Prepaid Interest	Interest on mortgage payable to lender from date of closing to end of 1st month	$_____
(16) Private Mortgage Insurance	PMI is required if mortgage is more than 80% of purchase price, generally, .004 of mortgage amount	$_____
(17) Recording Fees	Approximately $50–$75	$_____
(18) Survey	Depends on size of property, but ranges from $350–$500	$_____
(19) Title Insurance	Approximately $500 per $100,000 of coverage	$_____
(20) Title Search	Approximately $150–$200	$_____
Estimated Total Closing Costs:		$_____

APPENDIX 5:
UNIFORM RESIDENTIAL LOAN APPLICATION

Uniform Residential Loan Application

This application is designed to be completed by the applicant(s) with the Lender's assistance. Applicants should complete this form as "Borrower" or "Co-Borrower," as applicable. Co-Borrower information must also be provided (and the appropriate box checked) when □ the income or assets of a person other than the Borrower (including the Borrower's spouse) will be used as a basis for loan qualification or □ the income or assets of the Borrower's spouse or other person who has community property rights pursuant to state law will not be used as a basis for loan qualification, but his or her liabilities must be considered because the spouse or other person has community property rights pursuant to applicable law and Borrower resides in a community property state, the security property is located in a community property state, or the Borrower is relying on other property located in a community property state as a basis for repayment of the loan.

If this is an application for joint credit, Borrower and Co-Borrower each agree that we intend to apply for joint credit (sign below):

Borrower	Co-Borrower

I. TYPE OF MORTGAGE AND TERMS OF LOAN

Mortgage Applied for:	□ VA □ FHA	□ Conventional □ USDA/Rural Housing Service	□ Other (explain):	Agency Case Number	Lender Case Number
Amount $	Interest Rate %	No. of Months	Amortization Type:	□ Fixed Rate □ GPM	□ Other (explain): □ ARM (type):

II. PROPERTY INFORMATION AND PURPOSE OF LOAN

Subject Property Address (street, city, state & ZIP)					No. of Units
Legal Description of Subject Property (attach description if necessary)					Year Built

Purpose of Loan	□ Purchase □ Refinance	□ Construction □ Construction-Permanent	□ Other (explain):	Property will be: □ Primary Residence	□ Secondary Residence	□ Investment

Complete this line if construction or construction-permanent loan.

Year Lot Acquired	Original Cost $	Amount Existing Liens $	(a) Present Value of Lot $	(b) Cost of Improvements $	Total (a + b) $

Complete this line if this is a refinance loan.

Year Acquired	Original Cost $	Amount Existing Liens $	Purpose of Refinance	Describe Improvements □ made □ to be made
				Cost: $

Title will be held in what Name(s)	Manner in which Title will be held	Estate will be held in: □ Fee Simple □ Leasehold (show expiration date)
Source of Down Payment, Settlement Charges, and/or Subordinate Financing (explain)		

UNIFORM RESIDENTIAL LOAN APPLICATION

Borrower	III. BORROWER INFORMATION	Co-Borrower

Borrower's Name (include Jr. or Sr. if applicable).				Co-Borrower's Name (include Jr. or Sr. if applicable)			
Social Security Number	Home Phone (incl. area code)	DOB (mm/dd/yyyy)	Yrs. School	Social Security Number	Home Phone (incl. area code)	DOB (mm/dd/yyyy)	Yrs. School
☐ Married ☐ Unmarried (include ☐ Separated single, divorced, widowed)	Dependents (not listed by Co-Borrower) no. ages			☐ Married ☐ Unmarried (include ☐ Separated single, divorced, widowed)	Dependents (not listed by Borrower) no. ages		
Present Address (street, city, state, ZIP) ☐ Own ☐ Rent ___ No. Yrs.				Present Address (street, city, state, ZIP) ☐ Own ☐ Rent ___ No. Yrs.			
Mailing Address, if different from Present Address				Mailing Address, if different from Present Address			

If residing at present address for less than two years, complete the following:

Former Address (street, city, state, ZIP) ☐ Own ☐ Rent ___ No. Yrs.				Former Address (street, city, state, ZIP) ☐ Own ☐ Rent ___ No. Yrs.			

Borrower	IV. EMPLOYMENT INFORMATION	Co-Borrower

Name & Address of Employer	☐ Self Employed	Yrs. on this job	Name & Address of Employer	☐ Self Employed	Yrs. on this job
		Yrs. employed in this line of work/profession			Yrs. employed in this line of work/profession
Position/Title/Type of Business	Business Phone (incl. area code)		Position/Title/Type of Business	Business Phone (incl. area code)	

If employed in current position for less than two years or if currently employed in more than one position, complete the following:

Home Mortgage Law Primer

Borrower			IV. EMPLOYMENT INFORMATION (cont'd)		Co-Borrower	
Name & Address of Employer	☐ Self Employed	Dates (from – to)	Name & Address of Employer	☐ Self Employed	Dates (from – to)	
		Monthly Income $			Monthly Income $	
Position/Title/Type of Business	Business Phone (incl. area code)		Position/Title/Type of Business	Business Phone (incl. area code)		
Name & Address of Employer	☐ Self Employed	Dates (from – to)	Name & Address of Employer	☐ Self Employed	Dates (from – to)	
		Monthly Income $			Monthly Income $	
Position/Title/Type of Business	Business Phone (incl. area code)		Position/Title/Type of Business	Business Phone (incl. area code)		

V. MONTHLY INCOME AND COMBINED HOUSING EXPENSE INFORMATION

Gross Monthly Income	Borrower	Co-Borrower	Total	Combined Monthly Housing Expense	Present	Proposed
Base Empl. Income*	$	$	$	Rent	$	
Overtime				First Mortgage (P&I)		$
Bonuses				Other Financing (P&I)		
Commissions				Hazard Insurance		
Dividends/Interest				Real Estate Taxes		
Net Rental Income				Mortgage Insurance		
Other (before completing, see the notice in "describe other income," below)				Homeowner Assn. Dues		
				Other:		
Total	$	$	$	Total	$	$

* Self Employed Borrower(s) may be required to provide additional documentation such as tax returns and financial statements.

Describe Other Income   *Notice:* Alimony, child support, or separate maintenance income need not be revealed if the Borrower (B) or Co-Borrower (C) does not choose to have it considered for repaying this loan.

B/C		Monthly Amount
		$

VI. ASSETS AND LIABILITIES

This Statement and any applicable supporting schedules may be completed jointly by both married and unmarried Co-Borrowers if their assets and liabilities are sufficiently joined so that the Statement can be meaningfully and fairly presented on a combined basis; otherwise, separate Statements and Schedules are required. If the Co-Borrower section was completed about a non-applicant spouse or other person, this Statement and supporting schedules must be completed about that spouse or other person also.

Completed ☐ Jointly ☐ Not Jointly

ASSETS	Cash or Market Value	Liabilities and Pledged Assets. List the creditor's name, address, and account number for all outstanding debts, including automobile loans, revolving charge accounts, real estate loans, alimony, child support, stock pledges, etc. Use continuation sheet, if necessary. Indicate by (*) those liabilities, which will be satisfied upon sale of real estate owned or upon refinancing of the subject property.		
Description				
Cash deposit toward purchase held by:	$			
		LIABILITIES	Monthly Payment & Months Left to Pay	Unpaid Balance
List checking and savings accounts below				
Name and address of Bank, S&L, or Credit Union		Name and address of Company	$ Payment/Months	$
Acct. no.	$	Acct. no.		
Name and address of Bank, S&L, or Credit Union		Name and address of Company	$ Payment/Months	$
Acct. no.	$	Acct. no.		
Name and address of Bank, S&L, or Credit Union		Name and address of Company	$ Payment/Months	$
Acct. no.	$	Acct. no.		

Freddie Mac Form 65   7/05   Page 2 of 5   Fannie Mae Form 1003   7/05

UNIFORM RESIDENTIAL LOAN APPLICATION

VI. ASSETS AND LIABILITIES (cont'd)

Name and address of Bank, S&L, or Credit Union	Name and address of Company	$ Payment/Months	$
Acct. no. $	Acct. no.		
Stocks & Bonds (Company name/ number & description) $	Name and address of Company	$ Payment/Months	$
	Acct. no.		
Life insurance net cash value $	Name and address of Company	$ Payment/Months	$
Face amount: $			
Subtotal Liquid Assets $			
Real estate owned (enter market value from schedule of real estate owned) $			
Vested interest in retirement fund $			
Net worth of business(es) owned (attach financial statement) $	Acct. no.		
Automobiles owned (make and year) $	Alimony/Child Support/Separate Maintenance Payments Owed to:	$	
Other Assets (itemize) $	Job-Related Expense (child care, union dues, etc.)	$	
	Total Monthly Payments	$	
Total Assets a. $	**Net Worth** (a minus b) ► $	**Total Liabilities b.** $	

Schedule of Real Estate Owned (If additional properties are owned, use continuation sheet.)

Property Address (enter S if sold, PS if pending sale or R if rental being held for income) ▼	Type of Property	Present Market Value	Amount of Mortgages & Liens	Gross Rental Income	Mortgage Payments	Insurance, Maintenance, Taxes & Misc.	Net Rental Income
		$	$	$	$	$	$
Totals		$	$	$	$	$	$

List any additional names under which credit has previously been received and indicate appropriate creditor name(s) and account number(s):

Alternate Name	Creditor Name	Account Number

VII. DETAILS OF TRANSACTION

a.	Purchase price	$
b.	Alterations, improvements, repairs	
c.	Land (if acquired separately)	
d.	Refinance (incl. debts to be paid off)	
e.	Estimated prepaid items	
f.	Estimated closing costs	
g.	PMI, MIP, Funding Fee	
h.	Discount (if Borrower will pay)	
i.	Total costs (add items a through h)	

VIII. DECLARATIONS

If you answer "Yes" to any questions a through i, please use continuation sheet for explanation.

	Borrower		Co-Borrower	
	Yes	No	Yes	No
a. Are there any outstanding judgments against you?	☐	☐	☐	☐
b. Have you been declared bankrupt within the past 7 years?	☐	☐	☐	☐
c. Have you had property foreclosed upon or given title or deed in lieu thereof in the last 7 years?	☐	☐	☐	☐
d. Are you a party to a lawsuit?	☐	☐	☐	☐
e. Have you directly or indirectly been obligated on any loan which resulted in foreclosure, transfer of title in lieu of foreclosure, or judgment?	☐	☐	☐	☐

(This would include such loans as home mortgage loans, SBA loans, home improvement loans, educational loans, manufactured (mobile) home loans, any mortgage, financial obligation, bond, or loan guarantee. If "Yes," provide details, including date, name, and address of Lender, FHA or VA case number, if any, and reasons for the action.)

VII. DETAILS OF TRANSACTION		VIII. DECLARATIONS				
		If you answer "Yes" to any questions a through i, please use continuation sheet for explanation.	**Borrower**		**Co-Borrower**	
			Yes No		Yes No	
j.	Subordinate financing					
k.	Borrower's closing costs paid by Seller	f. Are you presently delinquent or in default on any Federal debt or any other loan, mortgage, financial obligation, bond, or loan guarantee? If "Yes," give details as described in the preceding question.	☐ ☐		☐ ☐	
l.	Other Credits (explain)	g. Are you obligated to pay alimony, child support, or separate maintenance?	☐ ☐		☐ ☐	
		h. Is any part of the down payment borrowed?	☐ ☐		☐ ☐	
m.	Loan amount (exclude PMI, MIP, Funding Fee financed)	i. Are you a co-maker or endorser on a note?	☐ ☐		☐ ☐	
		j. Are you a U.S. citizen?	☐ ☐		☐ ☐	
n.	PMI, MIP, Funding Fee financed	k. Are you a permanent resident alien?	☐ ☐		☐ ☐	
		l. Do you intend to occupy the property as your primary residence? If "Yes," complete question m below.	☐ ☐		☐ ☐	
o.	Loan amount (add m & n)	m. Have you had an ownership interest in a property in the last three years?	☐ ☐		☐ ☐	
p.	Cash from/to Borrower (subtract j, k, l & o from i)	(1) What type of property did you own—principal residence (PR), second home (SH), or investment property (IP)? (2) How did you hold title to the home—solely by yourself (S), jointly with your spouse (SP), or jointly with another person (O)?	_____		_____	

IX. ACKNOWLEDGEMENT AND AGREEMENT

Each of the undersigned specifically represents to Lender and to Lender's actual or potential agents, brokers, processors, attorneys, insurers, servicers, successors and assigns and agrees and acknowledges that: (1) the information provided in this application is true and correct as of the date set forth opposite my signature and that any intentional or negligent misrepresentation of this information contained in this application may result in civil liability, including monetary damages, to any person who may suffer any loss due to reliance upon any misrepresentation that I have made on this application, and/or in criminal penalties including, but not limited to, fine or imprisonment or both under the provisions of Title 18, United States Code, Sec. 1001, et seq.; (2) the loan requested pursuant to this application (the "Loan") will be secured by a mortgage or deed of trust on the property described in this application; (3) the property will not be used for any illegal or prohibited purpose or use; (4) all statements made in this application are made for the purpose of obtaining a residential mortgage loan; (5) the property will be occupied as indicated in this application; (6) the Lender, its servicers, successors or assigns may retain the original and/or an electronic record of this application, whether or not the Loan is approved; (7) the Lender and its agents, brokers, insurers, servicers, successors, and assigns may continuously rely on the information contained in the application, and I am obligated to amend and/or supplement the information provided in this application if any of the material facts that I have represented herein should change prior to closing of the Loan; (8) in the event that my payments on the Loan become delinquent, the Lender, its servicers, successors or assigns may, in addition to any other rights and remedies that it may have relating to such delinquency, report my name and account information to one or more consumer reporting agencies; (9) ownership of the Loan and/or administration of the Loan account may be transferred with such notice as may be required by law; (10) neither Lender nor its agents, brokers, insurers, servicers, successors or assigns has made any representation or warranty, express or implied, to me regarding the property or the condition or value of the property; and (11) my transmission of this application as an "electronic record" containing my "electronic signature," as those terms are defined in applicable federal and/or state laws (excluding audio and video recordings), or my facsimile transmission of this application containing a facsimile of my signature, shall be as effective, enforceable and valid as if a paper version of this application were delivered containing my original written signature.

Acknowledgement. Each of the undersigned hereby acknowledges that any owner of the Loan, its servicers, successors and assigns, may verify or reverify any information contained in this application or obtain any information or data relating to the Loan, for any legitimate business purpose through any source, including a source named in this application or a consumer reporting agency.

Borrower's Signature	Date	Co-Borrower's Signature	Date
X		X	

X. INFORMATION FOR GOVERNMENT MONITORING PURPOSES

The following information is requested by the Federal Government for certain types of loans related to a dwelling in order to monitor the lender's compliance with equal credit opportunity, fair housing and home mortgage disclosure laws. You are not required to furnish this information, but are encouraged to do so. The law provides that a lender may not discriminate either on the basis of this information, or on whether you choose to furnish it. If you furnish the information, please provide both ethnicity and race. For race, you may check more than one designation. If you do not furnish ethnicity, race, or sex, under Federal regulations, this lender is required to note the information on the basis of visual observation and surname if you have made this application in person. If you do not wish to furnish the information, please check the box below. (Lender must review the above material to assure that the disclosures satisfy all requirements to which the lender is subject under applicable state law for the particular type of loan applied for.)

BORROWER ☐ I do not wish to furnish this information		CO-BORROWER ☐ I do not wish to furnish this information	
Ethnicity: ☐ Hispanic or Latino ☐ Not Hispanic or Latino		Ethnicity: ☐ Hispanic or Latino ☐ Not Hispanic or Latino	
Race: ☐ American Indian or Alaska Native ☐ Native Hawaiian or Other Pacific Islander	☐ Asian ☐ Black or African American ☐ White	Race: ☐ American Indian or Alaska Native ☐ Native Hawaiian or Other Pacific Islander	☐ Asian ☐ Black or African American ☐ White
Sex: ☐ Female ☐ Male		Sex: ☐ Female ☐ Male	

To be Completed by Interviewer This application was taken by: ☐ Face-to-face interview ☐ Mail ☐ Telephone ☐ Internet	Interviewer's Name (print or type)	Name and Address of Interviewer's Employer
	Interviewer's Signature Date	
	Interviewer's Phone Number (incl. area code)	

Freddie Mac Form 65   7/05   Page 4 of 5   Fannie Mae Form 1003   7/05

UNIFORM RESIDENTIAL LOAN APPLICATION

CONTINUATION SHEET/RESIDENTIAL LOAN APPLICATION		
Use this continuation sheet if you need more space to complete the Residential Loan Application. Mark B f or Borrower or C for Co-Borrower.	Borrower:	Agency Case Number:
	Co-Borrower:	Lender Case Number:

I/We fully understand that it is a Federal crime punishable by fine or imprisonment, or both, to knowingly make any false statements concerning any of the above facts as applicable under the provisions of Title 18, United States Code, Section 1001, et seq.

Borrower's Signature	Date	Co-Borrower's Signature	Date
X		X	

APPENDIX 6:
BORROWER'S FINANCIAL STATEMENT

 **FannieMae.**

BORROWER'S FINANCIAL STATEMENT

			Servicer Loan Number	
Property Address				
Is your home listed for sale? Yes No		Agent's Name:	Agent's Phone Number:	
Borrower Name			Social Security Number	
Mailing Address (#, Street, Apt)				
Mailing Address (City, State, Zip)				
Total number of persons living at this address:			Number of dependents at this address:	
Home Phone:			Work Phone:	
Co-Borrower Name			Social Security Number	
Mailing Address (#, Street, Apt)				
Mailing Address (City, State, Zip)				
Total number of persons living at this address:			Number of dependents at this address:	
Home Phone:			Work Phone:	
Have you contacted credit counseling services? Yes No			Number of cars you own?	

Monthly Income (Wages): $ / mo. Additional income (not wages): $ /mo. * Source:
*Notice: Alimony, child support or separate maintenance income need not be revealed if the Borrower or
Co-Borrower does not choose to have it considered for approval of

Asset Type	Estimated Value	Liability Type	Payment/Month	Balance Due
Home		Alimony/Child Support		
Other Real Estate		Dependent Care		
Checking Accounts		Rent		
Savings/Money Market		Other Mortgage(s)		
IRA/Keogh Accounts		Personal Loan(s)		
401 k/ESOP Accounts		Medical Expenses		
Stocks, Bonds, CD's		HOA Fees/Dues		
Other Investments		Other		
Reason for delinquency:				

I (we) agree that the financial information provided is an accurate statement of my (our) financial status. I (we) understand and
acknowledge that any action taken by the lender of my (our) mortgage loan on my (our) behalf will be made in strict reliance on the financial
information provided. My (Our) signature(s) below grants the holder of my (our) mortgage the authority to confirm the information I (we
have disclosed in this financial statement, to verify that it is accurate by ordering a credit report, and to contact my real estate agent and/or
credit counseling service representative (if applicable).

Submitted this   day of

By: _____   Date: _____
        Signature of Borrower

By: _____   Date: _____
        Signature of Co-Borrower

Before mailing, make sure you have signed and dated the form and attached a copy of your most recent paystub.
If you are self-employed, attached a copy of your most recent Federal Tax returns.

Fannie Mae Form 1020
Jul-06

APPENDIX 7:
UNIFORM RESIDENTIAL APPRAISAL REPORT

Uniform Residential Appraisal Report
File #

The purpose of this summary appraisal report is to provide the lender/client with an accurate, and adequately supported, opinion of the market value of the subject property.

Property Address	City	State	Zip Code
Borrower	Owner of Public Record	County	
Legal Description			
Assessor's Parcel #	Tax Year	R.E. Taxes $	
Neighborhood Name	Map Reference	Census Tract	

Occupant ☐ Owner ☐ Tenant ☐ Vacant   Special Assessments $ ☐ PUD   HOA $ ☐ per year ☐ per month
Property Rights Appraised ☐ Fee Simple ☐ Leasehold ☐ Other (describe)
Assignment Type ☐ Purchase Transaction ☐ Refinance Transaction ☐ Other (describe)
Lender/Client   Address
Is the subject property currently offered for sale or has it been offered for sale in the twelve months prior to the effective date of this appraisal? ☐ Yes ☐ No
Report data source(s) used, offering price(s), and date(s).

I ☐ did ☐ did not analyze the contract for sale for the subject purchase transaction. Explain the results of the analysis of the contract for sale or why the analysis was not performed.

Contract Price $ Date of Contract   Is the property seller the owner of public record? ☐Yes ☐No Data Source(s)
Is there any financial assistance (loan charges, sale concessions, gift or downpayment assistance, etc.) to be paid by any party on behalf of the borrower? ☐ Yes ☐ No
If Yes, report the total dollar amount and describe the items to be paid.

Note: Race and the racial composition of the neighborhood are not appraisal factors.

Neighborhood Characteristics	One-Unit Housing Trends	One-Unit Housing	Present Land Use %
Location ☐ Urban ☐ Suburban ☐ Rural	Property Values ☐ Increasing ☐ Stable ☐ Declining	PRICE AGE	One-Unit %
Built-Up ☐ Over 75% ☐ 25–75% ☐ Under 25%	Demand/Supply ☐ Shortage ☐ In Balance ☐ Over Supply	$ (000) (yrs)	2-4 Unit %
Growth ☐ Rapid ☐ Stable ☐ Slow	Marketing Time ☐ Under 3 mths ☐ 3–6 mths ☐ Over 6 mths	Low	Multi-Family %
Neighborhood Boundaries		High	Commercial %
		Pred.	Other %

Neighborhood Description

Market Conditions (including support for the above conclusions)

Dimensions	Area	Shape	View

Specific Zoning Classification   Zoning Description
Zoning Compliance ☐ Legal ☐ Legal Nonconforming (Grandfathered Use) ☐ No Zoning ☐ Illegal (describe)
Is the highest and best use of the subject property as improved (or as proposed per plans and specifications) the present use? ☐ Yes ☐ No If No, describe

Utilities	Public	Other (describe)		Public	Other (describe)	Off-site Improvements—Type	Public	Private
Electricity	☐	☐	Water	☐	☐	Street	☐	☐
Gas	☐	☐	Sanitary Sewer	☐	☐	Alley	☐	☐

FEMA Special Flood Hazard Area ☐ Yes ☐ No FEMA Flood Zone   FEMA Map #   FEMA Map Date
Are the utilities and off-site improvements typical for the market area? ☐ Yes ☐ No If No, describe
Are there any adverse site conditions or external factors (easements, encroachments, environmental conditions, land uses, etc.)? ☐ Yes ☐ No If Yes, describe

General Description	Foundation	Exterior Description	materials/condition	Interior	materials/condition
Units ☐ One ☐ One with Accessory Unit	☐ Concrete Slab ☐ Crawl Space	Foundation Walls		Floors	
# of Stories	☐ Full Basement ☐ Partial Basement	Exterior Walls		Walls	
Type ☐ Det. ☐ Att. ☐ S-Det./End Unit	Basement Area sq. ft.	Roof Surface		Trim/Finish	
☐ Existing ☐ Proposed ☐ Under Const.	Basement Finish %	Gutters & Downspouts		Bath Floor	
Design (Style)	☐ Outside Entry/Exit ☐ Sump Pump	Window Type		Bath Wainscot	
Year Built	Evidence of ☐ Infestation	Storm Sash/Insulated		Car Storage ☐ None	
Effective Age (Yrs)	☐ Dampness ☐ Settlement	Screens		☐ Driveway # of Cars	

Attic	☐ None	Heating ☐ FWA ☐ HWBB ☐ Radiant	Amenities	☐ Woodstove(s) #	Driveway Surface	
☐ Drop Stair	☐ Stairs	☐ Other Fuel	☐ Fireplace(s) #	☐ Fence	☐ Garage # of Cars	
☐ Floor	☐ Scuttle	Cooling ☐ Central Air Conditioning	☐ Patio/Deck	☐ Porch	☐ Carport # of Cars	
☐ Finished	☐ Heated	☐ Individual ☐ Other	☐ Pool	☐ Other	☐ Att. ☐ Det. ☐ Built-in	

Appliances ☐ Refrigerator ☐ Range/Oven ☐ Dishwasher ☐ Disposal ☐ Microwave ☐ Washer/Dryer ☐ Other (describe)

Finished area **above grade** contains: Rooms   Bedrooms   Bath(s)   Square Feet of Gross Living Area Above Grade

Additional features (special energy efficient items, etc.)

Describe the condition of the property (including needed repairs, deterioration, renovations, remodeling, etc.)

Are there any physical deficiencies or adverse conditions that affect the livability, soundness, or structural integrity of the property? ☐ Yes ☐ No If Yes, describe

Does the property generally conform to the neighborhood (functional utility, style, condition, use, construction, etc.)? ☐ Yes ☐ No If No, describe

Uniform Residential Appraisal Report

File #

There are _____ comparable properties currently offered for sale in the subject neighborhood ranging in price from $ _____ to $ _____

There are _____ comparable sales in the subject neighborhood within the past twelve months ranging in sale price from $ _____ to $ _____

FEATURE	SUBJECT	COMPARABLE SALE # 1		COMPARABLE SALE # 2		COMPARABLE SALE # 3	
Address							
Proximity to Subject							
Sale Price	$		$		$		$
Sale Price/Gross Liv. Area	$ sq. ft.	$ sq. ft.		$ sq. ft.		$ sq. ft.	
Data Source(s)							
Verification Source(s)							
VALUE ADJUSTMENTS	DESCRIPTION	DESCRIPTION	+(-) $ Adjustment	DESCRIPTION	+(-) $ Adjustment	DESCRIPTION	+(-) $ Adjustment
Sale or Financing Concessions							
Date of Sale/Time							
Location							
Leasehold/Fee Simple							
Site							
View							
Design (Style)							
Quality of Construction							
Actual Age							
Condition							
Above Grade	Total Bdrms. Baths	Total Bdrms. Baths		Total Bdrms. Baths		Total Bdrms. Baths	
Room Count							
Gross Living Area	sq. ft.	sq. ft.		sq. ft.		sq. ft.	
Basement & Finished Rooms Below Grade							
Functional Utility							
Heating/Cooling							
Energy Efficient Items							
Garage/Carport							
Porch/Patio/Deck							
Net Adjustment (Total)		☐ + ☐ -	$	☐ + ☐ -	$	☐ + ☐ -	$
Adjusted Sale Price of Comparables		Net Adj. % Gross Adj. %	$	Net Adj. % Gross Adj. %	$	Net Adj. % Gross Adj. %	$

I ☐ did ☐ did not research the sale or transfer history of the subject property and comparable sales. If not, explain

My research ☐ did ☐ did not reveal any prior sales or transfers of the subject property for the three years prior to the effective date of this appraisal.

Data source(s)

My research ☐ did ☐ did not reveal any prior sales or transfers of the comparable sales for the year prior to the date of sale of the comparable sale.

Data source(s)

Report the results of the research and analysis of the prior sale or transfer history of the subject property and comparable sales (report additional prior sales on page 3).

ITEM	SUBJECT	COMPARABLE SALE # 1	COMPARABLE SALE # 2	COMPARABLE SALE # 3
Date of Prior Sale/Transfer				
Price of Prior Sale/Transfer				
Data Source(s)				
Effective Date of Data Source(s)				

Analysis of prior sale or transfer history of the subject property and comparable sales

Summary of Sales Comparison Approach

Indicated Value by Sales Comparison Approach $

Indicated Value by: Sales Comparison Approach $ _____ Cost Approach (if developed) $ _____ Income Approach (if developed) $ _____

This appraisal is made ☐ "as is", ☐ subject to completion per plans and specifications on the basis of a hypothetical condition that the improvements have been completed, ☐ subject to the following repairs or alterations on the basis of a hypothetical condition that the repairs or alterations have been completed, or ☐ subject to the following required inspection based on the extraordinary assumption that the condition or deficiency does not require alteration or repair:

Based on a complete visual inspection of the interior and exterior areas of the subject property, defined scope of work, statement of assumptions and limiting conditions, and appraiser's certification, my (our) opinion of the market value, as defined, of the real property that is the subject of this report is $ _____ , as of _____ , which is the date of inspection and the effective date of this appraisal.

Uniform Residential Appraisal Report

File #

ADDITIONAL COMMENTS

COST APPROACH TO VALUE (not required by Fannie Mae)

Provide adequate information for the lender/client to replicate the below cost figures and calculations.

Support for the opinion of site value (summary of comparable land sales or other methods for estimating site value)

ESTIMATED ☐ REPRODUCTION OR ☐ REPLACEMENT COST NEW	OPINION OF SITE VALUE	= $
Source of cost data	Dwelling Sq. Ft. @ $	=$
Quality rating from cost service Effective date of cost data	Sq. Ft. @ $	=$
Comments on Cost Approach (gross living area calculations, depreciation, etc.)	Garage/Carport Sq. Ft. @ $	=$
	Total Estimate of Cost-New	= $
	Less Physical Functional External	
	Depreciation	=$( )
	Depreciated Cost of Improvements......................................	=$
	"As-is" Value of Site Improvements....................................	=$
Estimated Remaining Economic Life (HUD and VA only) Years	Indicated Value By Cost Approach	=$

INCOME APPROACH TO VALUE (not required by Fannie Mae)

Estimated Monthly Market Rent $ X Gross Rent Multiplier   = $ Indicated Value by Income Approach

Summary of Income Approach (including support for market rent and GRM)

PROJECT INFORMATION FOR PUDs (if applicable)

Is the developer/builder in control of the Homeowners' Association (HOA)? ☐ Yes ☐ No Unit type(s) ☐ Detached ☐ Attached

Provide the following information for PUDs ONLY if the developer/builder is in control of the HOA and the subject property is an attached dwelling unit.

Legal name of project

Total number of phases	Total number of units	Total number of units sold
Total number of units rented	Total number of units for sale	Data source(s)

Was the project created by the conversion of an existing building(s) into a PUD? ☐ Yes ☐ No If Yes, date of conversion

Does the project contain any multi-dwelling units? ☐ Yes ☐ No Data source(s)

Are the units, common elements, and recreation facilities complete? ☐ Yes ☐ No If No, describe the status of completion.

Are the common elements leased to or by the Homeowners' Association? ☐ Yes ☐ No If Yes, describe the rental terms and options.

Describe common elements and recreational facilities

Uniform Residential Appraisal Report

This report form is designed to report an appraisal of a one-unit property or a one-unit property with an accessory unit; including a unit in a planned unit development (PUD). This report form is not designed to report an appraisal of a manufactured home or a unit in a condominium or cooperative project.

This appraisal report is subject to the following scope of work, intended use, intended user, definition of market value, statement of assumptions and limiting conditions, and certifications. Modifications, additions, or deletions to the intended use, intended user, definition of market value, or assumptions and limiting conditions are not permitted. The appraiser may expand the scope of work to include any additional research or analysis necessary based on the complexity of this appraisal assignment. Modifications or deletions to the certifications are also not permitted. However, additional certifications that do not constitute material alterations to this appraisal report, such as those required by law or those related to the appraiser's continuing education or membership in an appraisal organization, are permitted.

SCOPE OF WORK: The scope of work for this appraisal is defined by the complexity of this appraisal assignment and the reporting requirements of this appraisal report form, including the following definition of market value, statement of assumptions and limiting conditions, and certifications. The appraiser must, at a minimum: (1) perform a complete visual inspection of the interior and exterior areas of the subject property, (2) inspect the neighborhood, (3) inspect each of the comparable sales from at least the street, (4) research, verify, and analyze data from reliable public and/or private sources, and (5) report his or her analysis, opinions, and conclusions in this appraisal report.

INTENDED USE: The intended use of this appraisal report is for the lender/client to evaluate the property that is the subject of this appraisal for a mortgage finance transaction.

INTENDED USER: The intended user of this appraisal report is the lender/client.

DEFINITION OF MARKET VALUE: The most probable price which a property should bring in a competitive and open market under all conditions requisite to a fair sale, the buyer and seller, each acting prudently, knowledgeably and assuming the price is not affected by undue stimulus. Implicit in this definition is the consummation of a sale as of a specified date and the passing of title from seller to buyer under conditions whereby: (1) buyer and seller are typically motivated; (2) both parties are well informed or well advised, and each acting in what he or she considers his or her own best interest; (3) a reasonable time is allowed for exposure in the open market; (4) payment is made in terms of cash in U. S. dollars or in terms of financial arrangements comparable thereto; and (5) the price represents the normal consideration for the property sold unaffected by special or creative financing or sales concessions* granted by anyone associated with the sale.

*Adjustments to the comparables must be made for special or creative financing or sales concessions. No adjustments are necessary for those costs which are normally paid by sellers as a result of tradition or law in a market area; these costs are readily identifiable since the seller pays these costs in virtually all sales transactions. Special or creative financing adjustments can be made to the comparable property by comparisons to financing terms offered by a third party institutional lender that is not already involved in the property or transaction. Any adjustment should not be calculated on a mechanical dollar for dollar cost of the financing or concession but the dollar amount of any adjustment should approximate the market's reaction to the financing or concessions based on the appraiser's judgment.

STATEMENT OF ASSUMPTIONS AND LIMITING CONDITIONS: The appraiser's certification in this report is subject to the following assumptions and limiting conditions:

1. The appraiser will not be responsible for matters of a legal nature that affect either the property being appraised or the title to it, except for information that he or she became aware of during the research involved in performing this appraisal. The appraiser assumes that the title is good and marketable and will not render any opinions about the title.

2. The appraiser has provided a sketch in this appraisal report to show the approximate dimensions of the improvements. The sketch is included only to assist the reader in visualizing the property and understanding the appraiser's determination of its size.

3. The appraiser has examined the available flood maps that are provided by the Federal Emergency Management Agency (or other data sources) and has noted in this appraisal report whether any portion of the subject site is located in an identified Special Flood Hazard Area. Because the appraiser is not a surveyor, he or she makes no guarantees, express or implied, regarding this determination.

4. The appraiser will not give testimony or appear in court because he or she made an appraisal of the property in question, unless specific arrangements to do so have been made beforehand, or as otherwise required by law.

5. The appraiser has noted in this appraisal report any adverse conditions (such as needed repairs, deterioration, the presence of hazardous wastes, toxic substances, etc.) observed during the inspection of the subject property or that he or she became aware of during the research involved in performing this appraisal. Unless otherwise stated in this appraisal report, the appraiser has no knowledge of any hidden or unapparent physical deficiencies or adverse conditions of the property (such as, but not limited to, needed repairs, deterioration, the presence of hazardous wastes, toxic substances, adverse environmental conditions, etc.) that would make the property less valuable, and has assumed that there are no such conditions and makes no guarantees or warranties, express or implied. The appraiser will not be responsible for any such conditions that do exist or for any engineering or testing that might be required to discover whether such conditions exist. Because the appraiser is not an expert in the field of environmental hazards, this appraisal report must not be considered as an environmental assessment of the property.

6. The appraiser has based his or her appraisal report and valuation conclusion for an appraisal that is subject to satisfactory completion, repairs, or alterations on the assumption that the completion, repairs, or alterations of the subject property will be performed in a professional manner.

Uniform Residential Appraisal Report   File

APPRAISER'S CERTIFICATION: The Appraiser certifies and agrees that:

1. I have, at a minimum, developed and reported this appraisal in accordance with the scope of work requirements stated in this appraisal report.

2. I performed a complete visual inspection of the interior and exterior areas of the subject property. I reported the condition of the improvements in factual, specific terms. I identified and reported the physical deficiencies that could affect the livability, soundness, or structural integrity of the property.

3. I performed this appraisal in accordance with the requirements of the Uniform Standards of Professional Appraisal Practice that were adopted and promulgated by the Appraisal Standards Board of The Appraisal Foundation and that were in place at the time this appraisal report was prepared.

4. I developed my opinion of the market value of the real property that is the subject of this report based on the sales comparison approach to value. I have adequate comparable market data to develop a reliable sales comparison approach for this appraisal assignment. I further certify that I considered the cost and income approaches to value but did not develop them, unless otherwise indicated in this report.

5. I researched, verified, analyzed, and reported on any current agreement for sale for the subject property, any offering for sale of the subject property in the twelve months prior to the effective date of this appraisal, and the prior sales of the subject property for a minimum of three years prior to the effective date of this appraisal, unless otherwise indicated in this report.

6. I researched, verified, analyzed, and reported on the prior sales of the comparable sales for a minimum of one year prior to the date of sale of the comparable sale, unless otherwise indicated in this report.

7. I selected and used comparable sales that are locationally, physically, and functionally the most similar to the subject property.

8. I have not used comparable sales that were the result of combining a land sale with the contract purchase price of a home that has been built or will be built on the land.

9. I have reported adjustments to the comparable sales that reflect the market's reaction to the differences between the subject property and the comparable sales.

10. I verified, from a disinterested source, all information in this report that was provided by parties who have a financial interest in the sale or financing of the subject property.

11. I have knowledge and experience in appraising this type of property in this market area.

12. I am aware of, and have access to, the necessary and appropriate public and private data sources, such as multiple listing services, tax assessment records, public land records and other such data sources for the area in which the property is located.

13. I obtained the information, estimates, and opinions furnished by other parties and expressed in this appraisal report from reliable sources that I believe to be true and correct.

14. I have taken into consideration the factors that have an impact on value with respect to the subject neighborhood, subject property, and the proximity of the subject property to adverse influences in the development of my opinion of market value. I have noted in this appraisal report any adverse conditions (such as, but not limited to, needed repairs, deterioration, the presence of hazardous wastes, toxic substances, adverse environmental conditions, etc.) observed during the inspection of the subject property or that I became aware of during the research involved in performing this appraisal. I have considered these adverse conditions in my analysis of the property value, and have reported on the effect of the conditions on the value and marketability of the subject property.

15. I have not knowingly withheld any significant information from this appraisal report and, to the best of my knowledge, all statements and information in this appraisal report are true and correct.

16. I stated in this appraisal report my own personal, unbiased, and professional analysis, opinions, and conclusions, which are subject only to the assumptions and limiting conditions in this appraisal report.

17. I have no present or prospective interest in the property that is the subject of this report, and I have no present or prospective personal interest or bias with respect to the participants in the transaction. I did not base, either partially or completely, my analysis and/or opinion of market value in this appraisal report on the race, color, religion, sex, age, marital status, handicap, familial status, or national origin of either the prospective owners or occupants of the subject property or of the present owners or occupants of the properties in the vicinity of the subject property or on any other basis prohibited by law.

18. My employment and/or compensation for performing this appraisal or any future or anticipated appraisals was not conditioned on any agreement or understanding, written or otherwise, that I would report (or present analysis supporting) a predetermined specific value, a predetermined minimum value, a range or direction in value, a value that favors the cause of any party, or the attainment of a specific result or occurrence of a specific subsequent event (such as approval of a pending mortgage loan application).

19. I personally prepared all conclusions and opinions about the real estate that were set forth in this appraisal report. If I relied on significant real property appraisal assistance from any individual or individuals in the performance of this appraisal or the preparation of this appraisal report, I have named such individual(s) and disclosed the specific tasks performed in this appraisal report. I certify that any individual so named is qualified to perform the tasks. I have not authorized anyone to make a change to any item in this appraisal report; therefore, any change made to this appraisal is unauthorized and I will take no responsibility for it.

20. I identified the lender/client in this appraisal report who is the individual, organization, or agent for the organization that ordered and will receive this appraisal report.

Uniform Residential Appraisal Report   File

21. The lender/client may disclose or distribute this appraisal report to: the borrower; another lender at the request of the borrower; the mortgagee or its successors and assigns; mortgage insurers; government sponsored enterprises; other secondary market participants; data collection or reporting services; professional appraisal organizations; any department, agency, or instrumentality of the United States; and any state, the District of Columbia, or other jurisdictions; without having to obtain the appraiser's or supervisory appraiser's (if applicable) consent. Such consent must be obtained before this appraisal report may be disclosed or distributed to any other party (including, but not limited to, the public through advertising, public relations, news, sales, or other media).

22. I am aware that any disclosure or distribution of this appraisal report by me or the lender/client may be subject to certain laws and regulations. Further, I am also subject to the provisions of the Uniform Standards of Professional Appraisal Practice that pertain to disclosure or distribution by me.

23. The borrower, another lender at the request of the borrower, the mortgagee or its successors and assigns, mortgage insurers, government sponsored enterprises, and other secondary market participants may rely on this appraisal report as part of any mortgage finance transaction that involves any one or more of these parties.

24. If this appraisal report was transmitted as an "electronic record" containing my "electronic signature," as those terms are defined in applicable federal and/or state laws (excluding audio and video recordings), or a facsimile transmission of this appraisal report containing a copy or representation of my signature, the appraisal report shall be as effective, enforceable and valid as if a paper version of this appraisal report were delivered containing my original hand written signature.

25. Any intentional or negligent misrepresentation(s) contained in this appraisal report may result in civil liability and/or criminal penalties including, but not limited to, fine or imprisonment or both under the provisions of Title 18, United States Code, Section 1001, et seq., or similar state laws.

SUPERVISORY APPRAISER'S CERTIFICATION: The Supervisory Appraiser certifies and agrees that:

1. I directly supervised the appraiser for this appraisal assignment, have read the appraisal report, and agree with the appraiser's analysis, opinions, statements, conclusions, and the appraiser's certification.

2. I accept full responsibility for the contents of this appraisal report including, but not limited to, the appraiser's analysis, opinions, statements, conclusions, and the appraiser's certification.

3. The appraiser identified in this appraisal report is either a sub-contractor or an employee of the supervisory appraiser (or the appraisal firm), is qualified to perform this appraisal, and is acceptable to perform this appraisal under the applicable state law.

4. This appraisal report complies with the Uniform Standards of Professional Appraisal Practice that were adopted and promulgated by the Appraisal Standards Board of The Appraisal Foundation and that were in place at the time this appraisal report was prepared.

5. If this appraisal report was transmitted as an "electronic record" containing my "electronic signature," as those terms are defined in applicable federal and/or state laws (excluding audio and video recordings), or a facsimile transmission of this appraisal report containing a copy or representation of my signature, the appraisal report shall be as effective, enforceable and valid as if a paper version of this appraisal report were delivered containing my original hand written signature.

APPRAISER

Signature_____
Name _____
Company Name _____
Company Address_____
_____
Telephone Number _____
Email Address_____
Date of Signature and Report_____
Effective Date of Appraisal _____
State Certification #_____
or State License #_____
or Other (describe) _____ State # _____
State _____
Expiration Date of Certification or License _____

ADDRESS OF PROPERTY APPRAISED

_____
_____
APPRAISED VALUE OF SUBJECT PROPERTY $ _____
LENDER/CLIENT
Name _____
Company Name _____
Company Address_____
_____
Email Address _____

SUPERVISORY APPRAISER (ONLY IF REQUIRED)

Signature _____
Name_____
Company Name _____
Company Address_____
_____
Telephone Number _____
Email Address _____
Date of Signature _____
State Certification #_____
or State License #_____
State _____
Expiration Date of Certification or License _____

SUBJECT PROPERTY

☐ Did not inspect subject property
☐ Did inspect exterior of subject property from street
   Date of Inspection _____
☐ Did inspect interior and exterior of subject property
   Date of Inspection _____

COMPARABLE SALES

☐ Did not inspect exterior of comparable sales from street
☐ Did inspect exterior of comparable sales from street
   Date of Inspection _____

Freddie Mac Form 70 March 2005   Page 6 of 6   Fannie Mae Form 1004 March 2005

APPENDIX 8:
MORTGAGE PAYMENT ESTIMATION CHART

INTEREST RATE(%)	10 YEARS	15 YEARS	20 YEARS	25 YEARS	30 YEARS
5.00	$10.61	$7.91	$6.60	$5.85	$5.37
5.25	$10.73	$8.04	$6.74	$5.99	$5.52
5.50	$10.85	$8.17	$6.88	$6.14	$5.68
5.75	$10.98	$8.30	$7.02	$6.29	$5.84
6.00	$11.10	$8.44	$7.16	$6.44	$6.00
6.25	$11.23	$8.57	$7.31	$6.60	$6.16
6.50	$11.35	$8.71	$7.46	$6.75	$6.32
6.75	$11.48	$8.85	$7.60	$6.91	$6.49
7.00	$11.61	$8.99	$7.75	$7.07	$6.65
7.25	$11.74	$9.13	$7.90	$7.23	$6.82
7.50	$11.87	$9.27	$8.06	$7.39	$6.99
7.75	$12.00	$9.41	$8.21	$7.55	$7.16
8.00	$12.13	$9.56	$8.36	$7.72	$7.34
8.25	$12.27	$9.70	$8.52	$7.88	$7.51
8.50	$12.40	$9.85	$8.68	$8.05	$7.69
8.75	$12.53	$9.99	$8.84	$8.22	$7.87
9.00	$12.67	$10.14	$9.00	$8.39	$8.05

INTEREST RATE(%)	10 YEARS	15 YEARS	20 YEARS	25 YEARS	30 YEARS
9.25	$12.80	$10.29	$9.16	$8.56	$8.23
9.50	$12.94	$10.44	$9.32	$8.74	$8.41
9.75	$13.08	$10.59	$9.49	$8.91	$8.59
10.00	$13.22	$10.75	$9.65	$9.09	$8.78

DIRECTIONS FOR ESTIMATING MONTHLY MORTGAGE PAYMENTS

Select the interest rate and term for the mortgage loan you are considering to ascertain your monthly payment per $1000 of loan principal. For example, if you are considering a mortgage loan in the amount of $50,000 which carries an interest rate of 7.50% for a term of 30 years, multiply the indicated amount of $6.99 by 50 ($50,000/100). Thus $349.50 is the estimated monthly payment not including taxes, insurance or miscellaneous closing costs.

APPENDIX 9:
SPLIT RATE MORTGAGE CLAUSE

FOR VALUE RECEIVED, We, the undersigned, the Promisors and Mortgagors, jointly and severally promise and agree as follows:

To pay to the order of HOME SAVINGS AND LOAN ASSOCIATION, Promisee and Mortgagee, a New York corporation, hereinafter called the "Association," at its offices at New York, New York, or at such other place as may be designated by the holder of the mortgage note, the principal sum of $_____ and such additional sums as may be subsequently advanced to the Promisors and Mortgagors by the Association, together with interest at the rate *of* _____ *percent per annum* until _____, 20___, and _____ percent per annum for the remaining term of the loan, or until the loan shall have been fully paid, subject to the provisions hereinafter set forth.

Such principal and interest shall be due and payable in monthly installments of $_____ per month, until _____, 20___, and $_____ per month thereafter, subject to the provisions hereinafter set forth. Payments shall be due on the first day of each and every month, commencing _____, 20___.

Notwithstanding any other provisions in this note or the mortgage given as collateral security therefor, the entire sum due hereon, including any additional advances, shall be paid within the time prescribed by law.

APPENDIX 10:
DIRECTORY OF
STATE BANKING AGENCIES

Alabama Superintendent of Banks
Center for Commerce
401 Adams Avenue, Suite #680
Montgomery, AL 36130-1201
Phone: 334-242-3452
Fax: 334-242-3500

Alaska Director of Banking
Department of Commerce
P.O. Box 110807
Juneau, AK 99811-0807
Phone: 907-465-2521
Fax: 907-465-2549
E-mail: DBSC@COMMERCE.STATE.AK.US

Arizona Superintendent of Banks
Arizona State Banking Dept.
2910 North 44th Street, Suite 310
Phoenix, AZ 85018
Phone: 602-255-4421/1-800-352-8400
Fax: 602-381-1225

Arkansas, Bank Commissioner
Tower Building
323 Center Street, Suite 500
Little Rock, AR 72201-2613
Phone: 501-324-9019
Fax: 501-324-9028

California Department of Financial Institutions
111 Pine Street, Suite 1100
San Francisco, CA 94111-5613
Phone: 415-263-8507/1-800-622-0620
Fax: 415-989-5310
Website: www.dfi.ca.gov

Colorado, State Bank Commissioner
Division of Banking
1560 Broadway Street, Suite 1175
Denver, CO 80202
Phone: 303-894-7575
Fax: 303-894-7570
Website: www.dora.state.co.us/banking

Connecticut, Banking Commissioner
Connecticut Department of Banking
260 Constitution Plaza
Hartford, CT 06103
Phone: 860-240- 8100/1-800-831-7225
Fax: 860-240-8178
E-mail: john.burke@po.state.ct.us
Website: www.state.ct.us/dob

Delaware, State Bank Commissioner
555 E. Lockerman Street, Suite 210
Dover, DE 19901
Phone: 302-739-4235
Fax: 302-739-3609

District of Columbia
Superintendent of Banking
and Financial Institutions
717 14th Street, N.W., 11th Floor
Washington, D.C. 20005
Phone: 202-727-1563
Fax: 202-727-1588
E-mail: jromero@yahoo.com
Website: www.obfi.dcgov.org

Florida, State Comptroller
State Capitol
Tallahassee, FL 32399-0350
Phone: 904-488-0370/1-800-848-3792
Fax: 904-488-9818

E-mail: dbf@mail.dbf.state.fl.us,
Website: www.dbf.state.fl.us/banking.html

Georgia, Commissioner
Banking and Finance
2990 Brandywine Road, Suite 200
Atlanta, GA 30341-5565
Phone: 770-986-1633

Commissioner, Financial Institutions
State of Hawaii
P.O. Box 2054
Honolulu, HI 96805
Phone: 808-586-2820/1-800-974-4000
Fax: 808-586-2818
E-mail: DFI@LAVA.NET

Idaho, Department of Finance
700 West State Street, 2nd Floor
Boise, ID 83720-0031
Phone: 208-332-8098/1-888-346-3376,
Fax: 208-334-2216
E-mail: GGEE@FIN.STATE.ID.US
Website: www2.state.id.us

Illinois, Commissioner of Banks and Real Estate
500 E. Monroe Street
Springfield, IL 62701
Phone: 217-782-3000/312-793-3000
Fax: 217-524-5941
E-mail: BANKS@BRE084r1.state.il.us
Website: www.state.il.us/obr @p_flush_2 =

Indiana, Department of Financial Institutions
402 W. Washington Street, Room W-066
Indianapolis, IN 46204-2759
Phone: 317-232-3955/1-800-382-4880
Fax: 317-232-7655
E-mail: cphillips@dfi.state.in.us

Iowa, Superintendent of Banking
200 East Grand, Suite 300
Des Moines, IA 50309
Phone: 515-281-4014/1-800-972-2018
Fax: 515-281-4862
Website: www.idob.state.ia.us

Kansas, State Bank Commissioner
700 Jackson Street, Suite 300
Topeka, KS 66603-3714
Phone: 785-296-2266
Fax: 785-296-0168

Kentucky, Department of Financial Institutions
77 Versailles Road
Frankfort, KY 40601
Phone: 502-573-3390/1- 800-223-2579
Fax: 502-573-8787
Website: www.dfi.state.ky.us

Louisiana, Commissioner, Financial Institutions
P.O. Box 94095
Baton Rouge, LA 70804-9095
Phone: 504-925-4660
Fax: 504- 925-4524

Maine, Superintendent of Banking
36 State House Station
Augusta, ME 04333-0036
Phone: 207-624-8570
Fax: 207-624-8590
Website: www.state.me.us

Maryland, Commissioner of Financial Regulation
500 North Calvert Street
Baltimore, MD 21202
Phone: 410-333-6812/1-888-784-0136
Fax: 410-333-0475
E-mail: fin-reg@dllr.state.md.us
Website: www.dllr.state.md.us/finance

Massachusetts, Commissioner of Banks
100 Cambridge Street
Boston, MA 02202
Phone: 617-727-3145/1-800-495-2265
Fax: 617-727-7631

Michigan, Commissioner, Financial Institutions Bureau
P.O. Box 30224
Lansing, MI 48909
Phone: 517-373-3460, 515-335-1109
Fax: 517-335-0908
Website: www.cis.state.mi.us

Minnesota, Deputy Commissioner
Enforcement and Licensing Division
133 East 7th Street
St. Paul, MN 55101
Phone: 612-296- 2135/1-800-657-3602
Fax: 612-296-8591

Mississippi, Commissioner, Department of Banking and Consumer
Finance
P.O. Box 23729
Jackson, MS 39225-3729
Phone: 601-359-1031/1-800-844-2499
Fax: 601-359-3557

Missouri, Commissioner of Finance
P.O. Box 716
Jefferson City, MO 65102
Phone: 573-751-3242
Fax: 573-751-9192
E-mail: finance@mail.state.mo.us

Montana, Commissioner, Financial Institutions
846 Front Street
P.O. Box 200546
Helena, MT 59620-0546
Phone: 406-444-2091
Fax: 406-444-4186

Nebraska, Director of Banking and Finance
1200 N Street, Suite 311
Lincoln, NE 68508
Phone: 402-471-2171
Fax: 402-471-3062
Website: www.ndbf.org

Nevada, Commissioner, Financial Institutions
406 East Second Street, Suite 3
Carson City, NV 89701-4758
Phone: 702-687-4259
Fax: 702-687-6909

New Hampshire
Bank Commissioner
169 Manchester Street
Concord, NH 03301

Phone: 603-271-3561
Fax: 603-271-1090

New Jersey, Commissioner
Department of Banking and Insurance
20 West State Street
P.O. Box 040
Trenton, NJ 08625
Phone: 609-292-3420

New Mexico
Financial Institutions Division
P.O. Box 25101
Santa Fe, NM 87504
Phone: 505-827-7100
Fax: 505-827-7107

New York, Superintendent of Banking
New York State Banking Department
Two Rector Street, New York, NY 10006-1894
Phone: 212-618-6553/1-800-522-3330

North Carolina, Commissioner of Banks
P.O. Box 10709
Raleigh, NC 27605
Phone: 919-733-3016
Fax: 919-733-6918
Website: www.banking.state.nc.us

North Dakota, Commissioner of
Banking and Financial Institutions
2000 Schafer Street
Bismarck, ND 58501-1204
Phone: 701-328-9933
Fax: 701-328-9955
E-mail: banking@BTIGATE.com
Website: www.state.nd.us/bank

Ohio, Superintendent, Division of
Financial Institutions
77 South High Street, 21st Floor
Columbus, OH 43266-0121
Phone: 614- 644-1631

Oklahoma, Bank Commissioner
4545 North Lincoln Blvd., Suite 164
Oklahoma City, OK 73105

Phone: 405-521-2782
Fax: 405-525-9701
Website: www.state.ok.us

Oregon, Division of
Finance and Corporate Securities
350 Winter Street, NE, Room 21
Salem, OR 97310
Phone: 503-378-4140
Fax: 503-947-7862
Website: www.cbs.state.or.us/external/dfcs

Pennsylvania, Secretary of Banking
333 Market Street, 16th Floor
Harrisburg, PA 17101-2290
Phone: 717-787-6991/1-800-PA-BANKS
Fax: 717-787-8773

Puerto Rico, Commissioner of
Financial Institutions
1492 Ponce de Leon Avenue, Suite 600
San Juan, PR 00907-4127
Phone: 787- 723-3131
Fax: 787-723-4042

Rhode Island, Superintendent of Banking
233 Richmond Street, Suite 231
Providence, RI 02903-4231
Phone: 401-277-2405
Fax: 401-331-9123

South Carolina, Commissioner of Banking
1015 Sumter Street, Room 309
Columbia, SC 29201
Phone: 803-734-2001
Fax: 803-734-2013

South Dakota, Director of Banking
State Capitol Building
500 East Capitol Avenue
Pierre, SD 57501-5070
Phone: 605-773-3421
Fax: 605-773-5367

Tennessee, Commissioner
Financial Institutions
John Sevier Building

500 Charlotte Avenue, 4th Floor
Nashville, TN 37243-0705
Phone: 615-741-2236
Fax: 615-741-2883
E-mail: tsmith@mail.state.tn.us

Texas, Banking Commissioner
2601 North Lamar
Austin, TX 78705
Phone: 512-475-1300
Fax: 512-475-3300,
Website: www.banking.state.tx.us

Utah, Commissioner, Financial Institutions
P.O. Box 89
Salt Lake City, UT 84110-0089
Phone: 801-538-8854
Fax: 801-538-8894

Vermont, Commissioner
Banking, Insurance, Securities
and Health Care Administration
89 Main Street Drawer 20
Montpelier, VT 05620-3101
Phone: 802-828-3301
Fax: 802-828- 3306
Website: www.state.vt.us/bis

Virgin Islands
Commissioner of Insurance
Chairman of Banking Board
Kongen's Garden #18
Charlotte Amalie, St. Thomas, VI 00802
Phone: 340-774-2991
Fax: 340-774-6953

Virginia, Commissioner, Financial Institutions
1300 E. Main Street, Suite 800
P.O. Box 640
Richmond, VA 23218-0640
Phone: 804-371-9657/1-800-552-7945
Fax: 804-371-9416

Washington, Department of Financial
Institutions
P.O. Box 41200

Olympia, WA 98504-1200
Phone: 360-902-8707
Fax: 360-586-5068

West Virginia, Commissioner of Banking
State Capitol Complex, Building 3, Room 311
1900 Kanawha Blvd. East
Charleston, WV 25305-0240
Phone: 304-558-2294, 1-800-642-9056

Wisconsin, Department of Financial Institutions
345 W. Washington Ave, 5th Floor
P.O. Box 7876
Madison, WI 53707-7876
Phone: 608-261-9555/1-800-452-3328
Fax: 608-264-7968
E-mail: badger.state.wi.us/agencies/dfi

Wyoming, Division of Banking
Herschler Building, 3rd Floor East
Cheyenne, WY 82002
Phone: 307-777-7797
Fax: 307-777-3555

APPENDIX 11:
THE HOME OWNERSHIP AND EQUITY PROTECTION ACT [PUB. L. NO. 103-325, TITLE I, 9/23/1994]

SUBTITLE B - THE HOME OWNERSHIP AND EQUITY PROTECTION ACT

SEC. 151. SHORT TITLE

This subtitle may be cited as the "Home Ownership and Equity Protection Act of 1994".

SEC. 152. CONSUMER PROTECTIONS FOR CERTAIN MORTGAGES.

(a) Mortgage Definition.—Section 103 of the Truth in Lending Act (15 U.S.C. § 1602) is amended by adding at the end the following new subsection:

"(aa) (1) A mortgage referred to in this subsection means a consumer credit transaction that is secured by the consumer's principal dwelling, other than a residential mortgage transaction, a reverse mortgage transaction, or a transaction under an open end credit plan, if—

"(A) the annual percentage rate at consummation of the transaction will exceed by more than 10 percentage points the yield on Treasury securities having comparable periods of maturity on the fifteenth day of the month immediately preceding the month in which the application for the extension of credit is received by the creditor; or

"(B) the total points and fees payable by the consumer at or before closing will exceed the greater of—

"(i) 8 percent of the total loan amount; or

"(ii) $ 400.

"(2) (A) After the 2-year period beginning on the effective date of the regulations promulgated under section 155 of the Riegle Community Development and Regulatory Improvement Act of 1994, and no more frequently than biennially after the first increase or decrease under this subparagraph, the Board may by regulation increase or decrease the number of percentage points specified in paragraph (1)(A), if the Board determines that the increase or decrease is—

"(i) consistent with the consumer protections against abusive lending provided by the amendments made by subtitle B of title I of the Riegle Community Development and Regulatory Improvement Act of 1994; and

"(ii) warranted by the need for credit.

"(B) An increase or decrease under subparagraph (A) may not result in the number of percentage points referred to in subparagraph (A) being—

"(i) less that 8 percentage points; or

"(ii) greater than 12 percentage points.

"(C) In determining whether to increase or decrease the number of percentage points referred to in subparagraph (A), the Board shall consult with representatives of consumers, including low-income consumers, and lenders.

"(3) The amount specified in paragraph (1)(B)(ii) shall be adjusted annually on January 1 by the annual percentage change in the Consumer Price Index, as reported on June 1 of the year preceding such adjustment.

"(4) For purposes of paragraph (1)(B), points and fees shall include—

"(A) all items included in the finance charge, except interest or the time-price differential;

"(B) all compensation paid to mortgage brokers;

"(C) each of the charges listed in section 106(e) (except an escrow for future payment of taxes), unless—

"(i) the charge is reasonable;

"(ii) the creditor receives no direct or indirect compensation; and

"(iii) the charge is paid to a third party unaffiliated with the creditor; and

"(D) such other charges as the Board determines to be appropriate.

"(5) This subsection shall not be construed to limit the rate of interest or the finance charge that a person may charge a consumer for any extension of credit.".

(b) Material Disclosures.—Section 103(u) of the Truth in Lending Act (15 U.S.C. § 1602(u)) is amended—

(1) by striking "and the due dates" and inserting "the due dates"; and

(2) by inserting before the period ", and the disclosures required by section 129(a)".

(c) Definition of Creditor Clarified.—Section 103(f) of the Truth in Lending Act (15 U.S.C. § 1602(f)) is amended by adding at the end the following: "Any person who originates 2 or more mortgages referred to in subsection (aa) in any 12-month period or any person who originates 1 or more such mortgages through a mortgage broker shall be considered to be a creditor for purposes of this title.".

(d) Disclosures Required and Certain Terms Prohibited.—The Truth in Lending Act (15 U.S.C. § 1601 et seq.) is amended by inserting after section 128 the following new section:

"Sec. 129. REQUIREMENTS FOR CERTAIN MORTGAGES.

"(a) Disclosures.—

"(1) Specific disclosures.—In addition to other disclosures required under this title, for each mortgage referred to in section 103(aa), the creditor shall provide the following disclosures in conspicuous type size:

"(A) 'You are not required to complete this agreement merely because you have received these disclosures or have signed a loan application.'.

"(B) 'If you obtain this loan, the lender will have a mortgage on your home. You could lose your home, and any money you have put into it, if you do not meet your obligations under the loan.'.

"(2) Annual percentage rate.—In addition to the disclosures required under paragraph (1), the creditor shall disclose–

"(A) in the case of a credit transaction with a fixed rate of interest, the annual percentage rate and the amount of the regular monthly payment; or

"(B) in the case of any other credit transaction, the annual percentage rate of the loan, the amount of the regular monthly payment, a statement that the interest rate and monthly payment may increase, and the amount of the maximum monthly payment, based on the maximum interest rate allowed pursuant to section 1204 of the Competitive Equality Banking Act of 1987.

"(b) Time of Disclosures.—

"(1) In general.—The disclosures required by this section shall be given not less than 3 business days prior to consummation of the transaction.

"(2) New disclosures required.—

"(A) In general.—After providing the disclosures required by this section, a creditor may not change the terms of the extension of credit if such changes make the disclosures inaccurate, unless new disclosures are provided that meet the requirements of this section.

"(B) Telephone disclosure.—A creditor may provide new disclosures pursuant to subparagraph (A) by telephone, if—

"(i) the change is initiated by the consumer; and

"(ii) at the consummation of the transaction under which the credit is extended–

"(I) the creditor provides to the consumer the new disclosures, in writing; and

"(II) the creditor and consumer certify in writing that the new disclosures were provided by telephone, by not later than 3 days prior to the date of consummation of the transaction.

"(3) Modifications.—The Board may, if it finds that such action is necessary to permit homeowners to meet bona fide personal financial emergencies, prescribe regulations authorizing the modification or waiver of rights created under this subsection, to the extent and under the circumstances set forth in those regulations.

"(c) No Prepayment Penalty.—

"(1) In general.—

"(A) Limitation on terms.—A mortgage referred to in section 103(aa) may not contain terms under which a consumer must pay a prepayment penalty for paying all or part of the principal before the date on which the principal is due.

"(B) Construction.—For purposes of this subsection, any method of computing a refund of unearned scheduled interest is a prepayment penalty if it is less favorable to the consumer than the actuarial method (as that term is defined in section 933(d) of the Housing and Community Development Act of 1992).

"(2) Exception.—Notwithstanding paragraph (1), a mortgage referred to in section 103(aa) may contain a prepayment penalty (including terms calculating a refund by a method that is not prohibited under section 933(b) of the Housing and Community Development Act of 1992 for the transaction in question) if—

"(A) at the time the mortgage is consummated—

"(i) the consumer is not liable for an amount of monthly indebtedness payments (including the amount of credit extended or to be extended under the transaction) that is greater than 50 percent of the monthly gross income of the consumer; and

"(ii) the income and expenses of the consumer are verified by a financial statement signed by the consumer, by a credit report, and in the case of employment income, by payment records or by verification from the employer of the consumer (which verification may be in the form of a copy of a pay stub or other payment record supplied by the consumer);

"(B) the penalty applies only to a prepayment made with amounts obtained by the consumer by means other than a refinancing by the creditor under the mortgage, or an affiliate of that creditor;

"(C) the penalty does not apply after the end of the 5-year period beginning on the date on which the mortgage is consummated; and

"(D) the penalty is not prohibited under other applicable law.

"(d) Limitations After Default.—A mortgage referred to in section 103(aa) may not provide for an interest rate applicable after default that is higher than the interest rate that applies before default. If the date of maturity of a mortgage referred to in subsection 103(aa) is accelerated due to default and the consumer is entitled to a rebate of interest, that rebate shall be computed by any method that is not less favorable than the actuarial method (as that term is defined in section 933(d) of the Housing and Community Development Act of 1992).

"(e) No Balloon Payments.—A mortgage referred to in section 103(aa) having a term of less than 5 years may not include terms under which the aggregate amount of the regular periodic payments would not fully amortize the outstanding principal balance.

"(f) No Negative Amortization.—A mortgage referred to in section 103(aa) may not include terms under which the outstanding principal balance will increase at any time over the course of the loan because the regular periodic payments do not cover the full amount of interest due.

"(g) No Prepaid Payments.—A mortgage referred to in section 103(aa) may not include terms under which more than 2 periodic payments required under the loan are consolidated and paid in advance from the loan proceeds provided to the consumer.

"(h) Prohibition on Extending Credit Without Regard to Payment Ability of Consumer.—A creditor shall not engage in a pattern or practice of extending credit to consumers under mortgages referred to in section 103(aa) based on the consumers' collateral without regard to the consumers' repayment ability, including the consumers' current and expected income, current obligations, and employment.

"(i) Requirements for Payments Under Home Improvement Contracts.—A creditor shall not make a payment to a contractor under a home improvement contract from amounts extended as credit under a mortgage referred to in section 103(aa), other than–

"(1) in the form of an instrument that is payable to the consumer or jointly to the consumer and the contractor; or

"(2) at the election of the consumer, by a third party escrow agent in accordance with terms established in a written agreement signed by the consumer, the creditor, and the contractor before the date of payment.

"(j) Consequence of Failure To Comply.—Any mortgage that contains a provision prohibited by this section shall be deemed a failure to deliver the material disclosures required under this title, for the purpose of section 125.

"(k) Definition.—For purposes of this section, the term 'affiliate' has the same meaning as in section 2(k) of the Bank Holding Company Act of 1956.

"(l) Discretionary Regulatory Authority of Board.—

"(1) Exemptions.—The Board may, by regulation or order, exempt specific mortgage products or categories of mortgages from any or all of the prohibitions specified in subsections (c) through (i), if the Board finds that the exemption—

"(A) is in the interest of the borrowing public; and

"(B) will apply only to products that maintain and strengthen home ownership and equity protection.

"(2) Prohibitions.—The Board, by regulation or order, shall prohibit acts or practices in connection with—

"(A) mortgage loans that the Board finds to be unfair, deceptive, or designed to evade the provisions of this section; and

"(B) refinancing of mortgage loans that the Board finds to be associated with abusive lending practices, or that are otherwise not in the interest of the borrower.".

(e) Conforming Amendments.—

(1) Table of sections.—The table of sections at the beginning of chapter 2 of the Truth in Lending Act is amended by striking the item relating to section 129 and inserting the following:

"129. Requirements for certain mortgages.".

(2) Truth in lending act.—The Truth in Lending Act (15 U.S.C. § 1601 et seq.) is amended—

(A) in the second sentence of section 105(a), by striking "These" and inserting "Except in the case of a mortgage referred to in section 103(aa), these";

(B) in section 111(a)(2), by inserting before the period the following: ", and such State-required disclosure may not be made in lieu of the disclosures applicable to certain mortgages under section 129"; and

(C) in section 111(b)—

(i) by striking "This" and inserting "Except as provided in section 129, this"; and

(ii) by adding at the end the following: "The provisions of section 129 do not annul, alter, or affect the applicability of the laws of any State or exempt any person subject to the provisions of section 129 from complying with the laws of any State, with respect to the requirements for mortgages referred to in section 103(aa), except to the extent that those State laws are inconsistent with any provisions of section 129, and then only to the extent of the inconsistency.".

SEC. 153. CIVIL LIABILITY

(a) Damages.—Section 130(a) of the Truth in Lending Act (15 U.S.C. § 1640(a)) is amended—

(1) by striking "and" at the end of paragraph (2)(B);

(2) by striking the period at the end of paragraph (3) and inserting "; and"; and

(3) by inserting after paragraph (3) the following new paragraph:

"(4) in the case of a failure to comply with any requirement under section 129, an amount equal to the sum of all finance charges and fees paid by the consumer, unless the creditor demonstrates that the failure to comply is not material.".

(b) State Attorney General Enforcement.—Section 130(e) of the Truth in Lending Act (15 U.S.C. § 1640(e)) is amended by adding at the end the following:

"An action to enforce a violation of section 129 may also be brought by the appropriate State attorney general in any appropriate United States district court, or any other court of competent jurisdiction, not later than 3 years after the date on which the violation occurs. The State attorney general shall provide prior written notice of any such civil action to the Federal agency responsible for enforcement under section 108 and shall provide the agency with a copy of the complaint. If prior notice is not feasible, the State attorney general shall provide notice to such agency immediately upon instituting the action. The Federal agency may—

"(1) intervene in the action;

"(2) upon intervening—

"(A) remove the action to the appropriate United States district court, if it was not originally brought there; and

"(B) be heard on all matters arising in the action; and

"(3) file a petition for appeal.".

(c) Assignee Liability.—Section 131 of the Truth in Lending Act (15 U.S.C. § 1641) is amended by adding at the end the following new subsection:

"(d) Rights Upon Assignment of Certain Mortgages.—

"(1) In general.—Any person who purchases or is otherwise assigned a mortgage referred to in section 103(aa) shall be subject to all claims and defenses with respect to that mortgage that the consumer could assert against the creditor of the mortgage, unless the purchaser or assignee demonstrates, by a preponderance of the evidence, that a reasonable person exercising ordinary due diligence, could not determine, based on the documentation required by this title, the itemization of the amount financed, and other disclosure of disbursements that the mortgage was a mortgage referred to in section 103(aa). The preceding sentence does not affect rights of a consumer under subsection (a), (b), or (c) of this section or any other provision of this title.

"(2) Limitation on damages.—Notwithstanding any other provision of law, relief provided as a result of any action made permissible by paragraph (1) may not exceed—

"(A) with respect to actions based upon a violation of this title, the amount specified in section 130; and

"(B) with respect to all other causes of action, the sum of—

"(i) the amount of all remaining indebtedness; and

"(ii) the total amount paid by the consumer in connection with the transaction.

"(3) Offset.—The amount of damages that may be awarded under paragraph (2)(B) shall be reduced by the amount of any damages awarded under paragraph (2)(A).

"(4) Notice.—Any person who sells or otherwise assigns a mortgage referred to in section 103(aa) shall include a prominent notice of the potential liability under this subsection as determined by the Board.".

SEC. 154. REVERSE MORTGAGE DISCLOSURE

(a) Definition of Reverse Mortgage.—Section 103 of the Truth in Lending Act (15 U.S.C. § 1602) is amended by adding at the end the following new subsection:

"(bb) The term 'reverse mortgage transaction' means a nonrecourse transaction in which a mortgage, deed of trust, or equivalent consensual security interest is created against the consumer's principal dwelling—

"(1) securing one or more advances; and

"(2) with respect to which the payment of any principal, interest, and shared appreciation or equity is due and payable (other than in the case of default) only after—

"(A) the transfer of the dwelling;

"(B) the consumer ceases to occupy the dwelling as a principal dwelling; or

"(C) the death of the consumer.".

(b) Disclosure.—Chapter 2 of title I of the Truth in Lending Act (15 U.S.C. § 1631 et seq.) is amended by adding at the end the following new section:

"Sec. 138. REVERSE MORTGAGES.

"(a) In General.—In addition to the disclosures required under this title, for each reverse mortgage, the creditor shall, not less than 3 days prior to consummation of the transaction, disclose to the consumer in conspicuous type a good faith estimate of the projected total cost of the mortgage to the consumer expressed as a table of annual interest rates. Each annual interest rate shall be based on a projected total future credit extension balance under a projected appreciation rate for the dwelling and a term for the mortgage. The disclosure shall include—

"(1) statements of the annual interest rates for not less than 3 projected appreciation rates and not less than 3 credit transaction periods, as determined by the Board, including—

"(A) a short-term reverse mortgage;

"(B) a term equaling the actuarial life expectancy of the consumer; and

"(C) such longer term as the Board deems appropriate; and

"(2) a statement that the consumer is not obligated to complete the reverse mortgage transaction merely because the consumer has received the disclosure required under this section or has signed an application for the reverse mortgage.

"(b) Projected Total Cost.—In determining the projected total cost of the mortgage to be disclosed to the consumer under subsection (a), the creditor shall take into account—

"(1) any shared appreciation or equity that the lender will, by contract, be entitled to receive;

"(2) all costs and charges to the consumer, including the costs of any associated annuity that the consumer elects or is required to purchase as part of the reverse mortgage transaction;

"(3) all payments to and for the benefit of the consumer, including, in the case in which an associated annuity is purchased (whether or not required by the lender as a condition of making the reverse mortgage), the annuity payments received by the consumer and financed from the proceeds of the loan, instead of the proceeds used to finance the annuity; and

"(4) any limitation on the liability of the consumer under reverse mortgage transactions (such as nonrecourse limits and equity conservation agreements).".

(c) Home Equity Plan Exemption.—Section 137(b) of the Truth in Lending Act (15 U.S.C. § 1647(b)) is amended by adding at the end the following:"This subsection does not apply to reverse mortgage transactions.".

(d) Table of Sections.—The table of sections at the beginning of chapter 2 of the Truth in Lending Act is amended by inserting after the item relating to section 137 the following:

"138. Reverse mortgages.".

SEC. 155. REGULATIONS

Not later than 180 days after the date of enactment of this Act, the Board of Governors of the Federal Reserve System shall issue such regulations as may be necessary to carry out this subtitle, and such regulations shall become effective on the date on which disclosure regulations are required to become effective under section 105(d) of the Truth in Lending Act.

SEC. 156. APPLICABILITY

This subtitle, and the amendments made by this subtitle, shall apply to every mortgage referred to in section 103(aa) of the Truth in Lending Act (as added by section 152(a) of this Act) consummated on or after the date on which regulations issued under section 155 become effective.

SEC. 157. FEDERAL RESERVE STUDY

During the period beginning 180 days after the date of enactment of this Act and ending 2 years after that date of enactment, the Board of Governors of the Federal Reserve System shall conduct a study and submit to the Congress a report, including recommendations for any appropriate legislation, regarding–

(1) whether a consumer engaging in an open end credit transaction (as defined in section 103 of the Truth in Lending Act) secured by the consumer's principal dwelling is provided adequate protections under Federal law, including section 127A of the Truth in Lending Act; and

(2) whether a more appropriate interest rate index exists for purposes of subparagraph (A) of section 103(aa)(1) of the Truth in Lending Act (as added by section 152(a) of this Act) than the yield on Treasury securities referred to in that subparagraph.

SEC. 158. HEARINGS ON HOME EQUITY LENDING

(a) Hearings.—Not less than once during the 3-year period beginning on the date of enactment of this Act, and regularly thereafter, the Board of Governors of the Federal Reserve System, in consultation with the Consumer Advisory Council of the Board, shall conduct a public hearing to examine the home equity loan market and the adequacy of existing regulatory and legislative provisions and the provisions of this subtitle in protecting the interests of consumers, and low-income consumers in particular.

(b) Participation.—In conducting hearings required by subsection (a), the Board of Governors of the Federal Reserve System shall solicit participation from consumers, representatives of consumers, lenders, and other interested parties.

APPENDIX 12:
PMI ENFORCEMENT AUTHORITIES

NAME	ADDRESS	TELEPHONE	JURIDICTION
Federal Deposit Insurance Corporation (FDIC) Compliance and Consumer Affairs Division	550 17th Street NW Washington, D.C. 20429	877-275-3342	The FDIC handles questions about deposit insurance coverage and complaints about FDIC-insured state banks which are not members of the Federal Reserve System.
Office of Thrift Supervision (OTS) Division of Consumer and Civil Rights	1700 G Street NW Washington, D.C. 20552	800-842-6929	The OTS handles complaints about Federal savings and loans and Federal savings banks.
National Credit Union Administrative (NCUA)	1775 Duke Street Alexandria, VA 22314-3428	703-518-6330	The NCUA Shared Insurance Fund provides Federal insurance for nearly 13,000 credit unions.
Farm Credit Administration (FCA) Office of Congressional and Public Affairs Farm Credit Administration	1501 Farm Credit Dr. McLean, VA 22102-5090	703-883-4100	The FCA regulates banks, associations, and related entities that comprise the Farm Credit System, including the Federal Agricultural Mortgage Corporation (Farmer Mac).

NAME	ADDRESS	TELEPHONE	JURIDICTION
Comptroller of the Currency (OCC) Compliance Management	250 E. Street SW Mail Stop 309 Washington, D.C. 20219	800-613-6743	The OCC handles complaints and regulates National Banks, which usually have "National" in their name, or "N.A." after their name.
The Federal Reserve Board Division of Consumer and Community Affairs	20th and C Streets NW Mail Stop 801 Washington, D.C. 20551	202-452-3693	The Federal Reserve Board handles complaints. regulates state-chartered banks and trusts, and administers the Truth-in-Lending, Equal Credit Opportunity Act and Fair Credit Reporting Act.

Source: U.S. Department of Housing and Urban Development.

APPENDIX 13:
THE FAIR HOUSING
ACT—SELECTED PROVISIONS
[42 U.S.C. § 3601 *et seq.*]

TITLE 42 - THE FAIR HOUSING ACT [42 U.S.C. § 3601 *et seq.*]

Sec. 800. [42 U.S.C. § 3601 note] Short Title

This title may be cited as the "Fair Housing Act".

Sec. 801. [42 U.S.C. § 3601] Declaration of Policy

It is the policy of the United States to provide, within constitutional limitations, for fair housing throughout the United States.

***

Sec. 804. [42 U.S.C. § 3604] Discrimination in sale or rental of housing and other prohibited practices

As made applicable by section 803 of this title and except as exempted by sections 803(b) and 807 of this title, it shall be unlawful—

(a) To refuse to sell or rent after the making of a bona fide offer, or to refuse to negotiate for the sale or rental of, or otherwise make unavailable or deny, a dwelling to any person because of race, color, religion, sex, familial status, or national origin.

(b) To discriminate against any person in the terms, conditions, or privileges of sale or rental of a dwelling, or in the provision of services or facilities in connection therewith, because of race, color, religion, sex, familial status, or national origin.

(c) To make, print, or publish, or cause to be made, printed, or published any notice, statement, or advertisement, with respect to the sale or rental of a dwelling that indicates any preference, limitation, or discrimination based on race, color, religion, sex, handicap, familial status, or national origin, or an intention to make any such preference, limitation, or discrimination.

(d) To represent to any person because of race, color, religion, sex, handicap, familial status, or national origin that any dwelling is not available for inspection, sale, or rental when such dwelling is in fact so available.

(e) For profit, to induce or attempt to induce any person to sell or rent any dwelling by representations regarding the entry or prospective entry into the neighborhood of a person or persons of a particular race, color, religion, sex, handicap, familial status, or national origin.

(f) (1) To discriminate in the sale or rental, or to otherwise make unavailable or deny, a dwelling to any buyer or renter because of a handicap of—

(A) that buyer or renter,

(B) a person residing in or intending to reside in that dwelling after it is so sold, rented, or made available; or

(C) any person associated with that buyer or renter.

(2) To discriminate against any person in the terms, conditions, or privileges of sale or rental of a dwelling, or in the provision of services or facilities in connection with such dwelling, because of a handicap of—

(A) that person; or

(B) a person residing in or intending to reside in that dwelling after it is so sold, rented, or made available; or

(C) any person associated with that person.

(3) For purposes of this subsection, discrimination includes—

(A) a refusal to permit, at the expense of the handicapped person, reasonable modifications of existing premises occupied or to be occupied by such person if such modifications may be necessary to afford such person full enjoyment of the premises, except that, in the case of a rental, the landlord may where it is reasonable to do so condition permission for a modification on the renter agreeing to restore the interior of the premises to the condition that existed before the modification, reasonable wear and tear excepted.

(B) a refusal to make reasonable accommodations in rules, policies, practices, or services, when such accommodations may be necessary to afford such person equal opportunity to use and enjoy a dwelling; or

(C) in connection with the design and construction of covered multifamily dwellings for first occupancy after the date that is 30 months after the date of enactment of the Fair Housing Amendments Act of 1988, a failure to design and construct those dwelling in such a manner that–

(i) the public use and common use portions of such dwellings are readily accessible to and usable by handicapped persons;

(ii) all the doors designed to allow passage into and within all premises within such dwellings are sufficiently wide to allow passage by handicapped persons in wheelchairs; and

(iii) all premises within such dwellings contain the following features of adaptive design:

(I) an accessible route into and through the dwelling;

(II) light switches, electrical outlets, thermostats, and other environmental controls in accessible locations;

(III) reinforcements in bathroom walls to allow later installation of grab bars; and

(IV) usable kitchens and bathrooms such that an individual in a wheelchair can maneuver about the space.

(4) Compliance with the appropriate requirements of the American National Standard for buildings and facilities providing accessibility and usability for physically handicapped people (commonly cited as "ANSI A117.1") suffices to satisfy the requirements of paragraph (3)(C)(iii).

(5)(A) If a State or unit of general local government has incorporated into its laws the requirements set forth in paragraph (3)(C), compliance with such laws shall be deemed to satisfy the requirements of that paragraph.

(B) A State or unit of general local government may review and approve newly constructed covered multifamily dwellings for the purpose of making determinations as to whether the design and construction requirements of paragraph (3)(C) are met.

(C) The Secretary shall encourage, but may not require, States and units of local government to include in their existing procedures for the review and approval of newly constructed covered multifamily dwellings, determinations as to whether the design and construction of such dwellings are consistent with paragraph (3)(C), and shall provide technical assistance to States and units of local government and other persons to implement the requirements of paragraph (3)(C).

(D) Nothing in this title shall be construed to require the Secretary to review or approve the plans, designs or construction of all covered multifamily dwellings, to determine whether the design and construction of such dwellings are consistent with the requirements of paragraph 3(C).

(6)(A) Nothing in paragraph (5) shall be construed to affect the authority and responsibility of the Secretary or a State or local public agency certified pursuant to section 810(f)(3) of this Act to receive and process complaints or otherwise engage in enforcement activities under this title.

(B) Determinations by a State or a unit of general local government under paragraphs (5)(A) and (B) shall not be conclusive in enforcement proceedings under this title.

(7) As used in this subsection, the term "covered multifamily dwellings" means—

(A) buildings consisting of 4 or more units if such buildings have one or more elevators; and

(B) ground floor units in other buildings consisting of 4 or more units.

(8) Nothing in this title shall be construed to invalidate or limit any law of a State or political subdivision of a State, or other jurisdiction in which this title shall be effective, that requires dwellings to be designed and constructed in a manner that affords handicapped persons greater access than is required by this title.

(9) Nothing in this subsection requires that a dwelling be made available to an individual whose tenancy would constitute a direct threat to the health or safety of other individuals or whose tenancy would result in substantial physical damage to the property of others.

Sec. 805. [42 U.S.C. § 3605] Discrimination in Residential Real Estate-Related Transactions

(a) In General—It shall be unlawful for any person or other entity whose business includes engaging in residential real estate-related transactions to discriminate against any person in making available such a transaction, or in the terms or conditions of such a transaction, because of race, color, religion, sex, handicap, familial status, or national origin.

(b) Definition—As used in this section, the term "residential real estate-related transaction" means any of the following:

(1) The making or purchasing of loans or providing other financial assistance—

(A) for purchasing, constructing, improving, repairing, or maintaining a dwelling; or

(B) secured by residential real estate.

(2) The selling, brokering, or appraising of residential real property.

(c) Appraisal Exemption—Nothing in this title prohibits a person engaged in the business of furnishing appraisals of real property to take into consideration factors other than race, color, religion, national origin, sex, handicap, or familial status.

Sec. 806. [42 U.S.C. § 3606] Discrimination in provision of brokerage services

After December 31, 1968, it shall be unlawful to deny any person access to or membership or participation in any multiple-listing service, real estate brokers' organization or other service, organization, or facility relating to the business of selling or renting dwellings, or to discriminate against him in the terms or conditions of such access, membership, or participation, on account of race, color, religion, sex, handicap, familial status, or national origin.

Sec. 807. [42 U.S.C. § 3607] Religious organizations or private club exemption

(a) Nothing in this subchapter shall prohibit a religious organization, association, or society, or any nonprofit institution or organization operated, supervised or controlled by or in conjunction with a religious organization, association, or society, from limiting the sale, rental or occupancy of dwellings which it owns or operates for other than a commercial purpose to persons of the same religion, or from giving preference to such persons, unless membership in such religion is restricted on account of race, color, or national origin. Nor shall anything in this subchapter prohibit a private club not in fact open to the public, which as an incident to its primary purpose or purposes provides lodgings which it owns or operates for other than a commercial purpose, from limiting the rental or occupancy of such lodgings to its members or from giving preference to its members.

(b)(1) Nothing in this title limits the applicability of any reasonable local, State, or Federal restrictions regarding the maximum number of occupants permitted to occupy a dwelling. Nor does any provision in this title regarding familial status apply with respect to housing for older persons.

(2) As used in this section "housing for older persons" means housing—

(A) provided under any State or Federal program that the Secretary determines is specifically designed and operated to assist elderly persons (as defined in the State or Federal program); or

(B) intended for, and solely occupied by, persons 62 years of age or older; or

(C) intended and operated for occupancy by persons 55 years of age or older, and—

(i) at least 80 percent of the occupied units are occupied by at least one person who is 55 years of age or older;

(ii) the housing facility or community publishes and adheres to policies and procedures that demonstrate the intent required under this subparagraph; and

(iii) the housing facility or community complies with rules issued by the Secretary for verification of occupancy, which shall—

(I) provide for verification by reliable surveys and affidavits; and

(II) include examples of the types of policies and procedures relevant to a determination of compliance with the requirement of clause (ii). Such surveys and affidavits shall be admissible in administrative and judicial proceedings for the purposes of such verification.

(3) Housing shall not fail to meet the requirements for housing for older persons by reason of:

(A) persons residing in such housing as of the date of enactment of this Act who do not meet the age requirements of subsections

(2)(B) or (C): **Provided**, That new occupants of such housing meet the age requirements of sections (2)(B) or (C); or

(B) unoccupied units: **Provided**, That such units are reserved for occupancy by persons who meet the age requirements of subsections (2)(B) or (C).

(4) Nothing in this title prohibits conduct against a person because such person has been convicted by any court of competent jurisdiction of the illegal manufacture or distribution of a controlled substance as defined in section 102 of the Controlled Substances Act (21 U.S.C. § 802).

(5)(A) A person shall not be held personally liable for monetary damages for a violation of this title if such person reasonably relied, in good faith, on the application of the exemption under this subsection relating to housing for older persons.

(B) For the purposes of this paragraph, a person may only show good faith reliance on the application of the exemption by showing that—

(i) such person has no actual knowledge that the facility or community is not, or will not be, eligible for such exemption; and

(ii) the facility or community has stated formally, in writing, that the facility or community complies with the requirements for such exemption.

***

Sec. 810. [42 U.S.C. § 3610] Administrative Enforcement; Preliminary Matters

(a) Complaints and Answers.—

(1)(A)(i) An aggrieved person may, not later than one year after an alleged discriminatory housing practice has occurred or terminated, file a complaint with the Secretary alleging such discriminatory housing practice. The Secretary, on the Secretary's own initiative, may also file such a complaint.

(ii) Such complaints shall be in writing and shall contain such information and be in such form as the Secretary requires.

(iii) The Secretary may also investigate housing practices to determine whether a complaint should be brought under this section.

(B) Upon the filing of such a complaint—

(i) the Secretary shall serve notice upon the aggrieved person acknowledging such filing and advising the aggrieved person of the time limits and choice of forums provided under this title;

(ii) the Secretary shall, not later than 10 days after such filing or the identification of an additional respondent under paragraph (2), serve on the respondent a notice identifying the alleged discriminatory housing practice and advising such respondent of the procedural rights and obligations of respondents under this title, together with a copy of the original complaint;

(iii) each respondent may file, not later than 10 days after receipt of notice from the Secretary, an answer to such complaint; and

(iv) the Secretary shall make an investigation of the alleged discriminatory housing practice and complete such investigation within 100 days after the filing of the complaint (or, when the Secretary takes further action under subsection (f)(2) with respect to a complaint, within 100 days after the commencement of such further action), unless it is impracticable to do so.

(C) If the Secretary is unable to complete the investigation within 100 days after the filing of the complaint (or, when the Secretary takes further action under subsection (f)(2) with respect to a complaint, within 100 days after the commencement of such further action), the Secretary shall notify the complainant and respondent in writing of the reasons for not doing so.

(D) Complaints and answers shall be under oath or affirmation, and may be reasonably and fairly amended at any time.

(2) (A) A person who is not named as a respondent in a complaint, but who is identified as a respondent in the course of investigation, may be joined as an additional or substitute respondent upon written notice, under paragraph (1), to such person, from the Secretary.

(B) Such notice, in addition to meeting the requirements of paragraph (1), shall explain the basis for the Secretary's belief that the person to whom the notice is addressed is properly joined as a respondent.

(b) Investigative Report and Conciliation.—

(1) During the period beginning with the filing of such complaint and ending with the filing of a charge or a dismissal by the Secretary, the Secretary shall, to the extent feasible, engage in conciliation with respect to such complaint.

(2) A conciliation agreement arising out of such conciliation shall be an agreement between the respondent and the complainant, and shall be subject to approval by the Secretary.

(3) A conciliation agreement may provide for binding arbitration of the dispute arising from the complaint. Any such arbitration that results from a conciliation agreement may award appropriate relief, including monetary relief.

(4) Each conciliation agreement shall be made public unless the complainant and respondent otherwise agree and the Secretary determines that disclosure is not required to further the purposes of this title.

(5) (A) At the end of each investigation under this section, the Secretary shall prepare a final investigative report containing—

(i) the names and dates of contacts with witnesses;

(ii) a summary and the dates of correspondence and other contacts with the aggrieved person and the respondent;

(iii) a summary description of other pertinent records;

(iv) a summary of witness statements; and

(v) answers to interrogatories.

(B) A final report under this paragraph may be amended if additional evidence is later discovered.

(c) Failure to Comply With Conciliation Agreement.—Whenever the Secretary has reasonable cause to believe that a respondent has breached a conciliation agreement, the Secretary shall refer the matter to the Attorney General with a recommendation that a civil action be filed under section 814 for the enforcement of such agreement.

(d) Prohibitions and Requirements With Respect to Disclosure of Information.—

(1) Nothing said or done in the course of conciliation under this title may be made public or used as evidence in a subsequent proceeding under this title without the written consent of the persons concerned.

(2) Notwithstanding paragraph (1), the Secretary shall make available to the aggrieved person and the respondent, at any time, upon request following completion of the Secretary's investigation, information derived from an investigation and any final investigative report relating to that investigation.

(e) Prompt Judicial Action—

(1) If the Secretary concludes at any time following the filing of a complaint that prompt judicial action is necessary to carry out the purposes of this title, the Secretary may authorize a civil action for appropriate temporary or preliminary relief pending final disposition of the complaint under this section. Upon receipt of such authorization, the Attorney General shall promptly commence and maintain such an action. Any temporary restraining order or other order granting preliminary or temporary relief shall be issued in accordance with the Federal Rules of Civil Procedure. The commencement of a civil action under this subsection does not affect the initiation or continuation of administrative proceedings under this section and section 812 of this title.

(2) Whenever the Secretary has reason to believe that a basis may exist for the commencement of proceedings against any respondent under section 814(a) and 814(c) or for proceedings by any governmental licensing or supervisory authorities, the Secretary shall transmit the information upon which such belief is based to the Attorney General, or to such authorities, as the case may be.

(f) Referral for State or Local Proceedings.—

(1) Whenever a complaint alleges a discriminatory housing practice—

(A) within the jurisdiction of a State or local public agency; and

(B) as to which such agency has been certified by the Secretary under this subsection; the Secretary shall refer such complaint to that certified agency before taking any action with respect to such complaint.

(2) Except with the consent of such certified agency, the Secretary, after that referral is made, shall take no further action with respect to such complaint unless—

(A) the certified agency has failed to commence proceedings with respect to the complaint before the end of the 30th day after the date of such referral;

(B) the certified agency, having so commenced such proceedings, fails to carry forward such proceedings with reasonable promptness; or

(C) the Secretary determines that the certified agency no longer qualifies for certification under this subsection with respect to the relevant jurisdiction.

(3)(A) The Secretary may certify an agency under this subsection only if the Secretary determines that—

(i) the substantive rights protected by such agency in the jurisdiction with respect to which certification is to be made;

(ii) the procedures followed by such agency;

(iii) the remedies available to such agency; and

(iv) the availability of judicial review of such agency's action;

are substantially equivalent to those created by and under this title.

(B) Before making such certification, the Secretary shall take into account the current practices and past performance, if any, of such agency.

(4) During the period which begins on the date of the enactment of the Fair Housing Amendments Act of 1988 and ends 40 months after such date, each agency certified (including an agency certified for interim referrals pursuant to 24 CFR 115.11, unless such agency is subsequently denied recognition under 24 CFR 115.7) for the purposes of this title on the day before such date shall for the purposes of this subsection be considered certified under this subsection with respect to those matters for which such agency was certified on that date. If the Secretary determines in an individual case that an agency has not been able to meet the certification requirements within this 40-month period due to exceptional circumstances, such as the infrequency of legislative sessions in that jurisdiction, the Secretary may extend such period by not more than 8 months.

(5) Not less frequently than every 5 years, the Secretary shall determine whether each agency certified under this subsection continues to qualify for certification. The Secretary shall take appropriate action with respect to any agency not so qualifying.

(g) Reasonable Cause Determination and Effect.—

(1) The Secretary shall, within 100 days after the filing of the complaint (or, when the Secretary takes further action under subsection (f)(2) with respect to a complaint, within 100 days after the commencement of such further action), determine based on the facts

whether reasonable cause exists to believe that a discriminatory housing practice has occurred or is about to occur, unless it is impracticable to do so, or unless the Secretary has approved a conciliation agreement with respect to the complaint. If the Secretary is unable to make the determination within 100 days after the filing of the complaint (or, when the Secretary takes further action under subsection (f)(2) with respect to a complaint, within 100 days after the commencement of such further action), the Secretary shall notify the complainant and respondent in writing of the reasons for not doing so.

(2) (A) If the Secretary determines that reasonable cause exists to believe that a discriminatory housing practice has occurred or is about to occur, the Secretary shall, except as provided in subparagraph (C), immediately issue a charge on behalf of the aggrieved person, for further proceedings under section 812.

(B) Such charge—

(i) shall consist of a short and plain statement of the facts upon which the Secretary has found reasonable cause to believe that a discriminatory housing practice has occurred or is about to occur;

(ii) shall be based on the final investigative report; and

(iii) need not be limited to the facts or grounds alleged in the complaint filed under section 810(a).

(C) If the Secretary determines that the matter involves the legality of any State or local zoning or other land use law or ordinance, the Secretary shall immediately refer the matter to the Attorney General for appropriate action under section 814, instead of issuing such charge.

(3) If the Secretary determines that no reasonable cause exists to believe that a discriminatory housing practice has occurred or is about to occur, the Secretary shall promptly dismiss the complaint. The Secretary shall make public disclosure of each such dismissal.

(4) The Secretary may not issue a charge under this section regarding an alleged discriminatory housing practice after the beginning of the trial of a civil action commenced by the aggrieved party under an Act of Congress or a State law, seeking relief with respect to that discriminatory housing practice.

(h) Service of Copies of Charge.—After the Secretary issues a charge under this section, the Secretary shall cause a copy thereof, together with information as to how to make an election under section 812(a) and the effect of such an election, to be served–

(1) on each respondent named in such charge, together with a notice of opportunity for a hearing at a time and place specified in the notice, unless that election is made; and

(2) on each aggrieved person on whose behalf the complaint was filed.

Sec. 811. [42 U.S.C. § 3611] Subpoenas; Giving of Evidence

(a) In General.—The Secretary may, in accordance with this subsection, issue subpoenas and order discovery in aid of investigations and hearings under this title. Such subpoenas and discovery may be ordered to the same extent and subject to the same limitations as would apply if the subpoenas or discovery were ordered or served in aid of a civil action in the United States district court for the district in which the investigation is taking place.

(b) Witness Fees.—Witnesses summoned by a subpoena under this title shall be entitled to same witness and mileage fees as witnesses in proceedings in United States district courts. Fees payable to a witness summoned by a subpoena issued at the request of a party shall be paid by that party or, where a party is unable to pay the fees, by the Secretary.

(c) Criminal Penalties.—

(1) Any person who willfully fails or neglects to attend and testify or to answer any lawful inquiry or to produce records, documents, or other evidence, if it is in such person's power to do so, in obedience to the subpoena or other lawful order under subsection (a), shall be fined not more than $100,000 or imprisoned not more than one year, or both.

(2) Any person who, with intent thereby to mislead another person in any proceeding under this title—

(A) makes or causes to be made any false entry or statement of fact in any report, account, record, or other document produced pursuant to subpoena or other lawful order under subsection (a);

(B) willfully neglects or fails to make or to cause to be made full, true, and correct entries in such reports, accounts, records, or other documents; or

(C) willfully mutilates, alters, or by any other means falsifies any documentary evidence;

shall be fined not more than $100,000 or imprisoned not more than one year, or both.

Sec. 812. [42 U.S.C. § 3612] Enforcement by Secretary

(a) Election of Judicial Determination.—When a charge is filed under section 810, a complainant, a respondent, or an aggrieved person on whose behalf the complaint was filed, may elect to have the claims asserted in that charge decided in a civil action under subsection (o) in lieu of a hearing under subsection (b). The election must be made not later than 20 days after the receipt by the electing person of service under section 810(h) or, in the case of the Secretary, not later than 20 days after such service. The person making such election shall give notice of doing so to the Secretary and to all other complainants and respondents to whom the charge relates.

(b) Administrative Law Judge Hearing in Absence of Election.—If an election is not made under subsection (a) with respect to a charge filed under section 810, the Secretary shall provide an opportunity for a hearing on the record with respect to a charge issued under section 810. The Secretary shall delegate the conduct of a hearing under this section to an administrative law judge appointed under section 3105 of title 5, United States Code. The administrative law judge shall conduct the hearing at a place in the vicinity in which the discriminatory housing practice is alleged to have occurred or to be about to occur.

(c) Rights of Parties.—At a hearing under this section, each party may appear in person, be represented by counsel, present evidence, cross-examine witnesses, and obtain the issuance of subpoenas under section 811. Any aggrieved person may intervene as a party in the proceeding. The Federal Rules of Evidence apply to the presentation of evidence in such hearing as they would in a civil action in a United States district court.

(d) Expedited Discovery and Hearing.—

(1) Discovery in administrative proceedings under this section shall be conducted as expeditiously and inexpensively as possible, consistent with the need of all parties to obtain relevant evidence.

(2) A hearing under this section shall be conducted as expeditiously and inexpensively as possible, consistent with the needs and rights of the parties to obtain a fair hearing and a complete record.

(3) The Secretary shall, not later than 180 days after the date of enactment of this subsection, issue rules to implement this subsection.

(e) Resolution of Charge.—Any resolution of a charge before a final order under this section shall require the consent of the aggrieved person on whose behalf the charge is issued.

(f) Effect of Trial of Civil Action on Administrative Proceedings.–An administrative law judge may not continue administrative proceedings under this section regarding any alleged discriminatory housing practice after the beginning of the trial of a civil action commenced by the aggrieved party under an Act of Congress or a State law, seeking relief with respect to that discriminatory housing practice.

(g) Hearings, Findings and Conclusions, and Order.—

(1) The administrative law judge shall commence the hearing under this section no later than 120 days following the issuance of the charge, unless it is impracticable to do so. If the administrative law judge is unable to commence the hearing within 120 days after the issuance of the charge, the administrative law judge shall notify the Secretary, the aggrieved person on whose behalf the charge was filed, and the respondent, in writing of the reasons for not doing so.

(2) The administrative law judge shall make findings of fact and conclusions of law within 60 days after the end of the hearing under this section, unless it is impracticable to do so. If the administrative law judge is unable to make findings of fact and conclusions of law within such period, or any succeeding 60-day period thereafter, the administrative law judge shall notify the Secretary, the aggrieved person on whose behalf the charge was filed, and the respondent, in writing of the reasons for not doing so.

(3) If the administrative law judge finds that a respondent has engaged or is about to engage in a discriminatory housing practice, such administrative law judge shall promptly issue an order for such relief as may be appropriate, which may include actual damages suffered by the aggrieved person and injunctive or other equitable relief. Such order may, to vindicate the public interest, assess a civil penalty against the respondent—

(A) in an amount not exceeding $11,000 if the respondent has not been adjudged to have committed any prior discriminatory housing practice;

(B) in an amount not exceeding $27,500 if the respondent has been adjudged to have committed one other discriminatory housing practice during the 5-year period ending on the date of the filing of this charge; and

(C) in an amount not exceeding $55,000 if the respondent has been adjudged to have committed 2 or more discriminatory housing practices during the 7-year period ending on the date of the filing of this charge; except that if the acts constituting the discriminatory housing practice that is the object of the charge are committed by the same natural person who has been previously adjudged to have committed acts constituting a discriminatory housing practice, then the civil penalties set forth in subparagraphs (B) and (C) may be imposed without regard to the period of time within which any subsequent discriminatory housing practice occurred.

(4) No such order shall affect any contract, sale, encumbrance, or lease consummated before the issuance of such order and involving a bona fide purhaser, encumbrancer, or tenant without actual notice of the charge filed under this title.

(5) In the case of an order with respect to a discriminatory housing practice that occurred in the course of a business subject to a licensing or regulation by a governmental agency, the Secretary shall, not later than 30 days after the date of the issuance of such order (or, if such order is judicially reviewed, 30 days after such order is in substance affirmed upon such review)—

(A) send copies of the findings of fact, conclusions of law, and the order, to that governmental agency; and

(B) recommend to that governmental agency appropriate disciplinary action (including, where appropriate, the suspension or revocation of the license of the respondent).

(6) In the case of an order against a respondent against whom another order was issued within the preceding 5 years under this section, the Secretary shall send a copy of each such order to the Attorney General.

(7) If the administrative law judge finds that the respondent has not engaged or is not about to engage in a discriminatory housing practice, as the case may be, such administrative law judge shall enter an order dismissing the charge. The Secretary shall make public disclosure of each such dismissal.

(h) Review by Secretary; Service of Final Order.—

(1) The Secretary may review any finding, conclusion, or order issued under subsection (g). Such review shall be completed not

later than 30 days after the finding, conclusion, or order is so issued; otherwise the finding, conclusion, or order becomes final.

(2) The Secretary shall cause the findings of fact and conclusions of law made with respect to any final order for relief under this section, together with a copy of such order, to be served on each aggrieved person and each respondent in the proceeding.

(i) Judicial Review.—

(1) Any party aggrieved by a final order for relief under this section granting or denying in whole or in part the relief sought may obtain a review of such order under chapter 158 of title 28, United States Code.

(2) Notwithstanding such chapter, venue of the proceeding shall be in the judicial circuit in which the discriminatory housing practice is alleged to have occurred, and filing of the petition for review shall be not later than 30 days after the order is entered.

(j) Court Enforcement of Administrative Order Upon Petition by Secretary.—

(1) The Secretary may petition any United States court of appeals for the circuit in which the discriminatory housing practice is alleged to have occurred or in which any respondent resides or transacts business for the enforcement of the order of the administrative law judge and for appropriate temporary relief or restraining order, by filing in such court a written petition praying that such order be enforced and for appropriate temporary relief or restraining order.

(2) The Secretary shall file in court with the petition the record in the proceeding. A copy of such petition shall be forthwith transmitted by the clerk of the court to the parties to the proceeding before the administrative law judge.

(k) Relief Which May Be Granted.—

(1) Upon the filing of a petition under subsection (i) or (j), the court may—

(A) grant to the petitioner, or any other party, such temporary relief, restraining order, or other order as the court deems just and proper;

(B) affirm, modify, or set aside, in whole or in part, the order, or remand the order for further proceedings; and

(C) enforce such order to the extent that such order is affirmed or modified.

(2) Any party to the proceeding before the administrative law judge may intervene in the court of appeals.

(3) No objection not made before the administrative law judge shall be considered by the court, unless the failure or neglect to urge such objection is excused because of extraordinary circumstances.

(l) Enforcement Decree in Absence of Petition for Review.—If no petition for review is filed under subsection (i) before the expiration of 45 days after the date the administrative law judge's order is entered, the administrative law judge's findings of fact and order shall be conclusive in connection with any petition for enforcement—

(1) which is filed by the Secretary under subsection (j) after the end of such day; or

(2) under subsection (m).

(m) Court Enforcement of Administrative Order Upon Petition of Any Person Entitled to Relief.—If before the expiration of 60 days after the date the administrative law judge's order is entered, no petition for review has been filed under subsection (i), and the Secretary has not sought enforcement of the order under subsection (j), any person entitled to relief under the order may petition for a decree enforcing the order in the United States court of appeals for the circuit in which the discriminatory housing practice is alleged to have occurred.

(n) Entry of Decree.—The clerk of the court of appeals in which a petition for enforcement is filed under subsection (1) or (m) shall forthwith enter a decree enforcing the order and shall transmit a copy of such decree to the Secretary, the respondent named in the petition, and to any other parties to the proceeding before the administrative law judge.

(o) Civil Action for Enforcement When Election Is Made for Such Civil Action.—

(1) If an election is made under subsection (a), the Secretary shall authorize, and not later than 30 days after the election is made the Attorney General shall commence and maintain, a civil action on behalf of the aggrieved person in a United States district court seeking relief under this subsection. Venue for such civil action shall be determined under chapter 87 of title 28, United States Code.

(2) Any aggrieved person with respect to the issues to be determined in a civil action under this subsection may intervene as of right in that civil action.

(3) In a civil action under this subsection, if the court finds that a discriminatory housing practice has occurred or is about to occur, the court may grant as relief any relief which a court could grant with respect to such discriminatory housing practice in a civil action under section 813. Any relief so granted that would accrue to an aggrieved person in a civil action commenced by that aggrieved person under section 813 shall also accrue to that aggrieved person in a civil action under this subsection. If monetary relief is sought for the benefit of an aggrieved person who does not intervene in the civil action, the court shall not award such relief if that aggrieved person has not complied with discovery orders entered by the court.

(p) Attorney's Fees.—In any administrative proceeding brought under this section, or any court proceeding arising therefrom, or any civil action under section 812, the administrative law judge or the court, as the case may be, in its discretion, may allow the prevailing party, other than the United States, a reasonable attorney's fee and costs. The United States shall be liable for such fees and costs to the extent provided by section 504 of title 5, United States Code, or by section 2412 of title 28, United States Code.

Sec. 813. [42 U.S.C. § 3613] Enforcement by Private Persons

(a) Civil Action.—

(1)(A) An aggrieved person may commence a civil action in an appropriate United States district court or State court not later than 2 years after the occurrence or the termination of an alleged discriminatory housing practice, or the breach of a conciliation agreement entered into under this title, whichever occurs last, to obtain appropriate relief with respect to such discriminatory housing practice or breach.

(B) The computation of such 2-year period shall not include any time during which an administrative proceeding under this title was pending with respect to a complaint or charge under this title based upon such discriminatory housing practice. This subparagraph does not apply to actions arising from a breach of a conciliation agreement.

(2) An aggrieved person may commence a civil action under this subsection whether or not a complaint has been filed under section 810(a) and without regard to the status of any such complaint, but if the Secretary or a State or local agency has obtained a conciliation agreement with the consent of an aggrieved person, no action may

be filed under this subsection by such aggrieved person with respect to the alleged discriminatory housing practice which forms the basis for such complaint except for the purpose of enforcing the terms of such an agreement.

(3) An aggrieved person may not commence a civil action under this subsection with respect to an alleged discriminatory housing practice which forms the basis of a charge issued by the Secretary if an administrative law judge has commenced a hearing on the record under this title with respect to such charge.

(b) Appointment of Attorney by Court.—Upon application by a person alleging a discriminatory housing practice or a person against whom such a practice is alleged, the court may—

(1) appoint an attorney for such person; or

(2) authorize the commencement or continuation of a civil action under subsection (a) without the payment of fees, costs, or security, if in the opinion of the court such person is financially unable to bear the costs of such action.

(c) Relief Which May Be Granted.—

(1) In a civil action under subsection (a), if the court finds that a discriminatory housing practice has occurred or is about to occur, the court may award to the plaintiff actual and punitive damages, and subject to subsection (d), may grant as relief, as the court deems appropriate, any permanent or temporary injunction, temporary restraining order, or other order (including an order enjoining the defendant from engaging in such practice or ordering such affirmative action as may be appropriate).

(2) In a civil action under subsection (a), the court, in its discretion, may allow the prevailing party, other than the United States, a reasonable attorney's fee and costs. The United States shall be liable for such fees and costs to the same extent as a private person.

(d) Effect on Certain Sales, Encumbrances, and Rentals.—Relief granted under this section shall not affect any contract, sale, encumbrance, or lease consummated before the granting of such relief and involving a bona fide purchaser, encumbrancer, or tenant, without actual notice of the filing of a complaint with the Secretary or civil action under this title.

(e) Intervention by Attorney General.—Upon timely application, the Attorney General may intervene in such civil action, if the Attorney General certifies that the case is of general public importance. Upon such intervention the Attorney General may obtain such relief as would be available to the Attorney General under section 814(e) in a civil action to which such section applies.

Sec. 814. [42 U.S.C. § 3614] Enforcement by the Attorney General

(a) Pattern or Practice Cases.–Whenever the Attorney General has reasonable cause to believe that any person or group of persons is engaged in a pattern or practice of resistance to the full enjoyment of any of the rights granted by this title, or that any group of persons has been denied any of the rights granted by this title and such denial raises an issue of general public importance, the Attorney General may commence a civil action in any appropriate United States district court.

(b) On Referral of Discriminatory Housing Practice or Conciliation Agreement for Enforcement.—

(1)(A) The Attorney General may commence a civil action in any appropriate United States district court for appropriate relief with respect to a discriminatory housing practice referred to the Attorney General by the Secretary under section 810(g).

(B) A civil action under this paragraph may be commenced not later than the expiration of 18 months after the date of the occurrence or the termination of the alleged discriminatory housing practice.

(2)(A) The Attorney General may commence a civil action in any appropriate United States district court for appropriate relief with respect to breach of a conciliation agreement referred to the Attorney General by the Secretary under section 810(c).

(B) A civil action may be commenced under this paragraph not later than the expiration of 90 days after the referral of the alleged breach under section 810(c).

(c) Enforcement of Subpoenas.—The Attorney General, on behalf of the Secretary, or other party at whose request a subpoena is issued, under this title, may enforce such subpoena in appropriate proceedings in the United States district court for the district in which the person to whom the subpoena was addressed resides, was served, or transacts business.

(d) Relief Which May Be Granted in Civil Actions Under Subsections (a) and (b).—

(1) In a civil action under subsection (a) or (b), the court—

(A) may award such preventive relief, including a permanent or temporary injunction, restraining order, or other order against the person responsible for a violation of this title as is necessary to assure the full enjoyment of the rights granted by this title;

(B) may award such other relief as the court deems appropriate, including monetary damages to persons aggrieved; and

(C) may, to vindicate the public interest, assess a civil penalty against the respondent—

(i) in an amount not exceeding $55,000, for a first violation; and

(ii) in an amount not exceeding $110,000, for any subsequent violation.

(2) In a civil action under this section, the court, in its discretion, may allow the prevailing party, other than the United States, a reasonable attorney's fee and costs. The United States shall be liable for such fees and costs to the extent provided by section 2412 of title 28, United States Code.

(e) Intervention in Civil Actions.—Upon timely application, any person may intervene in a civil action commenced by the Attorney General under subsection (a) or (b) which involves an alleged discriminatory housing practice with respect to which such person is an aggrieved person or a conciliation agreement to which such person is a party. The court may grant such appropriate relief to any such intervening party as is authorized to be granted to a plaintiff in a civil action under section 813.

***

Sec. 816. [42 U.S.C. § 3615] Effect on State laws

Nothing in this subchapter shall be constructed to invalidate or limit any law of a State or political subdivision of a State, or of any other jurisdiction in which this subchapter shall be effective, that grants, guarantees, or protects the same rights as are granted by this subchapter; but any law of a State, a political subdivision, or other such jurisdiction that purports to require or permit any action that would be a discriminatory housing practice under this subchapter shall to that extent be invalid.

***

Sec. 818. [42 U.S.C. § 3617] Interference, coercion, or intimidation; enforcement by civil action

It shall be unlawful to coerce, intimidate, threaten, or interfere with any person in the exercise or enjoyment of, or on account of his having exercised or enjoyed, or on account of his having aided or encouraged any other person in the exercise or enjoyment of, any right granted or protected by section 803, 804, 805, or 806 of this title.

***

Section 901. (Title IX As Amended) [42 U.S.C. § 3631] Violations; bodily injury; death; penalties

Whoever, whether or not acting under color of law, by force or threat of force willfully injures, intimidates or interferes with, or attempts to injure, intimidate or interfere with—

(a) any person because of his race, color, religion, sex, handicap (as such term is defined in section 802 of this Act), familial status (as such term is defined in section 802 of this Act), or national origin and because he is or has been selling, purchasing, renting, financing occupying, or contracting or negotiating for the sale, purchase, rental, financing or occupation of any dwelling, or applying for or participating in any service, organization, or facility relating to the business of selling or renting dwellings; or

(b) any person because he is or has been, or in order to intimidate such person or any other person or any class of persons from—

(1) participating, without discrimination on account of race, color, religion, sex, handicap (as such term is defined in section 802 of this Act), familial status (as such term is defined in section 802 of this Act), or national origin, in any of the activities, services, organizations or facilities described in subsection (a) of this section; or

(2) affording another person or class of persons opportunity or protection so to participate; or

(c) any citizen because he is or has been, or in order to discourage such citizen or any other citizen from lawfully aiding or encouraging other persons to participate, without discrimination on account of race, color, religion, sex, handicap (as such term is defined in section 802 of this Act), familial status (as such term is defined in section 802 of this Act), or national origin, in any of the activities, services, organizations or facilities described in subsection (a) of this section, or participating lawfully in speech or peaceful assembly opposing any denial of the opportunity to so participate–shall be fined not more than $1,000, or imprisoned not more than one year, or both; and if bodily injury results shall be fined not more than $10,000, or imprisoned not more than ten years, or both; and if death results shall be subject to imprisonment for any term of years or for life.

APPENDIX 14:
DIRECTORY OF HUD
FAIR HOUSING REGIONAL OFFICES

REGIONAL OFFICE AND AREAS COVERED	ADDRESS	TELEPHONE	FAX	TTY
BOSTON REGIONAL OFFICE Connecticut Maine Massachusetts New Hampshire Rhode Island Vermont	Fair Housing Enforcement Center U.S. Department of Housing and Urban Development Thomas P. O'Neill, Jr. Federal Building 10 Causeway Street, Room 321 Boston, MA 02222-1092	617-994-8300 800-827-5005	617-994-8300	617-565-5453

REGIONAL OFFICE AND AREAS COVERED	ADDRESS	TELEPHONE	FAX	TTY
NEW YORK REGIONAL OFFICE New York New Jersey	Fair Housing Enforcement Center U.S. Department of Housing and Urban Development 26 Federal Plaza, Room 3532 New York, NY 10278-0068	212-264-1290 800-496-4294	212-264-9829	212-264-0927
PHILADELPHIA REGIONAL OFFICE Delaware District of Columbia Maryland Pennsylvania Virginia West Virginia	Fair Housing Enforcement Center U.S. Department of Housing and Urban Development The Wanamaker Building 100 Penn Square East Philadelphia, PA 19107-9344	215-656-0662 888-799-2085	215-656-3419	215-656-3450
ATLANTA REGIONAL OFFICE Alabama Caribbean Florida Georgia Kentucky Mississippi North Carolina South Carolina Tennessee	Fair Housing Enforcement Center U.S. Department of Housing and Urban Development Five Points Plaza 40 Marietta Street, 16th Floor Atlanta, GA 30303-2808	404-331-5140 800-440-8091	404-331-1021	404-730-2654

REGIONAL OFFICE AND AREAS COVERED	ADDRESS	TELEPHONE	FAX	TTY
CHICAGO REGIONAL OFFICE Illinois Indiana Michigan Minnesota Ohio Wisconsin	Fair Housing Enforcement Center U.S. Department of Housing and Urban Development Ralph H. Metcalfe Federal Building 77 West Jackson Blvd., Room 2101 Chicago, IL 60604-3507	312-353-6236 800-765-9372	312-886-2837	312-353-7143
FORT WORTH REGIONAL OFFICE Arkansas Louisiana New Mexico Oklahoma Texas	Fair Housing Enforcement Center U.S. Department of Housing and Urban Development 801 North Cherry, 27th floor Fort Worth, TX 76102	817-978-5900 888-560-8913	817-978-5876	817-978-5595
KANSAS CITY REGIONAL OFFICE Iowa Kansas Missouri Nebraska	Fair Housing Enforcement Center U.S. Department of Housing and Urban Development Gateway Tower II 400 State Avenue, Room 200, 4th Floor Kansas City, KS 66101-2406	913-551-6958 800-743-5323	913-551-6958	913-551-6972

REGIONAL OFFICE AND AREAS COVERED	ADDRESS	TELEPHONE	FAX	TTY
DENVER REGIONAL OFFICE Colorado Montana North Dakota South Dakota Utah Wyoming	Fair Housing Enforcement Center U.S. Department of Housing and Urban Development 633 17th Street Denver, CO 80202-3607	303-672-5437 800-877-7353	303-672-5026	303-672-5248
SAN FRANCISCO REGIONAL OFFICE Arizona California Hawaii Nevada	Fair Housing Enforcement Center U.S. Department of Housing and Urban Development 600 Harrison Street, 3rd Floor San Francisco, CA 94107-1387	415-489-6548 800-347-3739	415-489-6558	415-489-6564
SEATTLE REGIONAL OFFICE Alaska Idaho Oregon Washington	Fair Housing Enforcement Center U.S. Department of Housing and Urban Development 909 First Avenue, Room 205 Seattle, WA 98104-1000	206-220-5170 800-877-0246	206-220-5447	206-220-5185

Source: U.S. Department of Housing and Urban Development.

APPENDIX 15:
HUD FAIR HOUSING DISCRIMINATION COMPLAINT FORM

If you don't report discrimination,
it can't be stopped!

Housing Discrimination Information Form

- If you believe your rights have been violated, HUD or a State or local fair housing agency is ready to help you file a complaint.

- You have one year from the date of the alleged act of discrimination to file your complaint.

- After your information is received, we will contact you to discuss the concerns you raise.

Instructions: (Please type or print.) Read this form carefully. Try to answer all questions. If you do not know the answer or a question does not apply to you, leave the space blank. You have one year from the date of the alleged discrimination to file a complaint. Your form should be signed and dated. Use reverse side of this page if you need more space to respond.

Keep this information for your records.

Date you mailed your information to HUD:(mm/dd/yyyy)

Address to which you sent the information:
Street:

City: State: Zip Code:

If you have not heard from HUD or a fair housing agency within three weeks from the date you mail this form, you may call to inquire about the status of your complaint. See addresses and telephone listings on the last page.

Previous Versions Obsolete   Page 3 of 7   form **HUD-903.1** (7/2004)

Your Name:	Best time to call:	Your Daytime Phone No:
Your Address:		Evening Phone No:
City:	State:	Zip Code:

Who else can we call if we cannot reach you?

1 Contact's Name:	Daytime Phone No:
Best time to call:	Evening Phone No:
2 Contact's Name:	Daytime Phone No:
Best time to call:	Evening Phone No:

1. **What** happened to you? How were you discriminated against? For example: were you refused an opportunity to rent or buy housing? Denied a loan? Told that housing was not available when in fact it was? Treated differently from others seeking housing? State briefly what happened.

2. **Why** do you believe you are being discriminated against?

It is a violation of the law to deny you your housing rights for any of the following factors: • race • color • religion • sex • national origin • familial status (families with children under 18) • disability.

For example: were you denied housing **because of** your race? Were you denied a mortgage loan **because of** your religion? Or turned down for an apartment **because** you have children? Were you harassed because you assisted someone in obtaining their fair housing rights? Briefly explain why you think your housing rights were denied **because of** any the factors listed above.

Previous Versions Obsolete	Page 4 of 7	form **HUD-903.1** (7/2004)

3. **Who** do you believe discriminated against you? Was it a landlord, owner, bank, real estate agent, broker, company, or organization?

Name:

Address:

4. **Where** did the alleged act of discrimination occur? Provide the address. For example: Was it at a rental unit? Single family home? Public or Assisted Housing? A Mobile Home? Did it occur at a bank or other lending institution?

Address:

City: State: Zip Code:

5. **When** did the last act of discrimination occur?
   Enter the date (mm/dd/yyyy) _____

   Is the alleged discrimination continuous or on going? ☐ Yes ☐ No

Signature: Date:(mm/dd/yyyy)

X _____

Send this form to HUD or to the fair housing agency where the alleged act of discrimination occurred.

If you are unable to complete this form, you may call the office nearest you.

See addresses and telephone numbers listed on the back page.

The information collected here will be used to investigate and to process housing discrimination complaints. The information may be disclosed to the United States Department of Justice for its use in the filing of pattern and practice suits of housing discrimination or the prosecution of the person(s) who committed the discrimination where violence is involved; and to State or local fair housing agencies that administer substantially equivalent fair housing laws for complaint processing.

Public Reporting Burden for this collection of information is estimated to average 20 minutes per response, including the time for reviewing instructions, searching existing data sources, gathering and maintaining the data needed, and completing and reviewing the collection of information.

Disclosure of this information is voluntary. Failure to provide some or all of the requested information will result in delay or denial of HUD assistance.

This agency may not collect this information, and you are not required to complete this form, unless it displays a currently valid OMB control number.

Privacy Act Statement The Department of Housing and Urban Development is authorized to collect this information by Title VIII of the Civil Rights Act of 1968, as amended by the Fair Housing Amendments Act of 1988, (P.L. 100-430); Title VI of the Civil Rights Act of 1964, (P.L. 88-352); Section 504 of the Rehabilitation Act of 1973, as amended, (P.L. 93-112); Section 109 of Title I - Housing and Community Development Act of 1974, as amended, (P.L. 97-35); Americans with Disabilities Act of 1990, (P.L. 101-336); and by the Age Discrimination Act of 1975, as amended, (42 U.S.C. 6103).

For Connecticut, Maine, Massachusetts, New Hampshire, Rhode Island, and Vermont:

NEW ENGLAND OFFICE
(Marcella_Brown@hud.gov)

Fair Housing Enforcement Center
U.S. Department of Housing and Urban Development
Thomas P. O'Neill, Jr. Federal Building
10 Causeway Street, Room 321
Boston, MA 02222-1092
Telephone (617) 994-8300 or
1-800-827-5005
Fax (617) 565-7313 • TTY (617) 565-5453

For New Jersey and New York

New York/New Jersey Office
(Stanley_Seidenfeld@hud.gov)
Fair Housing Enforcement Center
U.S. Department of Housing and Urban Development
26 Federal Plaza, Room 3532
New York, NY 10278-0068
Telephone (212) 264-1290 or
1-800-496-4294
Fax (212) 264-9829 • TTY (212) 264-0927

For Delaware, District of Columbia, Maryland, Pennsylvania, Virginia, and West Virginia

MID-ATLANTIC OFFICE
(Wanda_Nieves@hud.gov)
Fair Housing Enforcement Center
U.S. Department of Housing and Urban Development
The Wanamaker Building
100 Penn Square East
Philadelphia, PA 19107-9344
Telephone (215) 656-0662 or
1-888-799-2085
Fax (215) 656-3419 • TTY (215) 656-3450

For Alabama, the Caribbean, Florida, Georgia, Kentucky, Mississippi, North Carolina, South Carolina, and Tennessee:

SOUTHEAST/CARIBBEAN OFFICE
(Gregory_L._King@hud.gov)
Fair Housing Enforcement Center
U.S. Department of Housing and Urban Development
Five Points Plaza
40 Marietta Street, 16th Floor
Atlanta, GA 30303-2806
Telephone (404) 331-5140 or
1-800-440-8091
Fax (404) 331-1021 • TTY (404) 730-2654

For Illinois, Indiana, Michigan, Minnesota, Ohio, and Wisconsin:

MIDWEST OFFICE
(Barbara_Knox@hud.gov)
Fair Housing Enforcement Center
U.S. Department of Housing and Urban Development
Ralph H. Metcalfe Federal Building
77 West Jackson Boulevard,
Room 2101
Chicago, IL 60604-3507
Telephone (312) 353-7776 or
1-800-765-9372
Fax (312) 886-2837 • TTY (312) 353-7143

For Arkansas, Louisiana, New Mexico, Oklahoma, and Texas:

SOUTHWEST OFFICE
(Thurman_G._Miles@hud.gov or Garry_L._Sweeney@hud.gov)
Fair Housing Enforcement Center
U.S. Department of Housing and Urban Development
801 North Cherry, 27th Floor
Fort Worth, TX 76102
Telephone (817) 978-5900 or
1-888-560-8913
Fax (817) 978-5876 or 5851 • TTY (817) 978-5595

For Iowa, Kansas, Missouri and Nebraska:

GREAT PLAINS OFFICE
(Robbie_Herndon@hud.gov)

Fair Housing Enforcement Center
U.S. Department of Housing and
Urban Development
Gateway Tower II
400 State Avenue, Room 200, 4th
Floor
Kansas City, KS 66101-2406
Telephone (913) 551-6958 or
1-800-743-5323
Fax (913) 551-6856 • TTY (913)
551-6972

For Colorado, Montana, North Dakota, South Dakota, Utah, and Wyoming:

ROCKY MOUNTAINS OFFICE
(Sharon_L._Santoya@hud.gov)

Fair Housing Enforcement Center
U.S. Department of Housing and
Urban Development
633 17th Street
Denver, CO 80202-3690
Telephone (303) 672-5437 or
1-800-877-7353
Fax (303) 672-5026 • TTY (303)
672-5248

For Arizona, California, Hawaii, and Nevada:

PACIFIC/HAWAII OFFICE
(Charles_Hauptman@hud.gov)

Fair Housing Enforcement Center
U.S. Department of Housing and
Urban Development
600 Harrison Street, 3rd Floor
San Francisco, CA 94107-1300
Telephone (415) 489-6524 or
1-800-347-3739
Fax (415) 489-6559 • TTY (415)
489-6564

For Alaska, Idaho, Oregon, and Washington:

NORTHWEST/ALASKA OFFICE
(Judith_Keeler@hud.gov)

Fair Housing Enforcement Center
U.S. Department of Housing and
Urban Development
Seattle Federal Office Building
909 First Avenue, Room 205
Seattle, WA 98104-1000
Telephone (206) 220-5170 or
1-800-877-0246
Fax (206) 220-5447 • TTY (206)
220-5185

If after contacting the local office nearest you, you still have questions – you may contact HUD further at:

U.S. Department of Housing and
Urban Development
Office of Fair Housing and Equal
Opportunity
451 7th Street, S.W., Room 5204
Washington, DC 20410-2000
Telephone (202) 708-0836 or
1-800-669-9777
Fax (202) 708-1425 • TTY 1-800-
927-9275

Previous Versions Obsolete Page 7 of 7 form **HUD-903.1** (7/2004)

           Home Mortgage Law Primer

APPENDIX 16:
NOTICE OF RIGHT TO CANCEL

BORROWER'S NAME	ACCOUNT NUMBER	TYPE OF TRANSACTION

Your Right to Cancel

You are entering into a transaction that will result in a deed of trust or mortgage on your home. You have a legal right under federal law to cancel this transaction, without cost, within three business days from whichever of the following events occurs last:

(1) The date of the transaction which is _____; or

(2) The date you received your Truth in Landing disclosures; or

(3) The date you received this notice of your right to cancel.

If you cancel the transaction, the deed of trust or mortgage is also canceled. Unless modified by court order, within 20 calendar days after we receive your notice, we must take the steps necessary to reflect the fact that the deed of trust or mortgage on your home has been canceled, and we must return to you any money or property you have given to us or to anyone else in connection with this transaction.

Unless modified by court order, you may keep any money we have given you until we have done the things mentioned above, but you must then offer to return the money. Money must be returned to the address below. If we do not take possession of the money within 20 calendar days of your offer, you must keep it without further obligation.

How to Cancel

If you decide to cancel this transaction, you may do so by notifying us in writing at

_____

_____

_____

(Name & Address of Branch)

You may use any written statement that is signed and dated by you and states your intention to cancel, or you may use this notice by dating and signing below. Keep one copy of this notice because it contains important information about your rights.

If you cancel by mail or telegram, you must send the notice no later than midnight of

_____

(Date)

(Or midnight of the third business day following the latest of the three events listed above). If you send or deliver your written notice to cancel some other way, it must be delivered to the above address no later than that time.

I WISH TO CANCEL

_____   _____

Consumer's Signature   Date

Acknowledgment of Receipt: Each of the undersigned hereby acknowledges receipt of two copies of this "Notice of Right to Cancel."

_____

Date

_____   _____

Signature

_____   _____

Signature

APPENDIX 17:
GOOD FAITH ESTIMATE CHART

NAME OF LENDER:

The information provided below reflects estimates of the charges that you are likely to incur at the settlement of your loan. The fees listed are estimates—the actual charges may be more or less. Your transaction may not involve a fee for every item listed. The numbers listed beside the estimates generally correspond to the numbered lines contained in the HUD-1 or HUD-1A settlement statement that you will be receiving at settlement. The HUD- 1 or HUD-1A settlement statement will show you the actual cost for items paid at settlement.

ITEM	HUD-1/HUD-1A	AMOUNT OR RANGE
Loan Origination Fee	801	$
Loan Discount Fee	802	$
Appraisal Fee	803	$
Credit Report	804	$
Inspection Fee	805	$
Mortgage Broker Fee	Use blank line in 800 section	$
CLO Access Fee	Use blank line in 800 section	$
Tax related service fee	Use blank line in 800 section	$
Interest for (x) days @ $____ per day	901	$
Mortgage Insurance Premium	902	$
Hazard Insurance Premiums	903	$

ITEM	HUD-1/HUD-1A	AMOUNT OR RANGE
Reserves	1000	$
Hazard Insurance	1001	$
Mortgage Insurance	1002	$
City Property Taxes	1003	$
County Property Taxes	1004	$
Annual Assessments	1005	$
Settlement Fee	1101	$
Abstract or Title Search	1102	$
Title Examination	1103	$
Document Preparation Fee	1105	$
Attorney's Fee	1107	$
Title Insurance	1108	$
Recording Fees	1201	$
City/County Tax Stamps	1202	$
State Tax	1203	$
Survey	1301	$
Pest Inspection	1302	$
Other Fees (list here)		

These estimates are provided pursuant to the Real Estate Settlement Procedures Act of 1974, as amended (RESPA). Additional information can be found in the HUD Special Information Booklet, which is to be provided to you by your mortgage broker or lender, if your application is to purchase residential real property and the Lender will take a first lien on the property.

APPENDIX 18:
AFFILIATED BUSINESS ARRANGEMENT DISCLOSURE STATEMENT

FROM:

PROPERTY:

DATE:

This is to give you notice that [referring party] has a business relationship with [settlement services providers(s)]. *[Describe the nature of the relationship between the referring party and the providers(s), including percentage of ownership interest, if applicable.]*

Because of this relationship, this referral may provide [referring party] a financial or other benefit.

1. Set forth below is the estimated charge or range of charges for the settlement services listed. You are NOT required to use the listed provider(s) as a condition for [settlement of your loan on] [or] [purchase, sale, or refinance of] the subject property.

(a) Provider:

(b) Settlement Service:

(c) Charge/Range of Charges:

THERE ARE FREQUENTLY OTHER SETTLEMENT SERVICE PROVIDERS AVAILABLE WITH SIMILAR SERVICES. YOU ARE FREE TO SHOP AROUND TO DETERMINE THAT YOU ARE RECEIVING THE BEST SERVICES AND THE BEST RATE FOR THESE SERVICES.

2. Set forth below is the estimated charge or range of charges for the settlement services of an attorney, credit reporting agency, or real estate appraiser that we, as your lender, will require you to use, as a

condition of your loan on this property, to represent our interests in the transaction.

(a) Provider:

(b) Settlement Service:

(c) Charge/Range of Charges:

ACKNOWLEDGMENT

I/we have read this disclosure form, and understand that [referring party] is referring me/us to purchase the above-described settlement service(s) and may receive a financial or other benefit as the result of this referral.

[Signature line]

INSTRUCTIONS TO PREPARER:

Use paragraph A for referrals other than those by a lender to an attorney, a credit reporting agency, or a real estate appraiser that a lender is requiring a borrower to use to represent the lender's interests in the transaction.

Use paragraph B for those referrals to an attorney, credit reporting agency, or real estate appraiser that a lender is requiring a borrower to use to represent the lender's interests in the transaction.

When applicable, use both paragraphs. Specific timing rules for delivery of the affiliated business disclosure statement are set forth in 24 CFR 3500.15(b)(1) of Regulation X.

Note: The "INSTRUCTIONS TO PREPARERS" section should not appear on the statement.

Source: United States Department of Housing and Urban Development.

APPENDIX 19:
HUD-1 SETTLEMENT STATEMENT

D. HUD-1 Settlement Statement

A.	U.S. DEPARTMENT OF HOUSING AND URBAN DEVELOPMENT	SETTLEMENT STATEMENT

B. TYPE OF LOAN		6. File Number	7. Loan Number
1. FHA 2. FmHA			
3. CONV. UNINS. 4. VA 5. CONV. INS.	8. Mortgage Insurance Case Number		

C. NOTE: This form is furnished to give you a statement of actual settlement costs. Amounts paid to and by the settlement agent are shown. Items marked "(p.o.c.)" were paid outside the closing; they are shown here for informational purposes and are not included in the totals.

D. NAME AND ADDRESS OF BORROWER:	E. NAME AND ADDRESS OF SELLER:	F. NAME AND ADDRESS OF LENDER:
G. PROPERTY LOCATION:	H. SETTLEMENT AGENT: NAME, AND ADDRESS	
	PLACE OF SETTLEMENT:	I. SETTLEMENT DATE:

J. SUMMARY OF BORROWER'S TRANSACTION		K. SUMMARY OF SELLER'S TRANSACTION	
100. GROSS AMOUNT DUE FROM BORROWER:		400. GROSS AMOUNT DUE TO SELLER:	
101. Contract sales price		401. Contract sales price	
102. Personal property		402. Personal property	
103. Settlement charges to borrower(line 1400)		403.	
104.		404.	
105.		405.	
Adjustments for items paid by seller in advance		Adjustments for items paid by seller in advance	
106. City/town taxes to		406. City/town taxes to	
107. County taxes to		407. County taxes to	
108. Assessments to		408. Assessments to	
109.		409.	
110.		410.	
111.		411.	
112.		412.	
120. GROSS AMOUNT DUE FROM BORROWER		420. GROSS AMOUNT DUE TO SELLER	

200. AMOUNTS PAID BY OR IN BEHALF OF BORROWER:	
201. Deposit of earnest money	
202. Principal amount of new loan(s)	
203. Existing loan(s) taken subject to	
204.	
205.	
206.	
207.	
208.	
209.	
Adjustments for items unpaid by seller	
210. City/town taxes to	
211. County taxes to	
212. Assessments to	
213.	
214.	
215.	
216.	
217.	
218.	
219.	
220. **TOTAL PAID BY/FOR BORROWER**	

500. REDUCTIONS IN AMOUNT DUE TO SELLER:	
501. Excess deposit (see instructions)	
502. Settlement charges to seller (line 1400)	
503. Existing loan(s) taken subject to	
504. Payoff of first mortgage loan	
505. Payoff of second mortgage loan	
506.	
507.	
508.	
509.	
Adjustments for items unpaid by seller	
510. City/town taxes to	
511. County taxes to	
512. Assessments to	
513.	
514.	
515.	
516.	
517.	
518.	
519.	
520. **TOTAL REDUCTION AMOUNT DUE SELLER**	

300. CASH AT SETTLEMENT FROM/TO BORROWER	
301. Gross amount due from borrower(line 120)	
302. Less amounts paid by/for borrower(line 220)	
303. **CASH (FROM) (TO) BORROWER**	

600. CASH AT SETTLEMENT TO/FROM SELLER	
601. Gross amount due to seller (line 420)	
602. Less reductions in amount due seller (line 520)	
603. **CASH (TO) (FROM) SELLER**	

L. SETTLEMENT CHARGES

		PAID FROM BORROWER'S FUNDS AT SETTLEMENT	PAID FROM SELLER'S FUNDS AT SETTLEMENT
700. **TOTAL SALES/BROKER'S COMMISSION** based on price $ @ %=			
Division of Commission (line 700) as follows:			
701. $ to			
702. $ to			
703. Commission paid at Settlement			
704.			
800. **ITEMS PAYABLE IN CONNECTION WITH LOAN**			
801. Loan Origination Fee %			
802. Loan Discount %			
803. Appraisal Fee to			
804. Credit Report to			
805. Lender's Inspection Fee			
806. Mortgage Insurance Application Fee to			
807. Assumption Fee			
808.			
809.			
810.			
811.			
900. **ITEMS REQUIRED BY LENDER TO BE PAID IN ADVANCE**			
901. Interest from to @$ /day			
902. Mortgage Insurance Premium for months to			
903. Hazard Insurance Premium for years to			
904. years to			
905.			
1000. **RESERVES DEPOSITED WITH LENDER**			
1001. Hazard Insurance months @ $ per month			
1002. Mortgage insurance months @ $ per month			
1003. City property taxes months @ $ per month			
1004. County property taxes months @ $ per month			
1005. Annual assessments months @ $ per month			
1006. months @ $ per month			
1007. months @ $ per month			
1008. Aggregate Adjustment months @ $ per month			
1100. **TITLE CHARGES**			
1101. Settlement or closing fee to			
1102. Abstract or title search to			
1103. Title examination to			
1104. Title insurance binder to			
1105. Document preparation to			
1106. Notary fees to			
1107. Attorney's fees to			
(includes above items numbers; *)*			
1108. Title Insurance to			
(includes above items numbers; *)*			
1109. Lender's coverage $			
1110. Owner's coverage $			
1111.			
1112.			
1113.			
1200. **GOVERNMENT RECORDING AND TRANSFER CHARGES**			
1201. Recording fees: Deed $; Mortgage $; Releases $			
1202. City/county tax/stamps: Deed $; Mortgage $			
1203. State tax/stamps: Deed $; Mortgage $			
1204.			
1205.			
1300. **ADDITIONAL SETTLEMENT CHARGES**			
1301. Survey to			
1302. Pest inspection to			
1303.			
1304.			
1305.			
1400. **TOTAL SETTLEMENT CHARGES** *(enter on lines 103, Section J and 502, Section K)*			

APPENDIX 20:
QUALIFIED WRITTEN REQUEST (RESPA)

RE: Name(s) on Loan Documents

        Property and/or Mailing Address

        Loan #_____

This is a "qualified written request" under Section 6 of the Real Estate Settlement Procedures Act (RESPA).

I am writing because:

    1. [Describe the issue or the question you have and/or what action you believe the lender should take].

    2. [Attach copies of any related written materials].

    3. [Describe any conversations with customer service regarding the issue and to whom you spoke].

    4. [Describe any previous steps you have taken or attempts to resolve the issue].

    5. [List a day time telephone number in case a customer service representative wishes to contact you].

I understand that under Section 6 of RESPA you are required to acknowledge my request within 20 business days, and must try to resolve the issue within 60 business days.

Sincerely,

[Your name]

GLOSSARY

Acceleration Clause—A common provision of a mortgage or note providing the holder with the right to demand that the entire outstanding balance is immediately due and usually payable in the event of default.

Acceptance of Deed—The physical taking of the deed by the grantee.

Acceptance of Offer—The seller's agreement to the terms of the agreement of sale.

Accrued Interest—Interest earned but not yet paid.

Acknowledgement—A formal declaration of one's signature before a notary public.

Adjustable Rate Mortgage Loans (ARM)—Loans with interest rates that are adjusted periodically based on changes in a pre-selected index.

Adjustment Interval—On an ARM loan, the time between changes in the interest rate or monthly payment.

Agreement of Sale—Contract signed by buyer and seller stating the terms and conditions under which a property will be sold.

Alternative Documentation—A method of documenting a loan file that relies on information the borrower is likely to be able to provide instead of waiting on verification sent to third parties for confirmation of statements made in the application.

Amortization—Repayment of a loan with periodic payments of both principal and interest calculated to payoff the loan at the end of a fixed period of time.

Amortized Mortgage—A mortgage in which repayment is made according to a plan requiring the payment of certain amounts at specified times so that all the debt is repaid at the end of the term.

Annual Percentage Rate (APR)—The cost of credit expressed as a yearly rate. The annual percentage rate is often not the same as the interest rate. It is a percentage that results from an equation considering the amount financed, the finance charges, and the term of the loan.

Annuity—An amount paid yearly or at other regular intervals, often at a guaranteed minimum amount. Also, a type of insurance policy in which the policy holder makes payments for a fixed period or until a stated age, and then receives annuity payments from the insurance company.

Application Fee—The fee that a mortgage lender or broker charges to apply for a mortgage to cover processing costs.

Appraisal—A written estimate of a property's current market value completed by an impartial party with knowledge of the real estate market.

Appraisal Fee—A fee charged by a licensed, certified appraiser to render an opinion of market value as of a specific date.

Appraiser—A professional who conducts an analysis of the property, including sales of similar properties, in order to develop an estimate of the value of the property, known as an appraisal.

Appreciation—An increase in the market value of a home due to changing market conditions and/or home improvements.

Arbitration—A process whereby disputes are settled by referring them to a fair and neutral third party, known as an arbitrator.

Arrears—Payments that are due but not yet paid.

Asbestos—A toxic material that was once used in housing insulation and fireproofing.

Asset—The entirety of a person's property, either real or personal.

Assessed Value—The value placed on property for the purpose of taxation.

Assessor—A public official who establishes the value of a property for taxation purposes.

Assignment—The transfer of ownership, rights, or interests in property by one person, the assignor, to another, the assignee.

Assignment of Mortgage—A document evidencing the transfer of ownership of a mortgage from one person to another.

Assumable Mortgage—A mortgage loan that can be taken over by the buyer when a home is sold.

Assumption—A method of selling real estate where the buyer of the property agrees to become responsible for the repayment of an existing loan on the property.

Assumption Fee—A fee a lender charges a buyer who will assume the seller's existing mortgage.

Automatic Stay—An injunction that automatically stops lawsuits, foreclosures, garnishments, and all collection activity against the debtor the moment a bankruptcy petition is filed.

Balance Sheet—A financial statement that shows assets, liabilities, and net worth as of a specific date.

Balloon Mortgage—Balloon mortgage loans are short-term fixed-rate loans with fixed monthly payments for a set number of years followed by one large final "balloon" payment for all of the remainder of the principal.

Balloon Payment—A final lump sum payment that is due, often at the maturity date of a balloon mortgage.

Bankruptcy—A legal procedure for resolving debt problems of individuals and businesses pursuant to Title 11 of the United States Code.

Bankruptcy Code—The informal name for Title 11 of the United States Code.

Bankruptcy Court—Refers to a division of the Federal District Court and/or the bankruptcy judges in regular active service in each District.

Bankruptcy Estate—All of the legal and equitable interests in property held by the debtor at the time he or she files the bankruptcy petition.

Bankruptcy Petition—A formal request for the protection of the federal bankruptcy laws.

Bankruptcy Plan—A debtor's detailed description of how the debtor proposes to pay creditors' claims over a fixed period of time.

Bargain and Sale Deed with Covenant—A deed conveying real property with a covenant which warrants title against grantor's acts.

Bargain and Sale Deed without Covenant—A deed conveying real property without any covenants warranting title.

Before-tax Income—Income before taxes are deducted, also referred to as "gross income."

Biweekly Payment Mortgage—A mortgage with payments due every two weeks.

Blanket Mortgage—A mortgage that covers more than one parcel of real estate.

Borrower—Also known as the mortgagor, refers to the individual who applies for and receives funds in the form of a loan and is obligated to repay the loan in full under the terms of the loan.

Bridge Loan—A short-term loan secured by the borrower's current home, that allows the proceeds to be used for building or closing on a new house before the current home is sold, also referred to as a "swing loan."

Broker—An individual who brings buyers and sellers together and assists in negotiating contracts for a client.

Building Code—Local regulations that set forth the standards and requirements for the construction, maintenance and occupancy of buildings.

Buydown—An arrangement whereby the property developer or another third party provides an interest subsidy to reduce the borrower's monthly payments typically in the early years of the loan.

Buydown Account—An account in which funds are held so that they can be applied as part of the monthly mortgage payment as each payment comes due during the period that an interest rate buydown plan is in effect.

Buyer's Market—Market conditions that favor buyers.

Call Option—A provision of a note which allows the lender to require repayment of the loan in full before the end of the loan term. The option may be exercised due to breach of the terms of the loan or at the discretion of the lender.

Cap—For an adjustable-rate mortgage (ARM), a limitation on the amount the interest rate or mortgage payments may increase or decrease.

Capacity—The buyer's ability to make their mortgage payments on time, which depends on certain factors, including income, assets and savings, and net income after deducting debts and other obligations.

Cash Out—Any cash received when you get a new loan that is larger than the remaining balance of your current mortgage, based upon the equity you have already built up in the house. The cash out amount is calculated by subtracting the sum of the old loan and fees from the new mortgage loan.

Cashier's Check—Also known as a bank check, refers to a check whose payment is guaranteed because it was paid for in advance and is drawn on the bank's account instead of the customer's.

Ceiling—The maximum allowable interest rate of an adjustable rate mortgage.

Certificate of Deposit—A document issued by a bank or other financial institution that is evidence of a deposit, with the issuer's promise to return the deposit plus earnings at a specified interest rate within a specified time period.

Certificate of Eligibility—Document issued by the Veterans Administration to qualified veterans that verifies a veteran's eligibility for a VA guaranteed loan.

Certificate of Title—Written opinion of the status of title to a property, given by an attorney or title company. This certificate does not offer the protection given by title insurance.

Certificate of Veteran Status—FHA form filled out by the VA to establish a borrower's eligibility for an FHA Vet loan.

Chain of Title—The chronological order of conveyance of a property from the original owner to the present owner.

Chapter 13—The chapter of the Bankruptcy Code providing for adjustment of debts of an individual with regular income.

Clear Title—Ownership that is free of liens, defects, or other legal encumbrances.

Closing—Also known as settlement, refers to the conclusion of a real estate transaction and includes the delivery of the security instrument, signing of legal documents and the disbursement of the funds necessary to the sale of the home or loan transaction.

Closing Agent—The person or entity that coordinates the various closing activities, including the preparation and recordation of closing documents and the disbursement of funds.

Closing Costs—Also known as settlement costs, refers to the costs for services that must be performed before the loan can be initiated, such as title fees, recording fees, appraisal fee, credit report fee, pest inspection, attorney's fees, and surveying fees.

Closing Date—The date on which the sale of a property is to be finalized and a loan transaction completed.

Closing Statement—A final listing of the closing costs of the mortgage transaction, including the sale price, down payment, total settlement costs required form the buyer and seller, also referred to as the HUD-1 Settlement Statement.

Co-borrower—Any borrower other than the first borrower whose name appears on the application and mortgage note.

Collateral—Assets pledged as security for a debt, such as a home.

Commission—Money paid to a real estate agent or broker for negotiating a real estate or loan transaction.

Commitment Letter—A binding offer from a lender that includes the amount of the mortgage, the interest rate, and repayment terms.

Common Areas—Those portions of a building, land, or improvements and amenities owned by a planned unit development or homeowner's association that are used by all of the unit owners who share in the common expenses of their operation and maintenance.

Comparables—Comparable properties that are used as a comparison in determining the current value of a property that is being appraised.

Condominium—A form of property ownership in which the homeowner holds title to an individual dwelling unit and a proportionate interest in common areas and facilities of a multi-unit project.

Conforming Loan—A mortgage loan which meets all requirements to be eligible for purchase by federal agencies such as the Federal National Mortgage Association (FNMA a/k/a "Fannie Mae") and the Federal Home Loan Mortgage Corporation (FHLMC a/k/a "Freddie Mac").

Consideration—Something of value exchanged between parties to a contract—a requirement for a valid contract.

Contingency—Condition which must be satisfied before a contract is legally binding.

Contract of Sale—The agreement between the buyer and seller on the purchase price, terms, and conditions of a sale.

Conventional Mortgage—A mortgage made by a financial institution which loan is not insured or guaranteed by the government.

Conversion Clause—A provision in some ARMs that allows you to change an ARM to a fixed-rate loan, usually after the first adjustment period. The new fixed rate will be set at current rates, and there may be a charge for the conversion feature.

Convertible ARMs—A type of ARM loan with the option to convert to a fixed-rate loan during a given time period.

Conveyance—The document used to effect a transfer, such as a deed, or mortgage.

Cooperative—Ownership of stock in a corporation which owns property that is subdivided into individual units.

Cost of Funds Index (COFI)—An index of the weighted-average interest rate paid by savings institutions for sources of funds, usually by members of the 11th Federal Home Loan Bank District.

Covenant—An undertaking by one or more parties to a deed.

Credit—The ability of a person to borrow money or buy goods by paying over time.

Credit Bureau—A company that gathers information on consumers who use credit, and then sell that information to lenders and other businesses in the form of a credit report.

Credit Life Insurance—A type of insurance that pays off a specific amount of debt or a specified credit account if the borrower dies while the policy is in force.

Creditor—A person who extends credit to whom a debtor owes money.

Credit Report—A report detailing the credit history of a prospective borrower that's used to help determine borrower creditworthiness.

Credit Score—A numerical value that ranks a borrower's credit risk.

Cushion—The excess balance a lender may require a borrower to maintain in their escrow account to cover unanticipated increases in the following year's real estate tax and insurance bills.

Debt—Money owed from one person or institution to another person or institution.

Debt-to-Income Ratio—The percentage of gross monthly income that goes toward paying for the borrower's monthly expenses.

Deed—A legal document by which title to real property is transferred from one owner to another. The deed contains a description of the property, and is signed, witnessed, and delivered to the buyer at closing.

Deed-in-Lieu of Foreclosure—The transfer of title from a borrower to the lender to satisfy the mortgage debt and avoid foreclosure, also referred to as a voluntary conveyance.

Deed of Trust—A legal document that conveys title to real property to a third party. The third party holds title until the owner of the property has repaid the debt in full.

Default—Failure to meet legal obligations in a contract, including failure to make payments on a loan.

Delinquency—Failure to make payments as agreed in the loan agreement.

Depreciation—A decline in the value of a house due to changing market conditions or lack of upkeep on the home.

Discharge—A court order that eliminates certain debts owed by the debtor for which the creditor may no longer seek payment.

Discount Point—A point is an up-front fee paid to the lender at the time that you get your loan. Each point equals one percent of your total loan amount. Points and interest rates are inherently connected: in general, the more points you pay, the lower the interest rate you get. However, the more points you pay, the more cash you need up front since points are paid in cash at closing.

Down Payment—The amount of a home's purchase price one needs to supply up front in cash to get a loan.

Due-on-Sale Clause—Provision in a mortgage or deed of trust allowing the lender to demand immediate payment of the loan balance upon sale of the property.

Earnest Money—Deposit made by a buyer towards the down payment in evidence of good faith when the purchase agreement is signed.

Easement—A right to the use of, or access to, land owned by another.

Encroachment—The intrusion onto another's property without right or permission.

Equal Credit Opportunity Act (ECOA)—Federal law requiring creditors to make credit equally available without discrimination based on race, color, religion, national origin, age, sex, marital status or receipt of income from public assistance programs.

Equity—The difference between the current market value of a property and the total debt obligations against the property. On a new mortgage loan, the down payment represents the equity in the property.

Escrow—A transaction in which a third party acts as the agent for seller and buyer, or for borrower and lender, in handling legal documents and disbursement of funds.

Escrow Account—Also known as an impound account, refers to an account held by the lender to which the borrower pays monthly installments, collected as part of the monthly mortgage payment, for annual expenses such as taxes and insurance. The lender disburses escrow account funds on behalf of the borrower when they become due.

Escrow Agent—A person with fiduciary responsibility to the buyer and seller, or the borrower and lender, to ensure that the terms of the purchase/sale or loan are carried out.

Eviction—The legal act of removing someone from real property.

Executor—A person named in a will and approved by a probate court to administer the deposition of an estate in accordance with the instructions of a will.

Executor's Deed—A deed given by an executor or other fiduciary who conveys real property.

Exempt Property—Certain property owned by an individual debtor that the Bankruptcy Code or applicable state law permits the debtor to keep from unsecured creditors.

Fair Market Value—The price at which property would be transferred between a willing buyer and willing seller, each of whom has a reasonable knowledge of all pertinent facts and is not under any compulsion to buy or sell.

Fannie Mae—A common nickname for the Federal National Mortgage Association.

Federal Deposit Insurance Corporation (FDIC)—Independent deposit insurance agency created by Congress to maintain stability and public confidence in the nation's banking system.

Federal Home Loan Mortgage Corporation (FHLMC)—Also known as "Freddie Mac," refers to the federal agency that buys loans that are underwritten to its specific guidelines, an industry standard for residential conventional lending.

Federal Housing Administration (FHA)—A federal agency within the Department of Housing and Urban Development (HUD), which insures residential mortgage loans made by private lenders and sets standards for underwriting mortgage loans.

Federal National Mortgage Association (FNMA)—Also known as "Fannie Mae," refers to the federal agency which buys loans that are underwritten to its specific guidelines, an industry standard for residential conventional lending.

Fee Simple—Absolute ownership of real property.

FHA-Insured Loan—A fixed or adjustable rate loan insured by the U.S Department of Housing and Urban Development.

First Mortgage—A mortgage which is in first lien position, taking priority over all other liens. In the case of a foreclosure, the first mortgage will be repaid before any other mortgages.

First-Time Home Buyer—A person with no ownership interest in a principal residence during the three-year period preceding the purchase of the security property.

Fixed-Period Adjustable-Rate Mortgage—An adjustable-rate mortgage (ARM) that offers a fixed rate for an initial period, typically three to ten years, and then adjusts every six months, annually, or at another specified period, for the remainder of the term.

Fixed Rate—An interest rate which is fixed for the term of the loan.

Fixed-Rate Mortgage—A mortgage with an interest rate that does not change during the entire term of the loan.

Flood Certification Fee—A fee charged by independent mapping firms to identify properties located in areas designated as flood zones.

Flood Insurance—Insurance that compensates for physical damage to a property by flood. Typically, this is not covered under standard hazard insurance.

Forbearance—The act by the lender of refraining from taking legal action on a mortgage loan that is delinquent.

Foreclosure—Legal process by which a mortgaged property may be sold to pay off a mortgage loan that is in default.

Forfeiture—The loss of money, property, rights, or privileges due to a breach of a legal obligation.

Full Covenant and Warranty Deed—A deed conveying real property that contains a covenant that warrants title by each previous holder of warranty deeds.

Fully Amortized Mortgage—A mortgage in which the monthly payments are designed to retire the obligation at the end of the mortgage term.

Good Faith Estimate—Written estimate of the settlement costs the borrower will likely have to pay at closing. Under the Real Estate Settlement Procedures Act (RESPA), the lender is required to provide this disclosure to the borrower within three days of receiving a loan application.

Grace Period—Period of time during which a loan payment may be made after its due date without incurring a late penalty. The grace period is specified as part of the terms of the loan in the Note.

Grantee—One who receives a conveyance of real property by deed.

Grantor—One who conveys real property by deed.

Gross Income—Total income before taxes or expenses are deducted.

Hazard Insurance—Protects the insured against loss due to fire or other natural disaster in exchange for a premium paid to the insurer.

Housing and Urban Development (HUD)—A federal government agency established to implement federal housing and community development programs; oversees the Federal Housing Administration.

HUD-1 Uniform Settlement Statement—A standard form which itemizes the closing costs associated with purchasing a home or refinancing a loan.

Impound Account—Also known as an escrow account, refers to an account held by the lender to which the borrower pays monthly installments, collected as part of the monthly mortgage payment, for annual expenses such as taxes and insurance. The lender disburses impound account funds on behalf of the borrower when they become due.

Index—A published rate used by lenders that serves as the basis for determining interest rate changes on ARM loans.

Initial Rate—The rate charged during the first interval of an ARM loan.

Interest—Charge paid for borrowing money, calculated as a percentage of the remaining balance of the amount borrowed.

Interest Rate—The annual rate of interest on the loan, expressed as a percentage of 100.

Interest Rate Cap—Consumer safeguards which limit the amount the interest rate on an ARM loan can change in an adjustment interval and/or over the life of the loan.

Joint Liability—Liability shared among two or more people, each of whom is liable for the full debt.

Joint Tenancy—A form of ownership of property giving each person equal interest in the property, including rights of survivorship.

Jumbo Loan—A mortgage larger than the $240,000 limit set by the Federal National Mortgage Association and the Federal Home Loan Mortgage Corporation.

Junior Mortgage—A mortgage subordinate to the claim of a prior lien or mortgage. In the case of a foreclosure, a senior mortgage or lien will be paid first.

Late Charge—Penalty paid by a borrower when a payment is made after the due date.

Legal Description—A means of identifying the exact boundaries of land.

Lender—The bank, mortgage company, or mortgage broker offering the loan.

LIBOR (London Interbank Offered Rate)—The interest rate charged among banks in the foreign market for short-term loans to one another. A common index for ARM loans.

Lien—A legal claim by one person on the property of another for security for payment of a debt.

Loan Application—An initial statement of personal and financial information required to apply for a loan.

Loan Application Fee—Fee charged by a lender to cover the initial costs of processing a loan application. The fee may include the cost of obtaining a property appraisal, a credit report, and a lock-in fee or other closing costs incurred during the process or the fee may be in addition to these charges.

Loan Origination Fee—Fee charged by a lender to cover administrative costs of processing a loan.

Loan Principal—The loan principal is the amount of the debt not including interest or any other additions.

Loan-to-Value Ratio (LTV)—The percentage of the loan amount to the appraised value (or the sales price, whichever is less) of the property.

Lock or Lock-In—A lender's guarantee of an interest rate for a set period of time. The time period is usually that between loan application approval and loan closing. The lock-in protects the borrower against rate increases during that time.

Margin—A specified percentage that is added to your chosen financial index to determine your new interest rate at the time of adjustment for ARM loans.

Mortgage—A written instrument, duly executed and delivered, that creates a lien upon real estate as security for the payment of a specific debt.

Mortgagee—The lender in a mortgage loan transaction.

Mortgage Banker—An individual or company that originates and/or services mortgage loans.

Mortgage Broker—An individual or company that arranges financing for borrowers.

Mortgage Loan—A loan for which real estate serves as collateral to provide for repayment in case of default.

Mortgage Note—Legal document obligating a borrower to repay a loan at a stated interest rate during a specified period of time. The agreement is secured by a mortgage or deed of trust or other security instrument.

Mortgagor—The borrower in a mortgage loan transaction.

Negative Amortization—A loan payment schedule in which the outstanding principal balance of a loan goes up rather than down because the payments do not cover the full amount of interest due. The monthly shortfall in payment is added to the unpaid principal balance of the loan.

Non-Assumption Clause—A statement in a mortgage contract forbidding the assumption of the mortgage by another borrower without the prior approval of the lender.

Note—Legal document obligating a borrower to repay a loan at a stated interest rate during a specified period of time. The agreement is secured by a mortgage or deed of trust or other security instrument.

Notice of Default—Written notice to a borrower that a default has occurred and that legal action may be taken.

Offer—The submittal of a set of terms for the purchase of real estate.

Origination Fee—Fee charged by a lender to cover administrative costs of processing a loan.

Partition—A division of real property among co-owners.

Payment Cap—Consumer safeguards which limit the amount monthly payments on an adjustable-rate mortgage may change. Since they do not limit the amount of interest the lender is earning, they may cause negative amortization.

Per Diem Interest—Interest calculated per day.

PITI—Abbreviation for Principal, Interest, Taxes and Insurance, the components of a monthly mortgage payment.

Points—Fees paid to the lender for the loan. One point equals 1 percent of the loan amount.

Power of Attorney—Legal document authorizing one person to act on behalf of another.

Pre-approval—The process of determining how much money a prospective homebuyer or refinancer will be eligible to borrow prior to application for a loan, including a preliminary review of a borrower's credit report.

Prepaid Expenses—Taxes, insurance and assessments paid in advance of their due dates.

Prepaid Interest—Interest that is paid in advance of when it is due which is typically charged to a borrower at closing to cover interest on the loan between the closing date and the first payment date.

Prepayment—Full or partial repayment of the principal before the contractual due date.

Prepayment Penalty—Fee charged by a lender for a loan paid off in advance of the contractual due date.

Pre-qualification—The process of determining how much money a prospective homebuyer will be eligible to borrow prior to application for a loan.

Principal—The amount of debt, not counting interest, left on a loan.

Private Mortgage Insurance (PMI)—Insurance to protect the lender in case you default on your loan, generally not required with conventional loans if the down payment is at least 20%.

Purchase Agreement—Contract signed by buyer and seller stating the terms and conditions under which a property will be sold.

Quitclaim Deed—A deed which conveys as much right, title and interest, if any, that the grantor may have in the property.

Real Estate—The land and all the things permanently attached to it.

Real Property—Real estate and the rights of ownership.

Recording—The process of filing of certain legal instruments or documents with the appropriate government office.

Reconveyance—The transfer of property back to the owner when a mortgage loan is fully repaid.

Recording—The act of entering documents concerning title to a property into the public records.

Referee's Deed—A deed given by a referee or other public officer pursuant to a court order for the sale of property.

Refinancing—The process of paying off one loan with the proceeds from a new loan secured by the same property.

RESPA—The Real Estate Settlement Procedures Act, a federal law that gives consumers the right to review information about loan settlement costs.

Right of Survivorship—The automatic succession to the interest of a deceased joint owner in a joint tenancy.

Right of Rescission—Under the provisions of the Truth-in-Lending Act, the borrower's right, on certain kinds of loans, to cancel the loan within three days of signing a mortgage.

Sales Agreement—Contract signed by buyer and seller stating the terms and conditions under which a property will be sold.

Second Mortgage—An additional mortgage placed on a property that has rights that are subordinate to the first mortgage.

Secured Creditor—An individual or business holding a claim against the debtor that is secured by a lien on property of the estate or that is subject to a right of setoff.

Secured Debt—Debt backed by a mortgage, pledge of collateral, or other lien.

Settlement—Also known as closing, refers to the conclusion of a real estate transaction and includes the delivery of the security instrument, signing of legal documents and the disbursement of the funds necessary to the sale of the home or loan transaction.

Settlement Costs—Also known as closing costs, refers to the costs for services that must be performed before the loan can be initiated, such as title fees, recording fees, appraisal fee, credit report fee, pest inspection, attorney's fees, and surveying fees.

Severalty—Ownership by a person in his own right.

Specific Performance—The requirement that a party must perform as agreed under a contract.

Statute of Frauds—Legal doctrine providing that all agreements concerning title to real estate must be in writing to be enforceable.

Survey—A measurement of land, prepared by a licensed surveyor, showing a property's boundaries, elevations, improvements, and relationship to surrounding tracts.

Sweat Equity—Value added to a property in the form of labor or services of the owner rather than cash.

Tax Impound—Money paid to and held by a lender for annual tax payments.

Tax Lien—Claim against a property for unpaid taxes.

Tax Sale—Public sale of property by a government authority as a result of non-payment of taxes.

Tenancy by the Entirety—An estate held by a husband and wife in which each have an undivided and equal right of possession during their joint lives, with the right of survivorship to the other spouse.

Tenancy in Common—An ownership of real estate by two or more persons, each of whom has an undivided fractional interest in the whole property, without any right of survivorship.

Term—The period of time between the beginning loan date on the legal documents and the date the entire balance of the loan is due.

Thrift institution—A general term for savings banks and savings and loan associations.

Title—Document which gives evidence of ownership of a property. Also indicates the rights of ownership and possession of the property.

Title Company—A company that insures title to property.

Title Insurance—Refers to an insurance policy which protects the lender and/or buyer against loss due to disputes over ownership of a property.

Title Search—Examination of municipal records to ensure that the seller is the legal owner of a property and that there are no liens or other claims against the property.

Transfer Tax—Tax paid when title passes from one owner to another.

Truth-in-Lending Act—Federal law requiring written disclosure of the terms of a mortgage by a lender to a borrower after application.

Underwriting—In mortgage lending, the process of determining the risks involved in a particular loan and establishing suitable terms and conditions for the loan.

Usury—Interest charged in excess of the legal rate established by law.

VA Loans—Fixed-rate loans guaranteed by the U.S. Department of Veterans Affairs. They are designed to make housing affordable for eligible U.S. veterans. VA loans are available to veterans, reservists, active-duty personnel, and surviving spouses of veterans with 100% entitlement. Eligible veterans may be able to purchase a home with no down payment, no cash reserve, no application fee, and lower closing costs than other financing options.

Variable Rate—Interest rate that changes periodically in relation to an index.

Variance—The authorization to improve or develop a particular property in a manner not authorized by the zoning ordinance.

Verification of Deposit (VOD)—Document signed by the borrower's bank or other financial institution verifying the borrower's account balance and history.

Verification of Employment (VOE)—Document signed by the borrower's employer verifying the borrower's position and salary.

Waiver—Voluntary relinquishment or surrender of some right or privilege.

Walk-through—A final inspection of a home to check for problems that may need to be corrected before closing.

Zoning Ordinances—Local law establishing building codes and usage regulations for properties in a specified area.

BIBLIOGRAPHY AND ADDITIONAL READING

Black's Law Dictionary, Fifth Edition. St. Paul, MN: West Publishing Company, 1979.

The Federal Housing Administration (Date Visited: July 2008) http://www.fha.gov/.

The Federal Reserve Board (Date Visited: July 2008) http://www.federalreserve.gov/.

The Federal Trade Commission (Date Visited: July 2008) http://www.ftc.gov/.

The Internal Revenue Service (Date Visited: July 2008) http://www.irs.gov/.

The Office of Fair Housing and Equal Opportunity (Date Visited: July 2008) http://www.fairhousingfirst.org/.

The U.S. Court System (Date Visited: July 2008) http://www.uscourts.gov/.

The U.S. Department of Housing and Urban Development (Date Visited: July 2008) http://www.hud.gov/.

The U.S. Department of Justice (Date Visited: July 2008) http://www.doj.gov/.

The U.S. Equal Opportunity Commission (Date Visited: July 2008) http://www.eeoc.gov/.

GAYLORD FG